BOYS, CHILDHOOD DOMESTIC ABUSE, AND GANG INVOLVEMENT

Violence at Home, Violence On-Road

Jade Levell

With a Foreword by
Marianne Hester

First published in Great Britain in 2026 by

Bristol University Press
University of Bristol
1–9 Old Park Hill
Bristol
BS2 8BB
UK
t: +44 (0)117 374 6645
e: bup-info@bristol.ac.uk

Details of international sales and distribution partners are available at bristoluniversitypress.co.uk

© Bristol University Press 2026

British Library Cataloguing in Publication Data
A catalogue record for this book is available from the British Library

ISBN 978-1-5292-1980-7 hardcover
ISBN 978-1-5292-5928-5 paperback
ISBN 978-1-5292-1981-4 ePub
ISBN 978-1-5292-1982-1 ePdf

The right of Jade Levell to be identified as the author of this work has been asserted by her in accordance with the Copyright, Designs and Patents Act 1988.

All rights reserved: no part of this publication may be reproduced, stored in a retrieval system, or transmitted in any form or by any means, electronic, mechanical, photocopying, recording, or otherwise without the prior permission of Bristol University Press.

Every reasonable effort has been made to obtain permission to reproduce copyrighted material. If, however, anyone knows of an oversight, please contact the publisher.

The statements and opinions contained within this publication are solely those of the author and not of the University of Bristol or Bristol University Press. The University of Bristol and Bristol University Press disclaim responsibility for any injury to persons or property resulting from any material published in this publication.

Bristol University Press works to counter discrimination on grounds of gender, race, disability, age and sexuality.

Cover design: Bristol University Press
Front cover image: 123RF/bialasiewicz

Bristol University Press' authorised representative in the European Union is:
Easy Access System Europe, Mustamäe tee 50, 10621 Tallinn, Estonia,
Email: gpsr.requests@easproject.com

For all child survivors of domestic violence and abuse

Contents

List of Figures and Tables	vi
Acknowledgements	vii
Foreword	viii
Preface	xi
Preface to the Paperback Edition	xiv
The Structure of the Book	xxi

PART I Foundations

1	Masculinity, Marginalization, and Patriarchal Violence	3
2	Invisible Victims of Domestic Abuse, Hypervisible in Gangs	16
3	Music as Method	33

PART II Life–History Research

4	Childhood Domestic Violence and Abuse	47
5	Learning How to Be a Man On-Road	64
6	'a man'/'The Man'	80
7	Love and Fear	97
8	The Road Ahead	113

PART III Joining the Dots

9	Policy Links: Why Is 'Domestic Abuse' not 'Serious Violence'? A False Dichotomy	135
10	Understanding the Pathways from Domestic Abuse to Gang Involvement	144
11	Masculinity, Vulnerability, and Violence	162

Notes	169
References	170
Index	193

List of Figures and Tables

Figure

10.1 Masculinities experienced by the participants 145

Tables

1.1   Participant demographics 14
3.1   Participants' interview track lists 42
10.1 Case features from Serious Case Reviews 147

Acknowledgements

My first thanks go to the men who told me their stories. I feel honoured you shared your memories with me and I treat your words with reverence.

I want to thank the Open University for funding my PhD and my academic supervisors who guided the study: Dr Rod Earle, Dr Chris Kubiak, Dr Johanna Motzkau, Dr Martin Robb. Thanks also to Dr. Lindsay O'Dell, Dr. Kier Irwin-Rogers, Professor Marianne Hester, Professor Ross Deuchar. Thank you to the practitioners who gave their time to discuss the front-line issues with me, especially Charlie Rigby. Thanks to Rebecca Tomlinson and the team at Policy Press for making the publishing process such a pleasure.

Lastly, a heart-warming thanks to my family and friends who have supported me throughout, especially Richard, my rock, and my children, whose love sustains me.

Foreword

Marianne Hester OBE

Jade Levell has written a powerful and important book on a topic that not only deserves attention but, as she says, has often been hidden in plain sight. Children's experiences of domestic abuse, where their mother is being abused by the father, and the children are abused and impacted in so many ways, began to be recognized by the feminist refuge movement in the 1970s. But it has taken a long time for society and services more generally to recognize that children are not mere 'bystanders' or 'witnesses', that their experiences have to be recognized, and that they are often in desperate need of safety and support. Even more tricky has been to acknowledge that boys are affected too, and that they also need a voice and support. Jade Levell provides boys with that voice.

Jade Levell's book confronts the realities of domestic abuse and tells it as it is. She shows how important it is not to sanitize or hide domestic violence and abuse through minimizing or not naming it for what it is, how crucial it is that we recognize and acknowledge the fears and abuse a child or young person experiences associated with violence against their mother, and highlights the threatening chaos of not knowing when it'll happen again. In many respects the experiences of Jade and her siblings mirror the wider research evidence we have with regard to children, young people, and domestic violence, where siblings can have different experiences, impacts, and resilience, and where these may be gendered (Hester et al, 2007; Devaney, 2015). It was Jade's brother who *'acted out and got in with the wrong crowd'*, was excluded from school, and consequently expelled, while she found support and validation in a school setting that helped her move forward.

The book confronts some key issues in feminist approaches to domestic violence and with regard to key support services and approaches, especially the tricky question of 'what about the boys and men?'. In this regard she is particularly critical of the refuge movement and the seeming lack of safe space for boys. Indeed there has always tended to be an age limit on boys staying in refuges with their mothers. Currently, the age limit is set by individual refuges. According to the Women's Aid Federation England some refuges allow sons up to the age of 16, while others cannot take boys over the age of 13 or 14. Very few refuges will accept male children up to the age of 18 (Women's Aid, 2022). But it has to be recognized that, since the start of the refuge movement in the early 1970s, refuges have always provided protection for both women and children, including boy children (Hester et al, 2007). Although there were initially few facilities in refuges specifically for children, this changed over the years with the development of policies on work with children, and with the employment of specific children's workers from the early 1980s. By 1986 Women's Aid Federation England had introduced an additional aim that refuges should provide specific support for children. This was followed in 1990 by the funding of a National Children's Officer post. By the 1990s most refuges saw the provision of services to children as an important priority, and that emphasis has continued to the present day.

We need of course to understand why refuges were set up by the women's movement to create safe spaces for women. This was and continues to be due to the overwhelming evidence that women experience most domestic violence, the most severe and life-threatening abuse, and do so from male partners. Moreover, as acknowledged in the statutory definition of domestic abuse (Domestic Abuse Act, 2021), parents may also be abused by their children, and this tends predominantly to be violence and abuse from boys and young men to their mothers (Miles and Condry, 2015). Such concerns, linked to the women's own experiences, informed the early rationale for placing age constraints on boys' access to refuges with their mothers.

However, these patterns of woman abuse by male partners and male children are not inevitable nor based on essentialist notions of biology. They are the unfortunate product of patriarchal and male-dominated societies. As expressed in the Council of Europe Convention on preventing and combating violence against women and domestic violence (the 'Istanbul Convention'), violence against women is both a cause and a consequence of gender inequality. The convention consequently places men and boys at the heart of the solution to domestic violence and abuse, positing that interventions to prevent gender-based violence against women must actively engage men as actors and agents for change. Jade Levell's book and her plea for spaces for boys and young men, where they can be safe and recover from growing up in contexts of domestic violence and learn new ways of relating, forms an important contribution to this approach, which will enable the involvement of boys and young men to be part of the solution to countering violence and abuse.

Another key feature of the book is Jade Levell's use of music elicitation as a method to engage with the men she interviews. Most of us find that music has some sort of emotional impact on us, and it is thus not surprising that this can be a highly effective approach to get at the difficult experiences and emotions of the men concerned. Jade Levell has created and taken this approach and application of music to a new level.

Preface

Tracy Chapman (1988)
'Behind the Wall'
This track talks about domestic abuse overheard by neighbours and of police inaction.

The context for this book began with my own lived experience of domestic violence and abuse (DVA) in childhood. This happened at a time when children were not recognized as direct victims. We were 'exposed', we bore witness. We were on the periphery of chaos, trying to keep the mirage of normality while living so close to the eye of the storm. Looking back, one of the things I found so difficult, apart from living with abuse and violence, was the taboo of DVA. The only place that I found explicit reference to DVA in my younger years was through music, which inspired the use of music elicitation interviews in this study. Whether lyrics were by P!nk, Tracy Chapman, or Eminem, I sought out mentions of DVA in music lyrics to give voice to what I was experiencing. Music offered me recognition, comfort, companionship, understanding, at a time when I never explicitly told anyone what we were going through at home. I didn't find the words to describe it myself until much later. Therein lies one of the stranger aspects of DVA; it is often a hidden in plain sight. Throughout my childhood it became clear that I and my siblings were processing our challenges differently, my brother and I in particular. While I found solace in the rhythm and distraction of school, he quickly acted out and *got in with the wrong crowd*. I was being offered extra-curricular opportunities at school, while my brother was excluded and later expelled.

I left home and went to university to study feminist theory. As bell hooks (1994, p 59) has so articulately expressed, 'I came to theory because I was hurting ... I came to theory desperate, wanting to comprehend – to grasp what was happening around and within me'. I wanted to make sense of the inequality I felt. The tolerance for violence. The social and cultural weight placed on enduring marriage over safety. I have worked in gender-based violence support services ever since; working in violence prevention has helped me make use of my pain. After a few years I got a job in a refuge for women and children fleeing abuse. I remember the nerves: would this be too close to home for me?

I found I thrived when working with feminist colleagues and embedding our practice in an explicit understanding of gender equality. However, it was in the refuge that I started thinking about how the boys who arrived would feel about the rules. In the refuge I worked in we had an upper age limit of 12 years old for sons of survivors, but 18 years for daughters. Technically older boys could go into care, although I imagine more often those mothers would have found another survival solution, such as sending sons to live with the perpetrator. I kept asking around for a reason. A colleague told me it was due to the statutory age for rape, which meant boys could not share a bunk bedroom with their families. Some said adolescent boys who were physically turning into men would scare the other residents. Or they were more likely to be perpetrators themselves. Women wanted a male-free space to recover. As a child survivor who had thrived in these spaces for my career, *I got it*. But I kept thinking about my brother, who had not received the privilege of an open-arms welcome to the domestic violence and abuse sector. He was invisible at best, feared and denigrated at worst. By this point he was living in a homeless hostel, with escalating addictions, getting into trouble with the police. It didn't make sense to me that boys like him, who seemed to need help the most, were the blind spot of the DVA movement. Not to say that girl child survivors were receiving excellent support in the services I was working within and around. The specialist children's support work was gradually cut down to nothing, reflecting the wider model which has gained traction (largely due to lack of funding) in community services that focuses on supporting the non-abusive parent as a proxy support for their children. As both a child survivor and a DVA professional I felt uneasy in my part in reproducing children's enduring invisibility.

Years later I had moved into policy and training work. I was working in the Coordinated Community Response (CCR) model and responsible for DVA children and health in West London. Through this work I reached out to the local gangs' and serious youth violence outreach worker. He estimated that 90 per cent of his caseload was made up of child survivors of DVA but they were seldom recognized or supported as such. By the time they came to the attention of services they were seen as a risk to others, which then eclipsed their own past traumas. My brother was still on my mind, his life still spiralling into chaos. Hearing about the boys on-road, many who were DVA survivors, yet so easily stigmatized by their criminality, fuelled me further. It struck me that adolescent boys are so far from the 'ideal victim' stereotype. They can be chaotic, noisy, rebellious, 'trouble'. But many are also traumatized children who have experienced abuse and violence.

In this book I aim to shine the light on the life stories of men who lived with childhood DVA and on-road and gang involvement. I highlight their pain, their struggle, and their survival through the lens of masculinity. These are some of the most marginalized boys and young men in the UK who are often failed by services. In many ways this book has evolved as both a beacon of recognition for child survivors, as well as an extended ode to my brother. I'm asking: what could have been done? How can we understand *how he understood it?* How can we help boys survive, thrive, and not self-destruct or harm others?

Jade Levell
February 2022

Preface to the Paperback Edition

Tom Walker (2017)
'Leave a Light On'

In the three years since the first publication of this book, I have presented the findings to hundreds of professionals working in grassroots practice and policy from across Europe. Often, I have shared the music tracks that the participants entrusted with me. Listening to soundtracks that reflect lives very different from those of the audience is helping to foster a movement of radical empathy. At times I have wondered if this has been the biggest contribution of the book. A theoretical understanding of male violence is vital but generating an emotional and compassionate response around the tangible impact of male violence is perhaps the most urgent and important driver of real-world change.

This preface tracks ripples of policy change and recent calls to action inspired by this book. We need to maintain urgency and hope, using these policy recommendations to leverage real change. It is vital that we continue imagining a future world that supports child survivors of domestic violence and abuse (DVA), rather than punishing youth violence in a silo.

Children as DVA victims in their own right

In April 2025 the office of the Domestic Abuse Commissioner (DAC) for England and Wales released a landmark report entitled *Victims in Their Own Right? Babies, Children and Young People's Experience of Domestic Abuse*. Section 6.7 was dedicated to the overlap of domestic abuse and 'serious violence' and became concrete recommendations for government. Specifically, the Commissioner recommended that (2025, p 122):

- The Home Office and Department for Education should publish joint guidance and a shared language framework to clarify roles in supporting children affected by domestic abuse. This must use gender-specific language to reflect differing needs, in line with the recommendation on page 125.

- The Home Office and Safer Streets Mission Board should fund gender-specific, masculinity-aware interventions for boys affected by domestic abuse. These must avoid implying future perpetration and instead address how abuse shapes identity and behaviour.
- The Department for Culture, Media and Sport should ensure the Youth Strategy improves collaboration between domestic abuse and youth services, recognising links between abuse exposure and serious youth violence.

The UK Government took up two of the DAC recommendations. Firstly, Recommendation 17: 'Ensure that the Youth Strategy includes content on how the Government will improve joint working between domestic abuse and youth organisations'. The government states that this will be considered within the upcoming 'National Youth Strategy' (HM Government, 2025, p 15). Secondly, Recommendation 27: 'Scope the development and availability of gender-specific and masculinity aware interventions for male child victims of domestic abuse', which will be considered as part of the upcoming (already delayed several times) Violence against Women and Girls Strategy (VAWG). The National Society for the Prevention of Cruelty to Children (NSPCC) has been tasked with developing learning materials, including a module on working with boy child survivors of DVA. How to maintain a feminist and gendered focus on VAWG while creating space for boys is an enduring challenge in this field. In 2025 I was invited to a VAWG round table hosted at the Home Office; several people raised the fact that the VAWG title renders boys less visible from the outset. In the response the government claims this strategy will include a funding uplift for child survivors which are, 'designed to support all children affected by domestic abuse, including boys' (HM Government, 2025, p 20).

Highlighting the enduring blind-spot of male victims

In 2025 I submitted written evidence to the UK Parliament which was published by the Home Affairs Select Committee. I emphasized that although children are legally recognized as direct victims of DVA in the Domestic Abuse Act (2021) ring-fenced funding has not followed, and there has also been no funding specifically for a gender-specific support approach to children. This point echoed the book's argument that Serious Violence Duty creates a hierarchy of violence, prioritizing public violence over private violence. Frontline practice has also been influenced by domestic homicide reviews (DHRs), which are investigations into the circumstances surrounding the death of individuals aged 16 or over that appear to have resulted from domestic abuse, with the aim of preventing future tragedies. In March 2023 the tragic murder of 'Paul' by his female partner in Liverpool resulted in a

Domestic Homicide Review (DHR) which cited this book: 'The current political strategic boundaries between domestic abuse, male victims, and serious youth violence policy does not support a full and humanizing approach to those affected' (Citysafe Liverpool, 2023, Line 1.29).

The DHR also reflected on the book's findings that both internal pressures linked to masculinity and external factors such as services framing sexual exploitation as a 'women and girls' issue can prevent male victims from recognizing or disclosing their experiences (Line 1.30). This DHR resulted in a city-wide action plan which highlighted the importance of service provision for male victims of DVA, with emphasis on early intervention.

Connections between boyhood DVA, public space violence including 'knife crime', and violent extremism

In 2025 the End Violence against Women Coalition (EVAW) published a report entitled, *New Paths to Prevention: Engaging More Boys and Men in Ending Violence against Women.* They picked up on the way the research supports gender-transformative approaches which recognize the interaction between trauma and boys' vulnerabilities in violence prevention. My research was cited in Recommendation 8: 'Make the connections between violence against women and other gendered policy issues, such as serious youth violence and knife crime (in which masculine norms also often play a central role), and bring agencies and organisations together to address them simultaneously' (Burrell and Westmarland, 2025, p 11).

This mantle has been picked up in pockets of practice across the UK. Wales has been focusing on a gender-transformative approach to male violence prevention which explicitly recognizes the need to 'challenge prevailing harmful masculine norms, as well as supporting routes for trauma-informed help seeking' (Snowdon et al, 2025, p 248).

An aspect of my recent work has been to critically explore young peoples' experiences of so-called 'serious violence' outside the controversial lens of 'knife crime'. I delivered lectures on the links between childhood domestic violence and knife crime in the winter of 2024 in a range of contexts, including the Youth Endowment Fund, the London Mayor's Office for Policing and Crime (MOPAC) and the office of the DAC. This talk highlighted several recent high-profile cases where the perpetrators of fatal stabbings were unsupported child survivors of DVA. I am mindful of the risks of 'himpathy' (Manne, 2017), whereby perpetrators are not held to account for their behaviour due to the perceived mitigation of past trauma. I am also aware of the recent rise of far-right populism and the increasing anti-feminist discourse which often co-opts discussions around youth masculinity and violence (Roberts et al, 2025). Despite this we have to have a reckoning about the general failure of early intervention within our current systems. The links between childhood experiences of violence and later violent extremism have been picked up in a UK Government report from July 2025 prepared by the Interim Independent Prevent Commissioner Lord Anderson of Ipswich KBE KC, entitled, 'Lessons for Prevent'. This report was instigated after the government announced a permanent oversight function for Prevent following the horrific attack in Southport in July 2024 by Axel Rudakubana. The report highlighted this book and the need for a focus on masculinities in relation to violent extremism that is much broader than just incel culture, which has gathered much media attention since the Netflix series *Adolescence* was released in March 2025; incel culture accounts for only 1% of Prevent referrals. This book was cited alongside 2021 research Project Starlight, commissioned by Counter Terrorism Policing, which revealed that over a third of 'vulnerable to radicalization' (V2R) referrals to Prevent had experience of DVA (as victim, child survivor or perpetrator, or at times a combination of all three). Speaking on these findings in 2021 the National Coordinator for Prevent, Detective Chief Superintendent Vicky Washington, said, 'This initial research has resulted in some statistically significant data which cannot, and should not, be ignored' (Counter Terrorism Policing, 2021).

'*Det har alltid funnits våld, alltså när det har funnits problem*'/'There has always been violence, that is, when there have been problems'

In a somewhat surprising turn of events this book has gained traction among policy makers and practitioners in Sweden. Sweden is seeing rising levels of gang-related youth crime, which is igniting a heated public debate around agency, responsibility and early intervention. I was first invited to Sweden to speak at the Brottsoffermyndigheten conference on the European Day for Victims of Crime in February 2024. This event was followed by many speaking engagements over the following months, including keynote lectures at the National Conference on Crime Prevention (Brå) by the Swedish National Council for Crime Prevention (2024); the Swedish Gender Equality Agency (2024); the Stockholm local government conference (2024); the Magelungen Conference (2025); and an opportunity to train prison chaplains (2025). In February 2025 I was invited to speak at the Swedish Parliament. This momentum led to *Dagens Nyheter*, the highest circulating newspaper in Sweden, featuring me on the front cover as well as on a double-page spread inside.

This book was used by the Ombudsman for Children in Sweden in their own 2025 research, *There Has Always Been Violence, That Is, When There Have Been Problems*. The report focused on the conditions and factors that contribute to an increased risk of later involvement in and exploitation by criminal networks and gangs. The report was based on 88 in-depth interviews with children and young people who were deprived of their liberty in detention centres, secure youth homes and prisons. The report's authors conducted a survey which garnered 543 responses. Their findings concurred with my own; many children who became involved in gangs and criminal networks had experienced domestic violence and abuse in earlier childhood but had not received timely identification and support. They also found similar challenges for boys that mediated their experiences of violence through a masculinity lens.

What next? The need for paradigm shifts around boyhood, male violence, masculinities and violence prevention

Despite this evidence of interest and traction over recent years there is still a lot of work to be done. We need a paradigm shift around how we think of boys and masculinity in terms of violence prevention. The problems I identified in this book remain. The policy recommendations that I have outlined here have not yet been addressed. There is still a reluctance to see young male violence as an issue that is often hinged on prior experiences of adult male violence and mediated through masculinity. Interventions that are highlighted as being masculinity-focused, such as certain sports including boxing, can lean and capitalize on a hyper/traditional version of masculinity which may be unhelpful for boy child survivors. Gender-transformative approaches are few and far between, but with notable pockets of work being rapidly developed, including by Public Health Wales and Islington Council. In conversations I've had, I feel that there is still discomfort about making connections between childhood violence and adolescent violence, as well as the complex overlap of victimization and perpetration, particularly when it crosses private and public spaces. Our criminal justice lens encourages clear differentiation between categorizations of victims and perpetrators, which promotes siloed thinking and a reluctance to identify the concurrent victimization that perpetrators may be experiencing. Clearly, childhood offending behaviour is a complex area where aspects of responsibility and accountability are complicated by immaturity and dependence.

We also seem to have failed to imagine a strategic framework for gender-based violence (GBV) that retains a feminist activist lens yet sits outside an umbrella of VAWG. We need to imagine more broadly how we maintain the focus on gender in the context of patriarchy, alongside the diverse axes of structural oppression individuals face, which enable us to illuminate the foundations of GBV without neglecting the experience of boys.

Gender-neutral services that claim to serve all are not the answer either, risking individualizing through a lens on risk factors, and disconnecting male violence from its roots in patriarchy. We often discuss GBV via a focus on its predominant victims (women and girls) or spatially (*domestic* violence) rather than highlighting the connecting thread of harmful masculinities. What would happen if we instead strategically framed DVA and serious youth violence (as well as other types of GBV) as both forms of majority-male-perpetrated violence (MMPV)? Could this approach be a vehicle to bring together experts and practitioners on different types of male violence and masculinity and reduce siloed thinking around harm that affect boys as both victims and perpetrators? I think this approach makes increasing sense.

This book has laid roots for a movement of radical empathy: one that centres a compassionate understanding of childhood experiences of domestic violence and their connections to broader patterns of harm; and one populated by professionals who can sit with the discomfort of boys' concurrent victimization and perpetration. There's growing recognition that current approaches are falling short and failing to reach boys early enough. We need to reimagine how we respond to this issue with care and concern and a gender-transformative lens. Hope lives in me, and in many others. Together, like ripples becoming waves, I believe we can shift the tide.

Jade Levell
November 2025

References

Burrell, S. R. and Westmarland, N. (2025) *Engaging More Boys and Men in Ending Violence against Women*, Available from: https://www.endviolenceagainstwomen.org.uk/new-how-to-engage-men-in-ending-vawg/ [Accessed 1 November 2025].

Citysafe Liverpool (2023) 'Domestic Homicide Review: "Paul" who died in March 2023', *LDHR29*, Available from: https://liverpool.gov.uk/media/ha4gprtb/ldhr29-overview-report-final.pdf [Accessed 1 November 2025].

Counter Terrorism Policing (2021) *Research Project Released Investigating Prevalence of Domestic Abuse Related Incidences within Prevent Referrals*, Available from: https://www.counterterrorism.police.uk/research-project-released-investigating-prevalence-of-domestic-abuse-related-incidences-within-prevent-referrals/ [Accessed 1 November 2025].

Domestic Abuse Commissioner (2025) *Victims in Their Own Right? Babies, Children and Young People's Experience of Domestic Abuse*, Available from: https://domesticabusecommissioner.uk/wp-content/uploads/2025/06/dac_bcyp_main-report_V6-DIGITAL.pdf [Accessed 1 November 2025].

Ewen, J. (2025) '*Boys, Childhood Domestic Abuse and Gang Involvement: Violence at Home, Violence On-Road* by Jade Levell (2022)', *Gender and Justice*, 1(1), pp 140–42.

Frances, T. (2023) '*Boys, Childhood Domestic Abuse and Gang Involvement: Violence at Home, Violence On-Road* by Jade Levell', *Children & Society*, 37(4), pp 1334–35.

HM Government (2025). *Domestic Abuse Commissioner's Report: Victims in Their Own Right? Babies, Children and Young People's Experience of Domestic Abuse – Government Response*, Available from: https://assets.publishing.service.gov.uk/media/68d3f8348c739d679fb1dd3e/UK_Government_Response_to__Victims_in_Their_Own_Right._Babies_children_and_young_people_s_experience_of_domestic_abuse_.pdf [Accessed 1 November 2025].

Manne, K. (2017) *Down Girl: The Logics of Misogyny*, Oxford: Oxford University Press.

Roberts, S., Fairchild, J., Keleher, H., Trott, V. and Wescott, S. (2025) '"Adolescence", manufactured outrage and instructed victimhood: how the discourse on boys' alienation is fuelled by anti-feminist agendas', *European Journal of Cultural Studies*, Available from: https://doi.org/10.1177/13675494251371661

Smith, D. (2023) 'Book Review: *Boys, Childhood Domestic Abuse, and Gang Involvement*'. *Resolution Online Magazine*, 73, pp 20–21.

Snowdon, L. C., Walker, A., Barton, E. R., Parry, B. and Pike, S. (2025). From individual interventions to structural change: Why public health leadership is needed to engage men and boys in violence prevention. *Public Health*, *248*. https://doi.org/10.1016/j.puhe.2025.105972

The Structure of the Book

The book is divided into three parts. The first lays the foundations of the work. In this I initially outline the parameters of the study; namely the focus on masculinities and male (patriarchal) violence. In Chapter 1 I will introduce the participants whose narratives feature later in the book and the method of music elicitation. In Chapter 2 we dig deeper into what is known about prevalence of young people who experience both childhood domestic violence and abuse (DVA) and later on-road and gang involvement. I also discuss why boys end up as invisible in DVA services, yet hypervisible in gang and youth offending services. Central to this is the 2010 paradigm shift from framing children as *exposed* to DVA, to people who *experience* it. The literature on gangs focuses largely on the criminality of young people through their time on-road and/or gang-involved (see Chapter 1 for a discussion of these terms). As such, there has been less research written about the lived experience of gang-involved men's lives in a holistic way while on-road, but also prior to their involvement. I then move on to focus on the gap in existing literature around the dual experiences of both DVA and on-road/gang involvement. Existing scholarship and policy work predominantly draw on quantitative studies with elements of the risk factor paradigm, which has become reframed in the adverse childhood experience literature. Although informative, both approaches are based on checklists of negative experiences, which are counted and thus equated with each other. These approaches do not get to the crux of each issue. DVA is a specific form of gender-based violence that has unique and nuanced effects on individuals.

The chapters in Part II of the book are organized chronologically, broadly focusing on three age ranges within the participants' narratives: childhood (living with DVA); adolescence (peak on-road/gang-involved period); adulthood (post-on-road/gang involvement). Chapter 4 deals with narratives from childhood, which focused on the construction of masculinity in relation to experience of both DVA and the perpetrator. Chapter 5 is focused on the emerging ways the participants discussed using violence and intimidation in the school context. Chapter 6 is centred on narratives of the participants' time on-road and gang involvement. In the period of adolescence, the participants alluded to the emergence of protest masculinity, enacting toughness and violence as they became connected to the gang and formed ties which for some functioned as an alternative to family bonds. In the narratives of this period in life I explore the varying masculine identities expressed by the participants: protest masculinity and vulnerable masculinity. These identities interacted and were foregrounded at different points in the life stories. Chapter 7 uses cathexis as a lens to explore the tensions between love and fear within intimate connections both inside and outside of the gang space. Chapter 8 is focused on the participants' accounts of the process of desistance and recovery from their time on-road and when gang-involved. They discussed strategies they employed to create alternative masculinities that supported and enabled their journeys to recovery and integrations into society in new ways; however, these were mostly typified as marginalized masculinities, as they experienced limitations due to criminal records and association with their past experiences.

Part III of the book brings together both the participants' life stories as well as the gaps in practice, to focus on the broader themes and implications for front-line practice and intervention work. Chapter 9 looks at broader UK government policy on the disparate areas of 'domestic abuse' and 'serious violence' (SV) as distinct and disconnected categories. I make a case that there is a gender-blind approach to both the SV duty and the public health approach to violence that is being foregrounded in several regions. Chapter 10 looks at the life trajectories of the participants and identified some common themes, such as school exclusion and sexual violence, which has implications for front-line practice. These claims are supported by further analysis of Serious Case Reviews, where children who also had similar life journeys have died in the UK. Analysis of these tragic cases reinforces the ways in which both DVA and 'gang involvement' are issues fraught with disparate language and a lack of timely support. Finally, Chapter 11 is centred around expanding the core themes that emerged in the book, in particular masculinity, vulnerability, and violence. These were threads that were woven through the narratives and revealed much about the tensions that arose between protest and vulnerable masculinity and being both victims and perpetrators of violence. Violence was shown to be, at different times, an expression of the pursuit of power and an expression of vulnerability. These almost contradictory tensions are discussed, and I argue that protest masculinity and vulnerable masculinity have a symbiotic relationship. To understand these elements though it is essential to look at the context of patriarchy. Ultimately, I argue that both DVA and on-road violence are defined by the ways in which marginalized young men navigate powerlessness within a White supremacist heteronormative capitalist patriarchal system. Part III of the book is threaded with recommendations for practice that have arisen through the study. These aim to turn academic theory into positive change in practice.

Note on the accompanying music

Unfortunately, it was very difficult to obtain permissions to reproduce song lyrics in this book. To give a sense of the tracks in places where I can't reproduce the lyrics, I have included a brief description. This is not ideal, and I would have much preferred the lyrics to speak for themselves. Where I have listed a track, I recommend you access the accompanying track and, in some cases, music video. This will help you get a sense of the multimodal aspect of the interview. For ease I have brought these together in a Spotify playlist and have embedded the videos on my website www.jadelevell.com.

PART I
Foundations

1

Masculinity, Marginalization, and Patriarchal Violence

'I was like [an] innocent young boy. Abused. Hurt, broken, not heard, crying out, crying out, crying out, not heard, not heard, not heard, and when someone's not heard they rebel, so [I] wasn't heard and then I rebelled and run to the streets.' (Sam)

This is a book about survival. How boys and young men survive violence, as well as how they survive through *using* violence. For the men whose life stories are included in this book, violence has punctuated their stories of childhood and adolescence. Initially they experienced it around them – perpetrated by their fathers or mothers' male partner. They felt the aching powerlessness of living with violence at home. However, as they grew older their role in relation to violence shifted. They learned to harness it themselves in school, among peers, before becoming embroiled in life on-road and involved with gangs. Experiences of violence in these contexts were not straightforward. At different moments they talked about victimization, exploitation, about their own perpetration. Of using violence as self-harm and protection, punctuated by seeing their close friends harmed and killed at close quarters. Violence was a visceral presence around them; some were abused and exploited, some abused and exploited others.

The complexity and proximity of the victim and perpetrator positions in relation to violence is a contentious crux with which to grapple. Stereotypes about both victims and perpetrators are mired in intersecting assumptions related to gender, race, class, age (among others). As Crenshaw (1991) noted, dual experiences of sexism and racism can render some victim/survivors invisible. Foregrounding both a gender, race, and class analysis has been central to this study – not least because there is substantial evidence that the young people most likely to be identified as in 'gangs' are poor, Black boys (Glynn, 2014; Amnesty International, 2018; Williams and Clarke, 2018). As Anthony Neal (2013, p 5) noted, the 'Black male body is often thought to be a criminal body and/or a body in need of policing and containment.' The men who took part in this study had all experienced marginalization for multiple reasons; however, many such reasons can be linked back to the impact of living in a White supremacist capitalist patriarchy (hooks, 1997). bell hooks coined this phrase as a way to describe the interlocking systems of power which structure hierarchies in our society. Focusing on systemic inequalities enables an analysis that goes beyond the material realities of individuals and instead to the systems of oppressions that surround us. In this book I apply Connell's (2005) theory of masculinity to show the ways in which these structural inequalities produce and maintain violence. This study has been rooted in feminist praxis. It constitutes a rallying cry in the feminist movement for deeper analysis on the ways in which we navigate the politics of gender, race, and class to reach out to some of the most marginalized victims.

I sought to hear the life stories of men who had lived with childhood domestic abuse (DA) and later went on-road and became involved in gangs. I wanted to understand how masculinity was developed in the context of violent childhoods within a racialized and patriarchal society. This goes deeper than searching for victimhood and perpetration; rather sitting with the tension of complex lives that do not fit into neat categories of harm. Young people who occupy this interface often fall through the gaps of support services. Importantly, though, these experiences all occurred in *childhood*. I am talking about *children's* lives. This is an important consideration to be placed at the forefront, always. The criminalization of young people who are, or who are thought to be, on-road and gang-involved, swiftly scoops them up in the discourse of the criminal justice system where they are seen as offenders first and as children second: innocence is lost. Stories of violence are not easy to share and the tool that was used in this study was music as an elicitation, or communication, tool. Participants were asked to bring three music tracks to help them tell parts of their life stories. As you will see throughout, music has provided a refuge, a supportive voice, a way to understand and articulate feelings throughout the difficulties of their lives. Music has been a powerful coping tool for the participants and was also a powerful listening tool in this study.

It is important to note from the outset that the men discussed in this book are a small minority of child survivors of domestic violence and abuse (DVA). Many boys who experience DVA grow up and have non-violent lives. This study has not sought to prove causation; that childhood DVA = gang involvement, but rather, to examine the *lived experiences* of men who have walked this path. I aimed to focus on these lives and go 'up-stream' to understand how the participants storied and understood their lives so far. DVA is a gendered crime, as shown by both prevalence statistics but also by the nature of the consequences. Women are more likely to be victimized

(Kimmel, 2002; Saunders, 2002; Walby and Allen, 2004), more likely to be at high risk of harm (Jones, 2016), to be hospitalized through injury (Barnish, 2004, p 12), or to be murdered (ONS, 2016). Indeed, Nicola Sturgeon, the Scottish First Minister, stated that 'We'll never have gender equality until we stop domestic violence' (Sanghani, 2015). Stark (2007, p 24) noted that 'unlike other capture crimes, coercive control is personalized, extends through social space as well as over time, and is gendered in that it relies for its impact on women's vulnerability as women due to sexual inequality.' If we accept that DVA is a form of patriarchal violence, most often carried out by men in households, then it helps us start to consider why gender may be an important consideration for boys who survive it.

Understanding boys and men's experiences of violence, which goes beyond the fictions of a clear-cut victim/perpetrator dichotomy, is essential. Until 2021, with the advent of the Domestic Abuse Bill in the UK, children had not been recognized as victims of DVA in their own right. Among this group, the gendered understanding of boys' and girls' lives remains less explored. The root of this lies in the historical essentialization of sexed (male) bodies and violence perpetration within mainstream feminist discourse. This has been grounded in the material reality of male violence; however, it resulted in an unintended blind spot around male child survivors. This has been changing throughout the 2010s, with supported men in the public eye sharing openly about their childhood experiences (for instance, Luke and Ryan Hart, David Challen, Ian Wright). This has occurred alongside an academic shift that has changed the emphasis from children previously being seen as 'witnesses' or 'bystanders', now increasingly recognized as individuals who *experience* DVA and are thus victims in their own right (Överlien and Hydén, 2009; Callaghan et al, 2015).

Using a masculinity lens

This study follows in a long line of feminist theorizing that views gender not as innate, but instead as a social construction. From the 1970s onwards there has been an increasing foregrounding on 'gender' as distinct from 'sex' (Oakley, 1972; West and Zimmerman, 1987; Butler, 1988). In these texts there was a differentiation made between the biological differences between men and women (sex) and the social practices and differences associated with each sex (gender). Connell (1987, 2005) followed in this tradition but focused in particular on the gendered conditions of masculinity, which she situated within a wider context of gender inequality. To examine the meanings of gendered practice theorists have referred to the *performativity* of gender, or how people *do gender* (Butler, 2004). This comes from the perspective that gender is performed in situational ways; it is context dependant (Messerschmidt, 2005). The understanding of how one goes about 'doing gender' is heavily influenced by the social structural constraints that exist in wider society. So, as individuals *do gender* they not only reproduce but sometimes change social structures. Through this gender can be viewed as 'structured action' or 'what people do under specific social-structural constraints' (Messerschmidt, 2005, p 197). In the same way that viewing femininity as a form of 'doing gender' rather than an essential characteristic has allowed for diverse and multiple conceptions of femininities, theorists such as Connell have highlighted the importance of discussing *masculinities* in plural. How men view women, and vice versa, form a key aspect of their gender construction efforts (Mullins, 2006). All forms of masculinities have been constructed in contrast to a feminine other, with those that are positioned at the bottom of the masculine hierarchy somehow symbolically assimilated to femininity (Swain, 2005).

Despite masculinity being historically essentialized as being only present in males (designated by sex), Connell (2000) has argued that masculinities are defined in relation to each other as well as in relation to femininities. She used the Gramscian notion of hegemony to describe the ways in which notions of hegemonic masculinity exist within social relations (Connell and Messerschmidt, 2005). Hegemonic masculinity is not assumed to be enacted by the majority of men; however, it is the normative and *most honoured* way of being a man, which 'ideologically legitimated the global subordination of women to men' (Connell and Messerschmidt, 2005, p 832). So, even if most men do not enact this, it is the masculine ideal in relation to which men position themselves. Men who receive the 'patriarchal dividend' without subscribing to hegemonic masculinity can be said to be presenting a 'complicit masculinity' (Connell and Messerschmidt, 2005, p 832).

Hegemonic masculinity does not necessarily equate to violence 'although it could be supported by force; it meant ascendancy achieved through culture, institutions, and persuasion' (Connell and Messerschmidt, 2005, p 832). Boys who participated in research on young masculinities, however, occupied 'troubled subject positions' in relation to hegemonic masculinity (Frosh et al, 2002, p 83). They knew the markers of hegemonic masculinity and took such masculinity as the standard that they compared themselves to; however, they did not generally aspire to achieving it in its totality. Boys sought to establish a masculine authenticity while diverging from the masculine ideal, with some even attempting to subvert hegemonic masculinity through claiming they were 'above it'. Thus, hegemonic masculinity is not a fixed ideal that all males have an ambition to achieve, it is a structural ideal. One discourse around masculine capital lies in a heterosexual assumption. Masculine performativity ('looking hard') has been structured around a presentation which is 'un-masculine', 'that is, "homosexual", being "womanly" (being a girl, a "puff", a "fag" and so forth, the routine and pervasive derogations of hetero-masculine culture)' (Collier, 1998, p 77). The masculine hierarchy is related to the amount of 'masculine capital' that the performance earns. Indeed, the deconstruction of the monolithic term 'masculinity' and its replacement with understanding of 'masculinities' was largely down to the advance of the gay liberation movement. It was men in this movement who sought to understand the experienced of the oppression both of men as well as *by men* (Connell and Messerschmidt, 2005).

Structured relations around masculinities exist in all local settings, which pivot around a localized version of hegemonic masculinity. One variation of masculinity that has said to occur within working-class or racialized and marginalized communities is *protest masculinity*, which 'embodies the claim to power typical of regional hegemonic masculinities in Western countries, but which lacks the economic resources and institutional authority that underpins the regional and global patterns' (Connell and Messerschmidt, 2005, p 847). A key problem with these as markers of masculine capital is that attainment of these becomes 'refracted in the prism of street life' when contextualized in heavily disadvantaged communities (Mullins, 2006, p 75). When situated in a society that values wealth, status, and capitalist achievement and power, some groups of minority young men realize that their marginal status creates insurmountable barriers to traditional masculine norms of success (Gibbs and Merighi, 1994). Thus, in on-road contexts, where much traditional masculine capital was unavailable, there has developed an adapted 'street' or on-road masculinity, which was derived from the resources available in that context, and which included violence and access to financial resources from the underground economy (Mullins, 2006). Similar sentiments have been shared by Harding (2014), who used social field theory to look at gangs in London and found that the gang context offers a fitting place to *do masculinity* in a way that aims to transcend race and class boundaries. However, as will be discussed in Chapter 2, violence that is associated with the on-road space or gangs often attracts more attention than other forms of violence. As bell hooks noted, male violence in its totality is a central problem, and is perpetrated by men of all races and ethnicities; however, Black male violence gets more attention from the dominant culture (hooks, 2003a). Black men are systematically stigmatized and rendered invisible (Glynn, 2014).

Protest masculinity is developed as a strategy to compensate for a variety of ontological threats: economic precarity, diminished status, emotional neglect. Invulnerability and omnipotence are the mythic symbols of masculine dominance and ascendance, so they are clutched at for the power they deliver to cancel the real weakness of the men's objective socio-economic and cultural position. By constructing tough and hard exteriors, young men who live on the edges of society aim to invert and subdue their internal vulnerabilities rendered by a childhood of abuse. This theme will be returned to throughout the book, where the life history narratives show how men (as boys) engaged in fighting, acting tough, being 'the nutter' in order both to express anger and resentment at their circumstances, but also as attempts to subvert the subordinate masculinity they developed in relation to the DVA perpetrator in childhood. In Maguire's (2021) study he explored the complexities of both protest and vulnerable masculinities among incarcerated men. He shone a light on the ways in which criminalized men negotiate their marginalization through navigating the tensions between 'subordinated and normalized prison masculinities' (Maguire, 2019, p 14). He found that the identities of those classified as *vulnerable prisoners* were 'loaded with risk, fear, failure, loss, shame, trauma, and guilt' (Maguire, 2019, p 16).

Vulnerability, as a concept, has been explored by Gilson (2014). She noted that vulnerability is one of the fundamentals of human experience and is something that can never be truly avoided. Her outline of some of the key features why vulnerability is so ethically pertinent is particularly good:

> The experience of vulnerability presents us with the reality of fallibility, mutability, unpredictability and uncontrollability. We are affected by forces outside our control, the effects of which we can neither fully know nor fully control. Thus, experiences of vulnerability can also prompt fear, defensiveness, avoidance, and disavowal. (Gilson, 2014, pp 3–4)

This definition of vulnerability shows why it is of integral importance to human subjectivity. I particularly appreciate the nuance in Gilson's approach: vulnerability is freed from the necessary association with victimization and harm. Instead, it is positioned as a universal experience that is a fundamental part of the human condition. Walklate (2011) looked at the ways in which connections can be made between vulnerability and resilience. In order to complicate static victim narratives, it is imperative to make space for resistance. Throughout the book I propose that vulnerable masculinity inevitably co-exists when there is protest masculinity. Gilson looks at the close relationship between vulnerability and violence. Specifically, she argues that 'violence is premised on vulnerability', as without vulnerability, violence would not be possible (Gilson, 2014, p 48). In that way, vulnerability could be seen as a condition which precipitates violence itself. Violence and vulnerability thus have a circular relationship, as once violence is perpetrated it then reveals the vulnerabilities of both the body and the mind. Violence, viewed through the lens of vulnerability, can show how violence is often perpetuated through the 'historical relay of violence' (Gilson, 2014, p 49). These theoretical conceptions of vulnerability and violence can illuminate the context of the men's lives.

The feeling of vulnerability can be exasperated by DVA in childhood. Stark and Hester (2019, p 98) noted that the 'child abuse' that children experience can cause 'existential vulnerability ("No one can protect me")' as well as 'tangential spouse abuse' whereby the child experiences the impact of the perpetrator's abuse of the mother. The concept of existential vulnerability is compelling. This term reveals a type of vulnerability that is much more than situational or circumstantial, but instead goes to the core of the child's idea of their own safety and ontological integrity. Gendered responses to the trauma of sexual violence have been explored by McGuffey (2005), who focused on the ways in which families create gender-reaffirming healing processes after sexual violence. The reassertion of traditional gender hierarchies post-sexual violence enables families to restore patriarchal norms, which are heavily influenced by the intersections of race, gender, and class. McGuffey (2008, p 217) found that marginalized men often respond to sexual violence by asserting their investment in traditional gender norms through 'athleticism, emotional detachment, the promotion of hetero-sexuality, and the construction of male space.' Iantaffi (2021) conceptualized 'gender trauma' to describe the ways in which individuals experience the weight of wider societal masculinity messages.

In Connell's original conceptualization of protest masculinity, she situated it as part of the wider gender order. Connell viewed this through a Marxist feminist lens, which drew on the Gramscian concept of 'hegemony' (used as a way to understand class relations) to understand structures of gender. Connell emphasized 'gender relations' over 'patriarchy' as a way to understand the 'interweaving of personal lives and social structure' (Messerschmidt, 2018, p 22). The term 'patriarchy' as a way to understand the structural organization of gendered practice has been central in feminist understandings of structural violence. However, the dominant focus shifted to 'gender' as the central focus of study rather than 'patriarchy' (Messerschmidt, 2018). This shift was part of the gradual mainstreaming of understandings of violence against women and also had the effect of removing this analysis from a broader understanding of patriarchy and gender inequality (Pease, 2019). This risks us missing the core foundation of DVA, which is that it is an expression of a patriarchal society in which violence against women is normalized and tolerated. In order to understand the hierarchy of masculinities and the reverence of hegemonic masculinity, it is essential to understand the social and structural dominance that this has as part of the wider gender order. By refocusing on masculinities within a broader structure of patriarchy we can be alert to the ways in which structure (gendered power) and ideology (the legitimation of gender inequality) interact as patriarchy (Tonsing, 2019).

There is an established body of knowledge that focuses on the patriarchal dynamic of DVA as a specific form of gender-based violence (Dobash and Dobash, 1979). I seek to extend the application of patriarchy to the on-road and gang context, which I suggest is also organized by the dynamics of gender inequality and patriarchal male violence. However, the focus in that context is as much focused on masculine hierarchies *between* men, as it is on male domination over women. It is important to note here that patriarchy is not only founded on male domination, but is also racialized, sexualized, and classed; it is a 'White supremacist capitalist patriarchy' (hooks, 1997). bell hooks originally coined this phrase in order to focus our attention on the dual systems of race and gender, which work together to form systems of domination, functioning simultaneously. The framing of interlocking oppressions was also typified in Crenshaw's (1991) writing on intersectionality; the main message is that you cannot view gender, race, class, and other axis of difference as disparate identities. They work together and fundamentally alter the individual experience of interlocking oppression.

The men I spoke to experienced patriarchal male violence at home, and then became involved in gangs and life on-road, an experience that was in many ways defined by patriarchal power structures and male violence, albeit largely against other men. What changed was their relationship to the violence as they grew up – moving from and between experiences of victimization to an agentic position. Any understanding of violence as a phenomenon is a fractured view: 'no one perspective "captures" violence' (Schinkel, 2010, p 3). Feminist theories of violence focus in particular on the function of violence from a 'means-end' perspective; that is, violence as a tool to maintain patriarchal power structures. This is pertinent in the context of the DVA in the participants' childhoods. Using a Duluth model of DVA outlines violence and abuse as a tool through which perpetrators seek and maintain power and control over their intimate partner and the wider family. An interesting link between the gang context and a patriarchal abusive relationship was made by Simon Harding (2014, 2020), who utilized the Duluth power and control wheel as an interview tool. He framed the gang as an abusive context by fitting the coercive tactics used by gangs as akin to an abusive relationship. The *gender regime* of patriarchy is key (Walby, 2020).

Analytic method: exploring the structure of gender relations

The analytic framework that I used is Connell's (1987, 2005) method for analysing masculinities in relation to the wider social structures of power relations, production relations, and cathexis. Connell noted that these together form the major structures of gender relations. Here she meant that they are: '(a) discoverable in current gender research and sexual politics, and (b) account for most of the structural dynamics currently understood' (Connell, 1987, p 97). When considering these three distinct areas of analysis, however, it is important to note that the structures are inherently connected. The analytic frame of power relations is particularly focused on the ways in which power is exchanged and transacted in ways that support the wider gender order. Production relations are focused on the allocation of tasks according to gender divisions and economic consequences, as well as the dividend that accrues as a result of the division. The last area of focus is cathexis, which looks at how both sexual and platonic relationships are constructed in the narratives, focusing on what they reveal about the wider gender order. Connell borrowed the concept of cathexis from Freud's psychodynamic theory. Connell outlined her interpretation of cathexis as meaning 'the construction of emotionally charged social relations with "objects" (i.e. other people) in the real world' (Connell, 1987, p 112). In practice this means a focus on interpersonal relationships, as well as ambivalent internal worlds, that reveal dynamics of the wider gender order.

Introduction to the study

This book has emerged from my multifaceted work in the gender-based-violence charity sector over ten years. I discovered this gap in understanding during front-line work and it grew from conversations with peers on the need for a deeper understanding on the issues. To dig deeper for the formal study, I contacted over 100 agencies who work in this field and ended up meeting with 12 expert contacts – from charity providers to council coordinators – to discuss this topic in more depth. This laid the groundwork for interviews with men who had lived experience. I faced difficulties in accessing onward referrals for younger active service users of support agencies and ultimately found it more fruitful to reach participants directly through online adverts. The criteria for inclusion was to identify as a male (over 16 years due to ethical constraints), who had experienced childhood DVA and also involvement on-road and/or a gang. All of the participants I finally met with identified as having been both on-road and gang-involved in their adolescence.

Large sections of narratives have been shared throughout to give a fuller sense of the stories in the participant's own words. The encouragement of long-form uninterrupted narratives was enabled with the use of music elicitation and unstructured interviews (see Chapter 3). At the end of each chapter key themes from across all the interviews are discussed. Narrative study is interdisciplinary and has touched all social science disciplines, reaching criminology in the 2010s, where a strand of 'narrative criminology' has been developing (Presser, 2016). The study of narratives within criminological research is not a new concept; however, it is one that is still emerging as a distinctive, self-declared perspective within the discipline (see Fleetwood et al, 2019). The first classic study was from the Chicago School, *The Jack-Roller* by Shaw (1930), where one life history was studied in order to seek to understand the lived experiences of a young man involved in various forms of illicit behaviour. This was followed much later by a special issue in *Theoretical Criminology*, which sought to revisit *The Jack-Roller* and use it to explore the concept of N = 1 and the way in which a full exploration of one case can be satisfactory for in-depth qualitative research (Maruna and Matravers, 2007). Narrative criminologists focus on the way in which self-narratives influence both harmful and criminal behaviour. Presser (2016) noted that narratives have been historically neglected by criminologists because mainstream and positivist criminology has marginalized culture and largely ignored the acculturated self. The narrative turn in criminology has widened the focus of stories of crime and encouraged a focus on the way individuals respond to, as well as interpret, their cultural framework, always acting within their own story of themselves.

This study was subject to clearance and approval from the Human Research Ethics Committee of the Open University. All names have been anonymized and identifiable data has been removed. Some participants asked me not to use their full stories, which I have respected. Others brought and discussed music they had made themselves, which unfortunately needed to be omitted to ensure their anonymity. The participants received reimbursement both for their travel and their time. I feel strongly that if consulting 'experts-by-experience', they should be compensated as expert consultants rather than volunteers. This was based on my experience in charity work of some practices that I felt were exploitative of survivor knowledge.

Definitions: 'on-road' and 'gang involvement'

The language around 'gang' is highly contentious both in academic as well as front-line practice. As will be discussed in Chapter 2, using both theoretical and practice examples from Serious Case Reviews, terminology around young people's street lives is highly contextual and has historically been connected with assumptions about race and class, and resulted in stigmatization and criminalization. For the purpose of this study, I chose to use both terms 'on-road' as well as 'gang-involved' in order to communicate the experiences of the target group with whom I met. In the end, the men who took part identified as having been both on-road and gang-involved, but that these terms referred to different aspects of their experiences. The term 'gang' was used by participants to describe experiences of organized criminality and coordinated violence. Classifying what constitutes a gang has been an ongoing task for academics, law enforcers, and governments since the turn of the century. There has been little consensus among experts on what the defining features are of a youth gang (O'Brien et al, 2013). Some gang scholars note that, although there are similarities between diverse gangs, no two are exactly alike (Deuchar, 2018). With this ambiguity in mind, I have cautiously drawn on the definition that the UK government uses as of 2022. According to this definition, a gang is:

A relatively durable, predominantly street-based group of young people who:

(1) see themselves (and are seen by others) as a discernible group,
(2) engage in a range of criminal activity and violence,
(3) identify with or lay claim over territory,
(4) have some form of identifying structural feature, and
(5) are in conflict with other, similar, gangs. (Centre for Social Justice, 2009, p 48)

The term 'on-road' is meaningful as an alternative phrase to gangs that resonate more for young people (Young, 2016). However, *on-road* not only refers to gang membership, but also serves as a broader term that depicts both a physical space and a *way of being in the world* for young people in disadvantaged urban neighbourhoods. It includes reference to the 'dark side' of street life, as 'on-road' was perceived by Gunter to refer to a subculture 'where a small minority of young men engage themselves into a world of badness' (Gunter, 2010, p 94). In a similar vein, Young and Hallsworth (2011, p 3) also discussed the nihilistic elements of life on-road, where survival instincts take over for young people 'worn down by marginalisation and exclusion ... [who] adopted a hood mentality, a fatalistic attitude to life that held "no dreams, no ambition, no drive; no nothing"'. For my sample though it was not all bleak. Being on-road also involved the hustle of urban life: drug dealing, hanging around, getting in trouble, creating and listening to rap music. This phrase resonated with the participants as it lacks the stigmatizing connotations of the gang.

Introduction to the participants

The interviews discussed in this book are the result of meeting with eight men who came from three large cities in England. All of the participants were mature, ranging from their twenties to their fifties. The majority identified as from Black or minoritized communities in the UK (see Table 1.1). All been brought up in gang-associated neighbourhoods. All of them had experienced violence or abuse at home; however, for some (Travis, Shaun) this was more on the periphery of their home lives, whereas for others, as children, they were experiencing DVA and family violence as well as being violently abused themselves (Sam, Eric). Some participants started disengaging with school, enacting violence with peers, whereas some found school an ongoing refuge and two of the participants had been to university (Eric, Jordan).

Those who went on-road all seemed to start getting involved by low-level drug dealing in order to make money, initially to make up for the pocket money they were not getting at home, or in some cases due to a

Table 1.1: Participant demographics

	City A B C	No. of interviews/ length (hour:min:seconds)	Race/ethnicity	Age (range)	Previously imprisoned?	Current employment situation
'Shaun'	A	1 1:44:24	White British	25–35	Yes	Employed
'Jordan'	B	1 00:37:42	Black British	25–35	No	Student
'Sam'	B	1 01:46:54	Black British	25–35	Yes	Employed
'Dylan'	A	2 00:58:20 00:20:21	Dual heritage (White British/Black Caribbean). Self-identifies as 'mixed race'	35–45	Yes	Self-employed
'Eric'	B	1 01:41:36	Black African refugee	25–35	No	Employed
'Dave'	C	2 01:35:17 00:24:07	White British	25–35	No	Unemployed
'Travis'	C	1 00:56:58	Dual heritage (White British/Black Caribbean)	15–25	No	Unemployed
'Lester'	B	1 01:48:53	Black British	45–55	Yes	Self-employed

Note: All of the names referenced in Table 1.1 and throughout the book are pseudonyms to ensure the participants' anonymity.

perceived pressure to provide for their families, in others to keep up with the fashions and activities of their peers. This then gradually escalated to gang involvement as they became more embroiled. They had varying experiences of gangs, from being on the periphery involved in drug dealing and low-level violence, to being at the heart of the organizational aspects, initiating projects, typified in being 'The Man' (see Chapter 6). Some of the participants (Sam, Lester, Dylan, Shaun) had then been incarcerated as a direct result of their involvement, which punctuated their eventual exit from on-road life. For others (Eric, Dave, Travis) there had been significant events within the gangs they had become involved in that instigated them disentangling themselves. These events ranged from bereavement, violent incidences that went 'too far', to escalating mental health problems. All of the participants were now engaged in alternative careers.

2

Invisible Victims of Domestic Abuse, Hypervisible in Gangs

Anecdotal reports from grass-roots service provision indicate that boys who experience domestic violence and abuse (DVA) and later on-road and gang involvement are largely invisible from the perspective of Child Protection and domestic violence/abuse DVA services in the early years, but then come to the attention of youth offending services in adolescence. This is gradually being reinforced through empirical research, which will be discussed in this chapter. As I will outline, boy child survivors of DVA have been sidelined within mainstream feminist discourse, which has resulted in their invisibility in services. This is in contrast with what can be seen in the criminal justice approaches to boys who are labelled as gang-involved, which at times has been used as a broad-brush label to characterize swathes of young people as either engaged in criminality, or 'at risk', sometimes prior to any conviction. It appears then that boys' experience of invisibility in relation to DVA as well as hypervisibility in relation to gangs, are both based on a pre-existing set of stereotypes and assumptions of what the 'ideal' victims and perpetrators look like. The labelling, and the stigma around this, which results in some young people being more readily identified as either 'at risk' or 'a risk', are reinforced by intersectional axis of oppression (Crenshaw, 1991). Race, class, and gender operate in a way which leaves Black urban young people more likely to be 'adultified' and seen as less in need of safeguarding support (Davis and Marsh, 2020), as well as more likely to be stopped, searched, and ultimately labelled and criminalized (Williams, 2015).

The polarization of victims and perpetrators as disparate identities has contributed to the invisibilities of young people. This is partly due to siloed language: services look for victims or perpetrators, or, in the case of gang-involved child survivors, victims or offenders, exploited or exploiters. This was typified in 2021 with the creation of a national Commission for Young Lives, aimed preventing the 'conveyor belt of vulnerable children falling into the hands of gangs and criminals' (Anne Longfield, quoted in Farrell, 2021).

This polarization between victim/perpetrator is problematic and creates an artificial divide between the young people whose experience is likely to be more nuanced. Commonly the predominant focus is on 'risk' over wellbeing; risks posed, risks to others, risk of further harm. Children who experience both are often situated as either children in need (if the threshold allows), or potential offenders, depending which agency becomes involved first, or who assesses and manages the greater risk of harm. As of the early 21st century, both academic and professional focus on DVA and gang work operate within distinct professional sectors or 'planets' (Hester, 2011), each with a differing language and culture, and varying assumptions about the young people involved. Siloed referral and funding routes operate according to resource allocation, which results in many young people falling through the gaps. Gangs outreach workers whom I have spoken to note estimated as much as 90 per cent of their caseload was made up of boys who had experienced DVA in childhood; however, these boys were seldom offered support, partly because the issue was hidden, or by the time anyone found out the perpetrator had left and so the imminent 'risk' had gone. This often means the abuse is left unrecorded, which is why it has been so difficult to find statistics on the actual prevalence of this issue. If the risk is not considered current, then young people are often rendered ineligible for Children's Services support. They then resurface in youth offending services a few years later. Seeing a victim of violence in those involved in criminality is a tricky task. Services are built to focus on the immediate risk of harm, so harm to others is understandably prioritized. There is little nuance in these polarized perspectives and the fact that we are talking about *children* can become lost. The extent to which children can be held accountable for their own violence, in the context of home and community violence, is contentious when they are framed as minors but are situated in a criminal justice system that treats them as fully culpable above the age of ten. By neglecting to provide services for boys at an earlier age we are failing in an attempt to understand their experiences at home – their experiences of childhood adversity become sidelined to the immediate risks presented. There is a danger of us leaning into lazy stereotypes, which are, of course, both gendered and racialized, nowhere more so than the classification of 'gang-involved' youth discussed in this chapter.

The invisibility of boys who experience domestic abuse in childhood

> By the time they reach eighteen years old, almost one quarter of children in the UK will have been exposed to DVA. (Bentley et al, 2016)

Experiencing DVA in childhood is a relatively common occurrence in the UK (and worldwide). A prevalence study in London estimated that one in seven (14.2 per cent) children and young people under the age of 18 will have lived with DVA at some point in their childhood (Radford et al, 2011). In 75 to 90 per cent of incidents of DVA, children are in the same or the next room, hearing the abuse and/or seeing the injuries and aftermath (Hughes, 1992; Abrahams, 1994; McGee, 2000). An estimated 130,000 children in the UK live in households with high-risk DVA; that is, where there is a significant risk of harm or death (Jones, 2016). Research has suggested that even very young children are affected by DVA experience. Hester and Pearson (1998) found instances where children who had experienced DVA when as young as two or three could recount episodes of abuse.

Children who have experienced DVA have been historically overlooked and seen as on the periphery to the abuse. Although the first published study into the negative effects of DVA exposure on children was in 1975 (Levine, 1975), early research focused on observational case studies recording the negative social, emotional, and behavioural impacts of DVA on children. From the turn of the 21st century there has been an increased focus on qualitative research that captures the child's own voice and perspectives, shifting from a deficit lens to a focus on the multi-faceted experiences of children who grow up with DVA (McGee, 2000; Mullender et al, 2002; Hester et al, 2007; Överlien and Hydén, 2009; Callaghan et al, 2015; Katz, 2016) as well as work into the effect on adult survivors of DVA (Hague et al, 2012). With the increase in research into children's lived experiences with DVA, there has been an adjoining paradigm shift. DVA scholarship and practice used to conceptualize children as 'witnesses' or as dealing with 'exposure' to DVA. However, this frames the primary victim as the adults, with the children merely viewing the abuse. This kept the enduring spotlight off them and on to the adults, which had a resulting impact on the provision of resources for children who experience DVA. Överlien and Hydén (2009) championed the shift to looking at 'experience' in order to focus on children's subjectivity and the multidimensional ways that children experience DVA. Callaghan et al (2015, p 5) noted that shifting to *experience* rather than *exposure* serves to disrupt a passive construction of childhood that historically framed children as 'collateral damage' who sit on the periphery of the violent relationship. This discursive shift has ignited a shift in policy, with the UK government having enshrined children's status as direct victims of DVA in law in 2021 (Home Office, 2020a). However, we are yet to see what this means in terms of improvements in practice. There are several key issues related to the purpose and design of child protection provision that means that the provision does not adequately fill the support gaps, despite the dual issues being increasingly recognized by policy. The first is high-risk thresholds for support. In a study of Domestic Homicide Reviews by Sharp-Jeff and Kelly (2016) they analysed the role of child protection and found that in many cases children were not meeting the threshold to be considered a child-in-need upon assessment. The second is the disparate 'planets' (Hester, 2011) in which different services operate, often with disparate languages, professional practice, and priorities, which can result in children falling through support gaps.

Gendered coping strategies have been explored in research. Some studies have found that boys who have been exposed to DVA present more externalizing problems than girls, such as disruptive behaviour and enacting violence (Wolfe et al, 1985, 1988, 2003) whereas other studies disagree (Jaffee et al, 2002; Bogat et al, 2006). Other research has suggested that age of exposure was a greater factor resulting in externalizing behavioural problems. Sternberg et al (2006) found that the detrimental effects of exposure to DVA on externalizing behavioural problems were greater for older children (aged seven to 14) than for their younger peers (aged four to six) (Chan and Yeung, 2009, p 315). However, neither meta-analysis of Wolfe et al (2003) nor Kitzmann et al (2003) showed that age moderated the effects of exposure to DVA (Chan and Yeung, 2009, p 315). It is clear from the research that experience of DVA affects children and young people differently but not always in a negative way. In a meta-analysis of research into the effects on children it was found that 63 per cent of children fared more poorly, across a range of social and emotional factors, than the average child who had not been exposed to DVA (Kitzmann et al, 2003). Notably this means that around 27 per cent of the children exposed to DVA showed similar outcomes to those who had not, presenting a conundrum.

A pervasive gendered social learning theory about the effects of witnessing DVA on children has been the 'cycle of violence' or 'cross-generational transmission of violence' (Butler et al, 2020, p 2). This theory states that violence is passed from one generation to the next through the family and that children who have witnessed DVA will themselves engage in violent relationships, either as victims or perpetrators (Jaffe et al, 1990; Peled et al, 1995; Cummings, 1998). This is often associated with gender dynamics, suggesting that girls will more likely become the victims, with boys becoming perpetrators. Evidence of intergenerational transmission of violence comes from longitudinal and ethnographic research that observes the relationships between childhood influences and later adult behaviour (Jewkes, 2002; Ehrensaft et al, 2003). Witnessing DVA as a child emerges as one of the strongest predictors of later perpetration (Hotaling and Sugarman, 1986; Saunders, 2002). This theory, however, has received criticism, mainly for the fact that it does not account for a large proportion of exposed children who do not follow this pattern (Lapierre, 2008, p 455). It also assumes a sense of violence or victimhood as destiny, which is a limiting prognosis for these children. The theory has been rejected by the majority of front-line agencies in that it does not explain why most children who have been exposed to DVA do not go on to perpetrate abuse, as well as the fact that many DVA perpetrators have not witnessed DVA in childhood (Mullender, 1996; Cunningham et al, 1998; Dutton, 1999).

Although these limitations have put the 'cycle of violence' into question, gendered assumptions have still had an impact on the perceptions of risk that male child survivors present in DVA provision. Feminist activism and scholarship highlighted the gendered nature of DVA, which disproportionately victimizes women. Women started grass-roots safe houses for survivors, which led to the development of refuges for *refugees from the patriarchal family* (Haaken and Yragui, 2003). Women-centric provision was framed as essential, centred upon safety, privacy, and dignity. The history of male exclusion in DVA front-line provision is typified in refuge exclusion criteria. Compared to female children, refuges typically do take in male children older than 12, and in some cases 16. Refuge age limitation policies often operate alongside the general 'no men' policy in many refuges (Baker, 2009). There are a variety of reasons that refuges state to support the exclusion of boys: instilling fear in traumatized residents fleeing male violence; risk of sexual violence in room sharing; potential future perpetration. These justifications have arisen as a response to the gendered nature of male violence, yet fail to give due recognition to boy-child-survivors' status as victims of male violence themselves. However, it is also worth pointing out that poor funding means that a refuge space for a whole family may be one room with multiple bunkbeds inside and the use of communal bathrooms. Refuge support providers are often working in incredibly austere conditions, trying to make the safest decisions with very limited resources. It is important to foreground that, despite my critique of the boundary work of DVA refuges, they have been delivering an essential service: providing fundamental safety for women fleeing violence. They began as services organized among women informally, through networks of houses (Pizzey, 1974). Although they have gradually become publicly funded over the years, they are still under-resourced. Since the austerity programme of the coalition and Conservative governments, one in every six refuges have closed, with many still at risk (Trickett, 2017). Essential infrastructure to support victims, both adults and children, are severely lacking. If a family has a son over the age limit of the refuge, then that child either cannot access the refuge space and would have to present as homeless to the local council, or could go into social services care, or live with their father (often the perpetrator), while the rest of the family enter the refuge (Sacks, 2008).

It is essential to note that families who access refuges are the tip of the iceberg in terms of DVA support. The majority will access community support services, which have been increasingly centred upon the provision of IDVAs (independent domestic violence advocates) who work with 'high-risk' cases. The use of IDVAs to assist survivors to navigate the legal system was initially promoted in Home Office-commissioned research in 2005; the report also emphasizes the necessity for more in-depth emotional support to be provided by a wider network of support workers alongside formal advocacy (Hester and Westmarland, 2005). However, the formalization of the IDVA role has developed alongside the development and roll-out of the Domestic Abuse Stalking and 'Honour'-Based Violence (DASH) risk assessment tool (Richards and Safelives, 2009). Since its widespread implementation by the police from 2009 it has become the customary tool used by DVA services, as well as statutory services, to assess DVA risk. An unintended consequence of the turn to high-risk provision is not only that it has accelerated the underfunding of informal community (non-'professionalized') support services, but also has focused resources on those identified as 'high risk' rather than the unfortunately named 'standard risk'. In reality, short-term advocacy for cases identified as at high risk of homicide/femicide have come to the forefront of localized commissioning, with longer-term or therapeutic support becoming rarer to find. The turn to high risk has also done nothing to improve support for children. In standard IDVA support, the children of survivors are seldom seen in person but are assumed to be made safer by proxy. This model has led to the further invisibility of child survivors, as the funding is increasingly redirected to a system that views children as add-ons rather than direct service users.

The discursive message this sends to boys is concerning and indeed Baker (2009, p 447) notes that existing studies indicate that teenage boys feel labelled as 'potentially violent men' by the operation of age limitation policies in many refuges. Furthermore, they state that these policies in refuges 'send mixed messages to them about their future as men and may exacerbate the anger, stress, mistrust and confusion they already feel after escaping or trying to escape a violent perpetrator' (Baker, 2009, p 442). This sense of distrust is even stronger in the case of Black families, who already face society's wider 'White gaze' on Black bodies, which render Black men physically and sexually dangerous (Phillips, 2020). This exclusionary practice has been documented as being particularly difficult for Black, Minority Ethnic, and Refugee (BAMER) families, as the 'assumption that males are inherently prone to violence is too close to the painful realities of living in a racist society where Black males are viewed as inherently "suspect"' (Haaken and Yragui, 2003, p 64). Black masculinity has 'commonly been pictured as a sexual and social threat in dominant White cultures' (Connell, 2002, p 254). Thus, the implications of excluding boys within BAMER families can bring up multiple issues. Bernard (2016) explored the ways in which interconnected inequalities, compounded by the experience of racism, shapes families' experiences of DVA.

The notion of women being inherently peaceful in opposition to male aggression has also been problematic for Black women. There has been a 'strong desire for innocence in many strands of feminist politics' (Volpp,

2005, p 46). This has led to the lack of acknowledgement of White women's complicity in violence against Black women, 'both directly and indirectly, in the support and maintenance of racism' (Segal, 1990, p 269). Krane and Davies (2002, p 188) noted that, 'as shelter intervention proceeds as if women were unencumbered with dependants, it will fail to acknowledge mothers and their considerations regarding their children'. Individuals' responses to violence and their experience of refuge provision are shaped by a range of factors, which include taking account of children's wishes.

The tension of the assumed victim/perpetrator overlap (both real and perceived) among young men child survivors has been explored by Gadd et al (2015). They conducted a multifaceted study into the experiences of young men who had 'witnessed', perpetrated, or been victimized themselves by DVA. It combined analyses of attitude surveys as well as narrative interviews to give a more in-depth picture of the situation. In their study they found that 13–14 year olds who had experienced DVA at home were 'almost three times more likely to report having perpetrated it (42%) than those who had not witnessed it (15%)' (Gadd et al, 2015, p 113). However, despite this high prevalence, there was also the fact that 58 per cent who had experienced DVA at home had not perpetrated any abuse. These findings 'open up the question of how long one should wait in anticipation of "effects" before one decides that there were none' (Gadd et al, 2015, p 113). This conundrum about the after-effects of DVA experience is one of focus points of Gadd et al's study, which seeks to further the debate – which they argue has been very Black and White, with feminist theorizing 'blurring the distinction between violent men and those who had not perpetrated assaults', resulting in a lack of focus on the factors that make some men violent and not others (Gadd et al, 2015, p 129). They sought to explain 'the differences between men', in particular, 'why most men are not violent most of the time, why some men are never abusive, and why many of those who have been strive not to be again' (Gadd et al, 2015, p 2).

Underlying the critique of sex essentialization there is a fundamental tension, which is that there is undoubtedly disproportionality among DVA perpetrators: the vast majority are male (Hester, 2013). The underlying fear of men which has permeated through the feminist organizing around DVA is in many ways a rational response to gender disproportionality, which is still pertinent to the discussion on single-sex support provision in contemporary debates. There are two questions that need to be considered to get to the heart of the tension. The first is to what extent should boys be conflated with men in terms of risk? Biologically speaking, boys will, through the process of puberty and socialization, become men. But at which point does their identity as child survivors, supported in 'women and children' services, end and their manhood begin? The second tension is that within a patriarchal society gender inequality permeates social and political structures, yet does not provide space for the diversity of men. Most men are not DVA perpetrators who commit violence, but most benefit from the patriarchal dividend. It is striking that it is precisely these boys who are perceived as likely future perpetrators who are then systematically excluded by DVA organizations, which thereby miss a critical opportunity of working with them to prevent them becoming this 'imminent risk'. This rejection, it could be argued, may well actively contribute to these boys learning that their inevitable fate is to become the aggressor, thereby inadvertently contributing to and perpetuating the dynamics that maintain the cycle of violence.

The hypervisibility of young men involved on-road and in gangs

Young men who have been on-road and/or gang-involved have had the opposite problem of being hidden as in the case of DVA victimization. If anything, young men who have been labelled in this way, often intersecting with race and class, have become hypervisible in youth offending and risk management support services. As will be discussed in this section, the gang academic sector has been fraught with tensions around definitional issues, the enhanced criminalization of young people, and the wider moral panic that has long endured about Black youth masculinities.

The labelling of men assumed to be in gangs is a highly racialized phenomena in the UK and has been recognized as such since the 1970s 'mugging' crisis analysed by Hall et al (2013) at the Birmingham Centre for Cultural Studies. Since the riots in England in 2011 the Metropolitan Police have been collecting a vast data set, called the Gangs Matrix, on young people who are perceived as being gang-involved, often despite no evidence or record of offending. Amnesty International (2018) released a report that claimed that the matrix is a highly racialized process which infringes on the individual's human rights, in particular the right to non-discrimination. They noted that it was based on a 'vague and ill-defined concept of "the gang" that has little objective meaning and is applied inconsistently' (Amnesty International, 2018, p 3). Amnesty noted that many of the indicators that the police use to define a gang member reflect more about urban youth culture rather than indication of serious crime. In fact, the vast majority (78 per cent) of people on the Gangs Matrix are Black, which is vastly disproportionate to London's Black population (13 per cent of the whole), as well as those Black people identified by the police as responsible for serious youth violence in London (27 per cent) (Amnesty International, 2018). This disproportionality means that many young people that are on the matrix have not committed a violent offence in the last two years (40 per cent) and some have never committed a serious offence at all (35 per cent). In addition to the Gangs Matrix, there is also a strong racial bias in the police's use of stop and search (Irwin-Rogers, 2018). In 2016, Black people were six times as likely to be stopped and searched and three times as likely to be arrested as White people. These statistics are not only a reflection of the intersections of race and ethnicity, but also of class, as there is a correlation between the young people identified on the Gangs Matrix and the most deprived areas (Williams, 2015). It is notable that, as my research participants were generally mature adults, some will have been on-road before any efforts to challenge police racism, particularly before the Macpherson Report upon Stephen Lawrence's death (Home Office, 1999).

There has been a moral panic around the existence of gangs in the UK since 2007, which was the year in which gang-related homicides peaked in London (Pearce and Pitts, 2011, p 21). In 2007 there were 28 young people under the age of 20 who were killed in 'gang-related murders' in London alone (Pearce and Pitts, 2011, p 15). In a Metropolitan Police survey, they identified 172 youth gangs in London, who were estimated to be responsible for 20 per cent of all the youth crime in the capital (Pearce and Pitts, 2011, p 15). After the London riots in 2011, Teresa May, the then Home Secretary, noted it served to 'bring home to the entire country just how serious a problem gang and youth violence has now become' (HM Government, 2011, p 3). In London, one in five of those arrested in connection with the riots were said to be known gang members (HM Government, 2011). At this time, it was becoming increasingly framed by government and policy makers that gangs were no longer just an American problem. However, subsequent research challenged the link between the London riots and gang activity, putting into question the way in which this 'link' was used to lever a huge amount of public and political interest in gang issues; with the police using media-generated fears of gangs as a 'dragnet', which led many uninvolved young people to criminalization (Cottrell-Boyce, 2013). Newburn et al (2018) asserted that the UK government's focus on criminality, troubled families, and gangs offered a distraction from looking at the socio-economic factors that played a part, as well as the impact of the Conservative government's austerity policy on the lives of urban young people. Gangs are most often found in areas made up of a large amount of social housing, particularly high-rise and high-density social housing. In London in particular there is a perfect correlation between 'gang neighbourhoods' and areas that are among the 20 per cent most deprived regions with high-density social housing (LSCB, 2009). In the majority of existing research, gangs are framed as male-dominated environments; however, there is increasing recognition of the experiences of women on-road too (Young, 2009; Deuchar et al, 2018).

The tendency for affluent societies to denote poor communities as constituting of cultures of crime and threatening disorder is functional, in that it allows the affluent majority to perceive the poor people as deserving of communities defined by criminality (McAuley, 2007). Dominant groups objectify poverty and gain from the inequality it creates, thus tolerate it at best, benefit from it at worst. The gang, through this lens, is a group of young people who choose 'to live and survive together' while being simultaneously stigmatized as a culture of crime by external agencies (McAuley, 2007, p 20). In an ethnographic study in the north of England, McAuley (2007) found perceptions that gangs had destroyed young people's work ethic, thus providing a cultural explanation, as opposed to focusing on the deep-seated structural factors that disadvantaged young people.

The sociological literature tells us that masculinities are produced from the available cultural and societal resources (Phoenix, 2004). Gunter (2017, p 134) focused on the 'ethnic penalty' and on why there are disproportionate numbers of young Black men in gangs and in prison. He emphasized the difficult task of highlighting this issue, while avoiding essentializing the experience of young Black men and reducing their lived experiences to macro-structural constraints. By being framed as predatory victimizers, they are alienated further. They are driven into a self-fulfilling cycle of deprivation that is predicated by their exclusion (Gibbs and Merighi, 1994). Williams and Clarke (2018, p 233) noted that 'gang-branding' results in 'hypercriminalisation' of BAME communities, 'which legitimises intrusive racist policing and surveillance, and justifies the imposition of deliberate harms upon racialised communities'. Young people in poor urban areas are more likely to be labelled in this way and this has a direct implication on issues of 'race'. Black youth styles and subcultures have long been stereotyped as occupying a negative space in popular culture, even while they have been commercially exploited: 'Black youth style and expressive cultures have been positioned as defensive, negative and oppositional, with an emphasis on authenticity and exclusion' (Alexander, 2000, p 19). Thus, it is somewhat unsurprising that, firstly, the activities of young Black boys are perceived as problematic, and, secondly, if a 'gang subculture' does exist then it is perceived as dangerous.

Despite the high levels of uncertainty around what constitutes a gang (introduced in Chapter 1), there has been a focus on two areas of gang activity as defining features due to public concern: crime and youth violence. The extent to which committing crime is an integral part of gang operations or 'membership' is widely debated. Although there appears to be a consensus in research that the existence of gangs contribute significantly to overall level of crime in the areas they populate (Krohn and Thornberry, 2008; Chu et al, 2012; O'Brien et al, 2013). O'Brien et al (2013) noted that, although there are regional and contextual variations between gangs, they have both criminal and antisocial behaviour in common. Densley (2012, p 47) asserted that gangs 'exist on a spectrum from the simple to the complex; thus, the search for one "catch all" statement on gangs may be a fruitless endeavour'. Instead, he notes that gangs should be seen as 'an evolving species of a broader genus, *organised crime*' (Densley, 2012, p 47, emphasis added). There is ongoing debate as to the number of connections gangs have to organized crime and this can partly be put down to perception. For instance, if a gang is dealing in drugs that they are sourcing illegally it is likely they are connected to larger criminal networks. The debate has essentially divided between those who believe gangs are organized entities with clear structures and those who argue that gangs are better understood as informal, loose, and episodic associational groupings of young people (Young, 2016).

Sullivan (2006, p 15) asserted that in some ways focusing on gangs as an object of study is 'a flawed enterprise' because 'the label is too vague and the focus on gangs distracts us from an object of study that is broader and more intrinsically problematic ... youth violence'. Serious youth violence is three times more likely to be committed by gang members than anti-social children who are not gang affiliated (LSCB, 2009, p 1). Indeed, this is the approach that the UK government is now taking, dealing with gangs under the strategy for 'Serious Violence' (SV) (Home Office, 2018). Densley et al (2020) noted that 2018 was a peak year for SV among young people in the UK. It is an issue attracting a lot of money and attention through an increasing advocation of a *public health approach*. However, it is notable that as of 2022 DVA is not included in the definition of SV and that public health approaches to SV are, for the most part, gender-blind and see DVA as a background issue (see Chapter 9 for further discussion on this).

Cross-cutting risk assessments identifying domestic abuse and gang involvement

> The Children's Commissioner for England found that children who were in gangs were 37% more likely to have experienced childhood domestic violence/abuse than other children. (Children's Commissioner, 2019, p 7)

There have been links made between DVA and gang involvement in academic and policy work. Both issues are considered to be safeguarding concerns. Children who experience DVA are considered, under statutory guidelines, to suffer emotional and psychological maltreatment, related to Section 31 of the Children Act 1989: impairment suffered from seeing or hearing the ill treatment of another. The child protection sector also holds safeguarding responsibility for minors who are involved in serious youth violence and gangs. Interestingly, the policy on safeguarding children and young people who may be affected by gang activity explicitly acknowledges that in this context 'children who harm others are both victims and perpetrators' (Department for Education and Home Office, 2010, p 6). In this document a reference is made to cycle of violence theories, as it outlines that 'being exposed to violence, either as a witness or victim, increases a child's propensity to violence later in life' (Department for Education and Home Office, 2010, p 13).

In the early 21st century there is an academic disconnect between the two spheres of DVA research and gang research. There has been an increasing body of work that is starting to look at these two factors, although it is predominantly within policy reports and social care fields rather than in academic research, but this is adding to the body of work which indicates a problematic connection. This link was made in the policy report, *Dying to Belong: An In-Depth Review of Street Gangs in Britain* by the Centre for Social Justice (2009). They used the statistical data that links DVA and criminality and then bolstered it with anecdotal reports from both offenders and practitioners who have experience with gangs. For instance, they interviewed Superintendent John Sutherland, who noted that he felt there was a high prevalence of DVA in the backgrounds of gang-involved young people. He stated that 'Much has been done [about domestic violence], but we still have an awful long way to go, and a huge proportion of our most troubled young people will have been victims or witnesses of abuse' (Centre for Social Justice, 2009, p 96). Another young offender was reported to state that 'Once you get used to living in that environment, of expecting violence, you recreate it when it's not there – because that's what you're used to' (Centre for Social Justice, 2009, p 96). This report frames the experience of DVA, as well as single-parent families (in particular 'fatherlessness') due to what is termed the 'breakdown of the family unit', as push factors for gang involvement. It posits that men then seek alternative father figures in the gang. It conflates the experience of DVA at home, as well as 'Poor parenting, particularly a lack of parental supervision', as factors that cause later gang involvement (Centre for Social Justice, 2009, p 27). It is important to consider, however, that the Centre for Social Justice is a centre-right-leaning political think-tank, founded by members of the Conservative Party. Thus, the overall denigration of single-parent families and the conflation of DVA with the relative term 'family dysfunction' raise warning signals about the way that this report is classifying the issues at hand. In the Home Office's own reports on gang issues in the UK, there is also mention of DVA as a risk factor. In the Home Office (2011) report *Ending Gang and Youth Violence*, it provides explicit examples outlining the 'lifecycle of a gang member', which places DVA as a core experience (HM Government, 2011, p 17). In a second example it traces the imagined life of 'Boy X', who experienced DVA at home (HM Government, 2011, p 21). These example cases were used to promote the increased funding of DVA services as early intervention against later gang involvement in the document.

Since 2019, there has been a flurry of reports which have emphasized that many young people in the youth justice system have experienced childhood

DVA. In 2019, Croydon Children's Services did a deep dive into 'vulnerable adolescent' (VA) cases with a focus on the relationship between childhood adversity and those who were identified as involved with gangs (Spencer et al, 2019). They looked at 60 cases that were part of a cohort identified as facing multiple adversity, 42 per cent of whom had experienced domestic violence in childhood: '38% (23/60) of children came to the notice of police due to reports of domestic abuse (primarily from aged 1 year to 12 years old – 13 were boys and 10 girls)' (Spencer et al, 2019, p 14). 'Domestic abuse or child to parent abuse, absent fathers or absence of both parents, compounded by the implications of the poor mental health of the remaining parent undoubtedly had a significant impact on the child's behaviour and relationship with figures of authority' (Spencer et al, 2019, p 47). In 2021, the *Punishing Abuse* report looked at the histories of 80 young people who were involved in the criminal justice system in the West Midlands. It found that 'in nearly a half of cases (46% of 80) the child witnessed domestic violence and this was suspected in nearly a third (29%) of cases; over three-quarters (79%) were confirmed as experiencing family violence or child abuse' (Chard, 2021, p 17). 'For nearly a half of these children (37 of 80 or 46%) the child was known to have been exposed to domestic violence, this was suspected for a further twenty-three (29%) children' (Chard, 2021, p 24). The *Vulnerability and Violence* report focused on the drivers for involvement in SV. It concluded there was a significant thread of childhood trauma; however, 'support often focuses on managing immediate risks rather than building trust over the longer term' (Crest Advisory, 2021, p 5).

Childhood DVA is often cited as a risk factor or 'adverse childhood experience' (ACE) in relation to later gang involvement. The Department of Education's risk factor diagram lists 56 potential risk factors that can lead to gang involvement (Department for Education and Home Office, 2010, p 19). Both 'conflict and violence in the home' and 'witness or victim of domestic violence' are deemed risk factors but are swamped by a myriad of other issues. Gang involvement has been said to result from an amalgamation of factors which constitute 'multiple marginalities' (Young et al, 2013, p 26). The newest iteration of the risk factor paradigm is in the ACE's approach. It originated in the CDC-Kaiser ACE study, which took place in the US in the late 1990s. The premise of the ACE approach is that it counts the types of adversity that a child experiences in childhood rather than the frequency. Scores range from 0–10, which refer not to the number of incidences, but rather the different types. All types of adversity are weighted equally in the score system (WHO, 2018). The focus is on the cumulative effect. People who have experienced in excess of four ACEs are at a heightened risk of 'chronic disease such as cancer, heart disease and diabetes as well as mental illness and health risk behaviours' (Boullier and Blair, 2018, p 132). McGavock and Spratt (2017) came to the conclusion that those who report

DVA are most likely to have an ACE score of at least four, which has been linked to an increased risk of spending a night in custody or in prison, as well as being involved in violence (Bellis et al, 2014). Thus, the presence of DVA itself on an ACE score can be seen as a proxy indicator for a higher ACE score overall.

There is a great risk when adopting a checklist-style approach in that it tends to pathologize the very people it seeks to help. There is an air of adversity-as-destiny that is inherent with a checklist that seeks to generalize complex human contexts based on simplistic cumulative score. The reductionist way in which the approach can be applied risks 'over-simplistic communication of risk/causality, determinism and stigma' (Lacey and Minnis, 2020, p 1). It does not account for all those with high scores who do not experience negative effects, nor offer information on the nuances of how people recover. A further concern about the use of ACE scores is that, by viewing adversities as cumulative factors, it fails to account for differences between them, as well as wider environmental factors or internal factors, such as resilience (McLaughlin and Sheridan, 2016). Children experience and construct their understanding of adversity in different ways, which may not be reflected in adversity's weighting on the ACE checklist. It also focuses on the experiences of the nuclear family while leaving wider structural inequalities unexamined. It is vital to consider the theoretical underpinnings and social history of DVA to understand how it is situated within a context of wider gender inequality. When looking at DVA as a specific form of gender-based violence, seeing childhood DVA as a risk factor outside of an understanding of gender inequality misses its fundamental dynamics.

Victim and perpetrator tension

Central to the tension among boys who both experience DVA as well as perpetrate violence in the on-road and gang context is the notion of the ideal victim. Work within the DVA practice community is predominantly approached from feminist activist perspectives and, in this context, the children who live with DVA (particularly girls) are traditionally considered as victims or 'survivors'. Conversely, work with on-road and/or gang-involved young people is located within a criminal justice risk management perspective, which places young people in the position of criminals, offenders, or 'at risk'. The conceptualization of young people, which is expressed through language, is significant in the construction of the victims and perpetrators in these cases. An issue for front-line policy work on DVA and gangs is that the external categorization of young people promotes a one-dimensional view of them and their behaviours. As Yates (2010, p 14) usefully noted, 'the "young offender" could just as readily be conceptualised as the "child in need" if child welfare assessments and provisions of the Children's Act

1989 were applied'. This is particularly important since many gang-involved individuals are children, who, if positioned as children, would traditionally be seen as vulnerable and in need of wider societal safeguarding (Motzkau, 2020). In gang discourse this rhetoric is often absent when referring to the problematic behaviours of the young people involved, as here they are positioned as offenders rather than children. As noted by Case (2021, p 2), '"Youth offending" is a pejorative label resulting from modernising processes of categorisation and "othering" of populations based on their assessed levels of risk of certain behaviours and the need to control, manage and punish these populations in order to protect the public.'

For the Norwegian criminologist Nils Christie, an example of the ideal victim is a little old lady who, on her way home from caring for her sick sister, is hit on the head by a large man who robs her to buy alcohol or drugs. Christie (1986) focused on the five aspects of the 'ideal' victim: (1) weak, (2) respectable, (3) blameless, and (4) attacked by a big, bad, (5) stranger. Schwöbel-Patel (2018) noted that the concept of the ideal victim amounts to a feminized, infantilized, and racialized stereotype of victimhood. The perceived racialized nature of gangs also fits into this reluctance to be constructed as vulnerable: young Black men are more likely to be at the centre of moral panics around youth-in-crisis than framed as victims. To add complexity to this discussion, what it means to be a 'survivor' is constructed differently between the DVA and gang sectors and, I suspect, is gendered. An ex-gang member is constructed as enacting a hypermasculine role, while to be a DVA survivor could be seen in contrast as a hyperfeminized role. Both the strengths and weaknesses of these gendered positions almost caricature the typical male/female stereotype – females as passive victims, helpless, weak, in contrast to a male in a gang: powerful, violent, alpha. This discussion highlights the limited empirical utility of mutually exclusive categories of perpetrator and victim, when the evidence points so consistently to young people being both.

The missing dimension in Christie's outline of the 'ideal victim' is race. Victimhood is gendered, classed, *and* racialized, which results in young Black men in the UK being again most marginalized from this discourse. Stereotypes of Black masculinity result not only in mixed-race and Black young men being less constructed as victims, but it also works in the opposite way in that they are more likely to be (sometimes wrongly) labelled as gang-involved and thus criminalized. Claire Alexander noted that the equation of Black masculine identities being defined and associated mainly with race has resulted in 'inscribing a hyper-visibility of Black masculinity, which disguises a more profound invisibility' (Alexander, 2000, p 17). In this way, Black masculinities are always positioned as subordinated to hegemonic ideals, which are implicitly 'White'. When viewed through this lens, the aspirational notion of hegemonic masculinity becomes another way to denigrate those who are not eligible for the contest. Thus, violence and criminality (protest masculinity) become alternatives for these men to pursue in lieu of the hegemonic masculinity. In the hierarchy, where working-class and poor males are seen as at the bottom, Black working-class boys occupy an even lower space than their White counterparts. The nature of racialization in child protection has been explored by Davis and Marsh (2020), who noted that Black young people are subject to a process of 'adultification'. In this process Black young people are assumed to be less vulnerable by professionals and are thus offered less safeguarding support. It also has an impact on the extent to which Black young people are constructed as primarily a risk to others, rather than at risk themselves.

We need to sit with the tension that young people who are gang-involved are often victims and perpetrators of violence. One of the issues that Gadd et al (2015, p 118) highlighted in their exploration of young men who had experienced DVA at home was that caution should be taken between the polarized concepts of children, either as '"done-to" victims' or 'brave survivors'. This was explored through the in-depth examination of the men's narratives, which showed how close many men are to occupying both roles, almost simultaneously. Gadd et al (2015, p 126) urge others to 'avoid constructing children's responses to exposure to domestic violence too narrowly, either as negative psychological effects or as positive acts of resilience with little ambiguity in-between'. They highlight how pertinent this is with the intersecting issue of gender. As noted in the social learning theory research, there has been a tendency to essentialize the gendered experience of boys who have experienced DVA, and assume that they will merely copy the male role model and enact DVA.

Change is on the horizon though. There has been a movement towards 'contextual safeguarding', which is an approach created by Carlene Firmin (2020) and team. It aims to shift the focus onto the contexts in which abuse occurs rather than simply taking an individualized approach. This focus on community context and impact on young people's experiences of safeguarding results in an understanding of adversity and harm that is wider than the individual experience. Many areas now have 'multi-agency safeguarding hubs' (MASH), which aim to co-locate services in order to provide a multidimensional safeguarding service. However, the contextual safeguarding academic team have raised a warning: 'we caution against Contextual Safeguarding becoming the next "Trojan horse" of child protection, facilitating the expansion and intrusion of surveillance into the lives of children and families' (Wroe and Lloyd, 2020, p 14). Multi-agency safeguarding approaches must navigate the politics of labelling and stigma, and the complexities of the role of the criminal justice system in safeguarding young people who may also be offending themselves.

Aligning with increased awareness of the intersection of exploitation is a more nuanced understanding of the way in which victims of exploitation then go on to exploit others. This is a significant shift from the reductive discourse that *gangs exploit young people* (with a very opaque description of what the gang means or who it consists of), to instead consider that organized crime groups can be akin to pyramid schemes of exploitation. To convey this intersection of power and vulnerability the police have coined the term 'alpha victim' to refer to exploited people who then exploit others (MSPTU, 2018). Originally this was developed to conceptualize victims of modern slavery. However, with increased focus on 'county lines' that span across young peoples' lives on-road, in gangs, or in serious organized crime (depending which level of the supply chain you are looking at), it has enabled a different focus on the young people involved. It is clear that taking a pure criminalization approach to county lines is inadequate, as so many young people are themselves incredibly vulnerable due to their wider circumstances. As will be described later in the book in the narratives of the men I spoke to, when boys live with a range of adversity, the push and pull factors that result in them going on-road are complex. Grooming is a complex process, and, as will become clear, several of the participants did not identify themselves as having been groomed or exploited. However, as highlighted in this chapter, this could be also because there is such a lack of societal space for criminalized boys to identify in this way.

3

Music as Method

'OK, so both of these songs, literally word for word, just everything, that I lived, 100 per cent.' (Sam)

Prior to the interview, I asked the participants to 'Bring three music tracks that help you tell part of your life story.' They knew the subject of the study was the experience of both DVA and gang involvement, so I did not need to emphasize which parts of their stories I was particularly interested in; however, I was open to hear whatever they wanted to share. Journalistically, this approach has been made famous through the BBC Radio 4 programme *Desert Island Discs*, where celebrities bring seven tracks to help discuss their life stories. We exist in a world where celebrities are asked about their lives and interests, but 'ordinary' people less so. Music used as a social research tool, alongside other expressive elicitation techniques, has been emerging in research for some time (DeNora, 1999; Keightley and Pickering, 2006). The term 'music elicitation', as a distinct method, was coined by Allett (2010) in a study about heavy metal fandom. In 2018, music elicitation has been used in group interview situations (dos Santos and Wagner, 2018).

The unusual research question piqued Eric's interest.

'It's heavy going back over it, back to the past?' (Jade)

'Yeah it is, it is, but those songs were the ones that made me, nobody ever asked me this question before, it got me excited in a sense like ooh yeah, I actually had to think about this.' (Eric)

As the fieldwork was being completed it became clear there were many other benefits to this approach, including increased participation and co-production of the interview as well as garnering deeper and multidimensional data, including music videos and lyrics. This approach was successful in creating a bridge between the worlds of the researcher and participant in a way that may not have otherwise been possible. It encouraged the participants to consider what they wanted to share, articulate it more fully through the use of lyrics, or music videos, or use music to evoke and complement a memory. Hip-hop and reggae were the dominant genres brought, and these will be peppered throughout this chapter as well as the whole book. Examples of these include the use of the track by the hip-hop artist OMI, called 'My Old Lady', chosen by Dylan, who used it to open up a heartfelt discussion about his love for his mother, highlighted by the lyric, 'she mothered and fathered me'. Several participants used music videos to literally illustrate elements of their lives, 'the music, the visuals [music video], is literally my life to a T', said Sam.

The movement towards more creative research methods to complement traditional interviews came from concerns that straightforward interviews can produce 'rational, sanitized, and self-conscious responses within the confines of language which, in and of itself, filters and limits expression of meaning' (Porr et al, 2011, p 31). Using creative methods in interviews, as forms of arts-based enquiry, aims to enable participants to 'express meaning embedded in the historical, cultural, and biographical contexts of their lives' (Porr et al, 2011, p 31). Music as an elicitation tool is powerful when used with a topic where it has played a role in the coping and recovery. In the case of DVA, listening to music is a tool that some children and young people who live with DVA use as a coping strategy, both as a 'form of self-expression, and self-soothing' (Callaghan et al, 2017, p 339). It offers a mechanism for comfort and enables young people to *get lost in the music*, which helps them stop thinking about their difficulties. It is worth considering that, if music has been used by a child as a coping mechanism to deal with their home life, then using it as an elicitation tool could be a very powerful way to enable the participant to locate their memories. DeNora (1999, p 31) noted that music is used by people as a 'device for on-going identity work and for spinning a biographical thread of self-remembrance'.

Music is an ideal lens through which to explore cathexis, in part because the tensions of complex and contradictory emotional relationships are so often explored and expressed through 'popular' music. It allows for sensitive topics to be shared and explored in accessible and lateral ways. The men selected, without prompting, hip-hop tracks produced by relatively mainstream artists that dealt with sexual violence and abuse. The process of listening to the music provided a connection between the lead author and participants – they were able to share and explore their respective stories in their own language and style. The communicative, narrative, and community component of the music of the Black Atlantic, whether it is blues or jazz, soul or funk, reggae or rap, has become deeply embedded in UK youth cultures (Gilroy, 1993, 2011). There is great emotional affect in music. Both Gilroy (2011) and Back (2015) have explored the way that music can both evoke and imply a form of 'planetary humanism' by communicating universal experiences of human feelings, from anguish to ecstasy, from love to hate, and everything in-between and beyond that may not be fully or adequately expressible in words alone. Back (2015) focused on B.B. King's prison performances and the ways in which these reached into the souls of incarcerated men, giving hope and catharsis in troubled times. bell hooks has written about the way in which this type of emotional outlet was found historically in blues music. She notes how the blues articulate pain, hopelessness, and lamentation, and opened up a space for honesty and vulnerability. hooks contrasted this with rap music, which instead conveyed the 'aggressive presentation of invulnerability … the false self' (hooks, 2003, p 93). Looking to the way in which the men used music in this study, I suggest that rap (and its contemporary and local variants) offers an analogous expressive vehicle for masculine vulnerabilities, conflicts, tensions, and confusions. I suggest that the exterior *aggressive invulnerability* projected in (some) rap music and its 'gangsta' stylings draws from more complex wells of inspiration than the two-dimensional dismissal allowed for by a dominant White culture. The transnational commercial culture that surrounds hip-hop fosters such flattened images that reflect historic White fears of Black masculinity, repackaged for consumption and profit (Neal, 2013). Other music genres of Black origin, notably trip-hop and R&B music, have developed in such a way as to provide a form of 'quiet', an expression of interior lives amid wider structural and racial inequalities (Allen and Randolph, 2020). This sonic, auditory space may be more vital in contexts where there is a lack of other safe spaces or supportive friendships for refuge from wider experiences of marginalization. In such contexts, people retreat into their interior selves to find inner refuge: 'African American inner selves are places that they fully control and that can serve as bulwarks from the ravages of racism, sexism, poverty, and other social storms' (Allen and Randolph, 2020, p 57). Music became a vibrant element in this study due to the emotional affect it produced.

Music as a narrative tool

Music elicitation, when combined with an unstructured interview space, gave greater control to the participant to determine the pace, length, and structure of the sessions. It enabled the participant to offer up different information than they would have in a words-only interview, as some complex concepts or feelings were communicated through the music or via video format. By offering an alternative way for the participants to convey or illustrate their experiences they could instead bring the music track and say 'that was what happened to me'. The participants all curated the way music featured in the interviews in different ways. One way this was done was to choose three songs to represent childhood years, then the teenage years or the years on-road, and then a song that represented their lives at the time of the interview. By choosing songs in this way some participants set a chronological structure to the interview, although they didn't necessarily start with the younger years first. The second way that songs were chosen to offer structure was to use them to highlight three distinct key messages that the participant wanted to share. Dylan chose Bob Marley, 'One Love', and then straight after it played said:

'The one love. That's the way I feel right about now.' (Dylan)

This opened up the opportunity for him to talk about the youth outreach work he is currently doing. When he had said what he wanted to in this section, he signified this by concluding, 'So that's why I chose that one love song', which then prompted me to put on his next song. He used the music as a narrative break, to chapter his story, and to signify a change of topic aligning with his next track choice.

The choice of music as an elicitation tool was motivated by a desire to enable participants to express their own meanings, while using music to embed their stories in the cultural contexts of their lives (Porr et al, 2011). As dos Santos and Wagner (2018) found in their use of music elicitation, it put participants at ease and acted as a springboard for discussion. Keightley and Pickering (2006, p 153) noted how popular music can connect a person in a very direct way to their own past, finding that music can 'recreate for us the texture of a specific experience [which is then] … felt in a quality that we never quite put into words'. In this way music becomes an aid to memory. Music is particularly emotive when used in this way, as it captures both a personal memory and a wider sense of popular culture and trends of the past. Music is often a product of its time, therefore it becomes an anchor to the time in which it was produced and can help memory recall (Laughey, 2006). This was highlighted in the interview by Eric, who noted:

'I've stayed away from listening to this song because … I feel sad, I hear that song and there's just so much, it's like I actually feel like crying that's the weird thing … it takes you to a different place.' (Eric)

This passage clearly shows that, for Eric, the music brought back varied emotions about his past and took him back to memories. This point is illustrated by him noting he has avoided listening to certain music tracks in his own life due to this.

Music as an anchor to memories

In music elicitation interviews it became clear early on that music functioned as an anchor to past memories. This is something that is part of the human condition; music can bring back visceral memories of the past, both good and bad experiences. As noted earlier, when music has been used as a self-soothing or tool of comfort, it can provide an even more poignant connection, without the use of invasive interview questions.

In this way it provides participants with a 'scaffolding for self-constitution' (DeNora, 1999, p 31). So, through bringing in music to the interview I asked the participant to expose some of their scaffolding and locate and express different parts of their identity through their music choices.

One of the reasons that music was such a powerful elicitation tool is that it helped the participants locate their past memories, as discussed. It became clear that for many the music had provided a supportive function in the past, as a supportive voice, providing inspiration, and making them feel less alone. In this way music was, for many, a fundamental coping mechanism.

DMX (2002)
'I Miss You'

This track is an ode to DMX's late grandmother. The lyrics focus on grief and bereavement, as well as missing the reassuring voice of his grandmother.

This track was selected by Eric as a way to talk about his grief around the death of his mother in his childhood. With this song – an ode to the rapper's late grandmother – Eric would listen to the lyrics and imagine his late mother saying the words to him. In this way the function of the music was to help articulate his memories of his mother. It also conveyed an empathic and supportive voice from a distance and from within, laden with the personal affect the music carried and aroused:

> 'When my mum died we never really mourned her, and then when we grew up we grew up with a step mum who was getting beaten up every day … So literally as sad as it may sound I play that to hear it's gonna be OK, you listen to it imagining someone is saying it to you, someone who cares for you.' (Eric)

Eric constructed his stepmum's beating and her lack of love in a matter-of-fact way, as inevitable, displaying a sad and pragmatic sense of what happened. Framing it using the passive construction 'who was beaten up every day' serves to erase the perpetrator from the description, does not name him, and implies his stepmum was suffering from an inevitable mishap. Crucially what the music provided was the reassurance of a mother. Dylan also used the song lyrics as a substitute for a reassuring voice. He chose a song that his mother used to play to him and her advice was woven into the lyrics. He noted that he chose Bob Marley's 'Three Little Birds', because:

> 'As a kid growing up my mum used to always play it and she always used to say we shouldn't be worrying about things.' (Dylan)

The main chorus line in the song is 'Don't worry about a thing, 'Cause every little thing gonna be alright.' So in a similar way to the others, playing the music served as a mantra, repeating, with affect, the advice of his mother who had passed away and was no longer there to give it. This example also shows how the participants were using the music elicitation as a tool, which enabled them to get to the heart of a story that may not have surfaced in a traditional interview setting. These excerpts not only reveal the way in which music was used as a coping strategy in the past by the participants, but also that music was a vehicle through which they were able to express different aspects of their former lives, which indicated a presence of vulnerable masculinity, as distinct from the foregrounded subordinate masculinity constructed in relation to the perpetrator or the emergent protest masculinity as expressed in relation to on-road activity or school. The way they conveyed their music choices during the interview indicated music helped them express and reflect on their emotions from childhood.

Musicians as masculine role models

> DMX conveyed 'lyrical flow, menacing swagger, wicked sense of humour and aching vulnerability' ... [DMX]'s public persona reflected the kaleidoscopic nature of Black masculinity in the late 1990s ... [He] raged against stereotypes of Black criminality even as he invoked, then subverted, the tropes of thug, gangsta and hoodlum into a showcase for Black artistry. (Joseph, 2021)

It became apparent in the interviews that music consumption was often about the artist as much as the art. The symbolic selves of musicians were used as malleable role models. As noted in the passage just quoted, sometimes in rap this means challenging as well as reinforcing masculinity stereotypes, sometimes simultaneously. The participants in this study were keen to share the ways in which certain music role models created a space whereby they were able to draw on the wider cultural capital of both hegemonic and protest masculinities as they rapped about (and sometimes were involved in) life on-road. However, as musicians and artists they were also able to be role models of artistic sensitivity, sharing vulnerable feelings through their music. This was shown in the tracks that the participants brought to the interview space that varied from those which talked positively about protest masculinity and gang involvement: by far the majority of songs were those which revealed emotions, insecurities, and tales of adversity.

Several participants referred to the role models within the music that they selected for the research interviews. A central reason cited was that rappers (in particular DMX and 2Pac) offered the participants an alternative model of masculinity. Eric noted that they showed him that men could be open with their emotions. There were two DMX songs and two 2Pac songs chosen during the fieldwork. They offered a dual masculinity, one where men had street capital but were also able to articulate their emotions and show a sensitive side:

> 'I think for me coz it's always been about DMX and 2Pac, for me they did it for me and they're like one of the two rappers were these hard guys but they're very very soft and very open about their emotions.' (Eric)

The rappers had street credibility as well as pursuing creative outlets. One participant explained how 2Pac's music played a big role in his youth, while 2Pac himself was a role model that he looked up to, which gave him the confidence to pursue education as well as manage the street life at that time. His explanation of why he chose the song really highlights the use of music as a support and coping mechanism, as he noted that listening to 2Pac allowed him 'to go to school instead of crying'. He noted that 2Pac 'played a big role in my life':

> 'When you are, it's like, I don't want to say depressed, but when you are down and when you can't tell no one, his music was always so good, like an escapism when this person feels you as well, especially with someone who was at some points living such a hard life … He made me realize I could be both, I could be out here doing whatever and still be educated, I can go and read a book, he allowed me to go and spend time in a library actually, let me go and find a book to read, let me go find this and this, let me educate myself, and 2Pac, changes was definitely the first song to me that kind of, introduced me to who he is … he played a big role in my life … sometimes I'd feel so alone … [when I listened to 2Pac] I would wake up in the morning and go to school instead of crying … it was so therapeutic.' (Eric)

The element of permission is evocative in this passage. 2Pac offered a model of performing a type of protest masculinity, living on the margins and gang-involved yet highly successful, while also offering a sense of permission for the artistic and sensitive outlets that Eric so deeply wanted to express. Jordan also felt an affiliation with 2Pac as a role model. Interestingly, the two participants who mentioned 2Pac were the two who, despite time in a gang-involved/on-road life, had also managed to gain university degrees. 2Pac offered that positive role model and was perceived by these two men as offering a model way of being that balanced street life and an educated and/or artistic life:

> '2Pac has been very big inspiration not only on a musical term, but as a person, as a survivor, as a Black man, as a man on the streets and

the roads, and as a role model, just for what he stood for, the content of his lyrics and his perspective and vision and how real he kept it and the same struggles that I believe I have lived to face.' (Jordan)

Here Jordan is explicitly referring to the multifaceted dimensions of 2Pac as a role model who inspired him. 2Pac is a complex public figure because in some senses he performed protest masculinity through emulating 'the mob image of power, toughness, ruthlessness, elite, ruggedly classy, wealthy, and womanizing ways' (Iwamoto, 2003, p 46). Iwamoto noted that he presented an idealized model of on-road protest masculinity, due to the lack of male role models in his own life. This idealized version was characterized by 'exaggerated toughness and physical strength that equated to respect and power – all characteristics of what he considered as defining a real man' (Iwamoto, 2003, p 46). Iwamoto (2003, p 45) noted that this performance of 'hyper-masculinity' is attractive to young Black men, who adopt these behaviours 'to combat the degrading effects of racism on their self-esteem'. In this discussion Iwamoto analysed the lack of role model options for 2Pac to choose from, and how, in turn, he himself became a role model for the men to whom I spoke. 2Pac also conveyed positive messages about being Black in his music. 2Pac felt a sense of 'pride, empathy and appreciation for Black culture' (Iwamoto, 2003, p 48). 2Pac was not only about promoting gang stereotypes, however. Iwamoto noted that his music often took an empowering stance for young Black men as well as for women. His music often portrayed 'narrations of the struggles and intense hardships people in poverty face on a daily basis' (Iwamoto, 2003, p 46). Similar themes can be found in the music of grime artists such as Stormzy, who has talked about wanting to be a positive role model, with his music presenting the hardships of life on-road, but also invests in the #Merky Foundation to fund university scholarships for Black students (University of Cambridge, 2021).

Grass-roots music creation

Localized music creation has long been a form of youth self-expression. Various forms of hip-hop related genres have existed and been consumed by urban youth. The contemporary localized iteration in the UK has been the emergence of grime and drill music, which was foregrounded by two of the participants as being an important part of their subculture. Joy White (2020, p 41) explored the way that grime music is linked to music of the Black diaspora, and has developed as 'a sonic representation of the spaces their creators occupy'. Central to the flourishing of the grime music scene is the way in which music can be created, recorded, and shared without the need for intermediaries such as record labels and management structures.

White (2020, p 42) noted, 'In a socio-economic landscape that is beset by racism and inequality, this emancipatory aspect cannot be ignored.' Perhaps unsurprisingly, given the complex context of marginalization discussed in Chapter 2, the connection between grime music, violence, and criminality has come more to the fore in the public discourse. Andell (2019) pointed out that the performance aspect of grime music can be on a continuum from positive expressions of creativity to negative portrayals of gang life. The broad range of outputs can make it difficult to extrapolate the real from the performative. Some scholars point to the ways in which music is used as a communication tool by gangs, as a vehicle to publicly convey their culture and identity (Lozon and Bensimon, 2017). Rap music that explores the reality of urban life on-road can end up in discursive loops, whereby 'everyday life recreates itself in its own image' (Ferrell, 2008, p 130). As gang-involved young people use social media platforms to showcase their lives and interests, this imagery loops back into their own lived lives (Pinkey and Robinson-Edwards, 2018). This apparent crossover has been emphasized in the inclusion of music videos in criminal courts, as evidence of wrongdoing. Critical scholars (Williams, 2015; Fatsis, 2019) also note that the target of specific forms of Black urban subculture is also part of a wider criminalization of certain groups. In this context, the 'gang' label can serve as a folk devil to target young people who are just trying to express themselves through music and get by.

Two of the participants in my study discussed their own involvement in the grime scene, Travis and Shaun. Shaun was an established artist, having produced and released several tracks. Shaun brought his own music to the interview and talked me through his own lyrics (which unfortunately can't be shared due to confidentiality). Both he and Travis emphasized the importance of music and lyric writing/performing as powerful forms of expression.

> 'My music just from the past, if someone tells me to speak about something I say listen to my music ... listen to my music if you want me to open up. Opening up to someone's face is very different, like I express myself through my music.' (Shaun)

Shaun uses his own music to tell his story so that it can explain his perspective without the need for constant disclosure. Interestingly, the same approach was used by the artist DMX when he had his day in court. In a music track ('Slippin''), which also features in this book as a track chosen by Sam, DMX shares his young life story, revealing hardship and adversity. When DMX was in court in 2018 for tax fraud he actually played his own track in court in order to convey the difficulties he had faced in childhood and to foreground the impact that this had on his life and subsequent criminality (BBC News, 2018).

Table 3.1: Participants' interview track lists

Participant	Music Track 1 + narrative theme	Music Track 2 + narrative theme	Music Track 3 + narrative theme
'Dylan'	**Current day** Inspiration, positivity Bob Marley and the Wailers, 'One Love' (1977b)	**Adolescence** Gang involvement Bob Marley and the Wailers, 'Three Little Birds' (1980)	**Childhood** DVA OMI, 'My Old Lady' (2013)
'Sam'	**Conveys entire life story** DMX, 'Slippin'' (1998)	**Conveys entire life story** Akon, 'Ghetto' (2004)	**Realities of gang life** Cormega, 'The Saga (The Remix)' (2007)
'Eric'	**Childhood** Grief over death of mother DMX, 'I Miss You' (2002)	**Adolescence** Gang involvement 2Pac, 'Changes' (1998)	**Current day** Mainstream life R. Kelly, 'The World's Greatest' (2002)
'Lester'	**Society inequality, racism** Bob Marley and the Wailers, 'Natural Mystic' (1977a)	**Power, politics** Leroy Smart, 'Ballistic Affair' (1976)	**Concerns for youths in gangs** Popcaan, 'Unruly Prayer' (2013)
'Jordan'	**Childhood** Young Dolph, '100 Shots' (2017)	**Adolescence** Gang involvement Westside Gunn ft Tiona D, 'Never Coming Homme' (2014)	**Current day** Inspiration, positivity 2Pac ft Danny Boy, 'I Ain't Mad At Cha' (1996)

Table 3.1: Participants' interview track lists (continued)

Participant	Music Track 1 + narrative theme	Music Track 2 + narrative theme	Music Track 3 + narrative theme
	Childhood/adolescence	**Adolescence**	**Current day**
'Shaun'		Gang involvement	Recovery
	Participant F: Music titles not shared to protect anonymity		
	Knife crime	**Suicide**	**Child sexual abuse**
'Dave'	Devlin, 'Mother's Son' (2013) Also discussed Dave, 'Lesley' (2019)	Ludacris ft Mary J. Blige, 'Runaway Love' (2007)	Logic ft Alessia Cara and Khalid, '1-800-273-8255' (2017)
	DVA and child abuse	**Knife crime**	**DVA**
'Travis'	Coleen McMahon, 'Beautiful Boy' (2012)	Depzman, 'Reality' (2013)	Joyner Lucas, 'I'm Sorry' (2016)

Travis noted, 'it's like poetry essentially'. Shaun was actively involved in writing and performing his music, although said it was a struggle to make money from it. However, he also discussed the difficulties around producing grime music with the risks of having to back up the tough image you portray in your tracks. An interesting theme that arose when both Travis and Shaun discussed their own music production is the fear of getting involved in gang rivalries or feeling a pressure to 'back up' the claims you make in the music and ending up in prison. For Travis, involvement in street-based rap music nearly got him involved unwittingly in gang rivalries as he got involved in a project for the social media impact, which he referred to as for the 'likes', however hadn't realized he had unwittingly provoked a gang rivalry and ended up being involved in a local dispute.

Participant music choices

In Table 3.1 I have outlined the music tracks that the participants brought to the interview, as well as an indication of the narrative theme that they used the track for in the interview.

PART II

Life–History Research

4

Childhood Domestic Violence and Abuse

Dave (2019)
'Lesley'
This hip-hop track is centred upon advice the artist gave to a woman named 'Lesley' who he befriended on a train and who discloses she is experiencing domestic abuse.

> 'This is a guy called Dave he's a rapper from the roads himself ... *he speaks a lot about essentially what I'm trying to say but in music form*. Giving the message that he's putting out there and who he is and where he comes from like, he's really making a difference to young people, road people as well, making them realize you can speak now.' (Travis)

As can be seen in this example, some of the music tracks that were discussed in the interviews dealt directly with issues of abuse. Talking to men about their experiences of childhood domestic violence was a sensitive and delicate process. They had all come to take part in the research because they identified with the study context; however, it became clear that the label did not resonate with everyone. Nowhere was this more poignant than in the case of Lester, who noted, 'I didn't experience the domestic part of the violence.' However, he disclosed how his mother had in fact been strangled to death by her partner when he was a young child. In addition to Lester feeling his experiences did not come under the domestic violence and abuse (DVA) label, there were also several men who considered DVA as incorporating their own direct experiences of physical and sexual child abuse. What became clear in the men's stories was that there was often a conflation between domestic violence/abuse and child maltreatment: 'domestic abuse' was interpreted more broadly as 'abuse in the home'. Travis shared the tragic story of his nephew who was killed by his parents. He was in tears as he spoke to me about his regret at not realizing the abuse that was occurring, which was brought up using this music track:

> **Coleen McMahon (2012)**
> **'Beautiful Boy'**
> Young beautiful boy
> Making his way up to the golden doors
> Time will not erase all the tears streaming
> down our faces for you
> We'll miss you baby boy.[1]

Sam, Jordan, and Eric all spoke about their own experiences of neglect and physical abuse from their parents, which occurred alongside the DVA. So, there was a diversity of experiences that were shared under the umbrella of DVA. In this chapter we will hone on the narratives of Dylan, Eric, and Dave, as they present three quite different stories. Dylan was a mixed-race man who saw and heard high-level violence from an early age; indeed, he had the perspective that this was usual within his wider family and community. Eric was a Rwandan refugee who explained the DVA in terms of his family's struggle to adjust due to their asylum-seeking journey. Dave was a White man who had seen his mother being abused by her boyfriend, whom he later tried to confront. It became clear that the presence of the DVA in the participants' lives was far greater than acting as witnesses or being exposed to it. Instead, they internalized the abuse, manifesting DVA emotionally and relationally to the extent that it reshaped their relationships with family, school, and friends. If we accept that children experience DVA viscerally, then we have to acknowledge that it has the potential to be as damaging as for the intimate partner of the perpetrator. Experiencing the DVA was characterized by a sense of powerlessness, both to understand and to stop the abuse. Children who live with DVA are 'experiencing it' (Callaghan et al, 2015), yet are not always privy to the rules of the game. They experience different aspects of the DVA, but that may vary from seeing, hearing, and sensing it, as well as living with the aftermath of it. As the nature of their experience varied, the boys were not likely to be privy to the underlying justifications, rules, or dynamics at play within the abusive adult relationship (McGee, 2000). This is not to say that there is not a pattern to the abuse for the victim, but that the children will, most likely, not be aware of it. This then follows that, for many children, the DVA they experience is a somewhat unknown quantity and they will be unaware of the justifications (however flawed). This means that they lack an awareness about the nature of and underlying basis of the violence. McGee (2000, p 107) noted that children often developed a 'fear of the unknown' and are often 'further traumatised by their absolute loss of control over the situation'. This suggests that there is another level of trauma by proxy, where it is not only the direct experience of the abuse that causes harm, but the lack of control or ability to intervene which causes further distress. In my study the participants tried to make sense of the DVA in order to predict the violence, for instance in Eric noting his own abuse came when the DVA ceased, or Dylan attributing his father's abuse to alcohol use. However, ultimately, the children found the DVA both unpredictable and incomprehensible. Children have an emerging sense of the world and how interpersonal relationships work and DVA disrupts any sense of regularity or fairness as anyone can get victimized at any time. This leads to a code of random domination and abuse. In this chapter we will read testimony that emphasizes different aspects of the DVA experience: the incomprehensibility of the DVA, the anxieties around intervening, and the general fear and unease that living with DVA provoked.

Dylan's story

OMI (2013)
'My Old Lady'

This track is dedicated to single mothers who have struggled and took on the dual parenting role. It expresses gratitude and recognition of the struggles of single parenting.

'This song is kinda like sums up my mum to a T, I don't know if you have listened to the lyrics, so you know, this is my mum because my mum mothered and fathered me, do you know, my mum done everything she could for us … and she still kept her house and home together, we always had the best of everything, she had to go to work and do everything but she done what she done for us, but she always had that heartache … so yeah this last song is … it kinda like encompasses how my mum was, she raised us, as she know she told us not to worry about anything she was always gonna be there, she taught us everything except how to live without her, and I still struggle to this day.

The word mum is a really powerful word innit, it's the most lovely do you know, none of us could have been here without our mum, do you know, some of our mums might not keep us, some of us might go into care or whatever, but without our mum we wouldn't be here, so it's the most important thing. I think women are the most important thing in the world to be honest. To have to go through all that pain and heartache and then get treated how they get treated. After my dad died, I found out I had been conceived through rape. He hurt my mum, I know he hurt my mum years after, but he actually raped my mum for me to be conceived. Rape ruins people's lives doesn't it, it ruins whole families, it ruins generations, women shouldn't have to go through that, men shouldn't have to go through that, but obviously it's the worst thing that can happen. I think it's worse than death to be honest, because you're living with what's happened, at least if you kill someone they're not here no more, so they're not having to live with it, it's just the families. It's like a death, living with death for the victim innit. Taking someone's power, abusing them, and making them do something they don't want to do, hurting them, assaulting them, raping them. Its vile it's disgusting; I think all rapists should be castrated slowly.

If I was to say I am Black that would be to deny my mum's heritage. I would rather accept my mum's heritage that my rapist dad's heritage … Everybody looks at me being Black but I'm mixed race. But even though he raped her numerous times, he tried to throw an iron in the bath when she was in the bath, do you know, that's what he would do, I could hear as a kid the water splashing and all that, coz he'd put her in the bath and then he'd beat her while she was in the bath. He was the nicest man ever when he hadn't had a drink and I'm not saying it coz, I don't call him dad no more because of what I'd found out, but honestly you wouldn't meet a nicer man, and my mum would say the same thing, it's once he had a drink he would turn into a devil, he'd turn into a monster. I'm not saying this because it should be said but if you've got a Black parent or parent from the Caribbean, back in the days like its acceptable for them to beat their partner. Where I come from its like acceptable where Black men hit Black women, do you know? Because my dad learned that from his dad because my gran, she's still alive now, she's nearly 100 and my granddad used to beat her, and my dad used to see it, and my gran, she was blind from when she was like in her 40s through the beatings she got from my granddad. Mums and people used to make up them excuses, I walked into the door and things like that. It's not just what my mum went through, my mum went through the worst thing I can imagine, so when my mum was saying that to them, they might not have been getting raped, they might have been getting beaten, one of my ex-girlfriends who I was with, she used to get beaten by her ex-partner, and he'd never hit her face, he'd hit her body or in her head where you couldn't see it, so there's a lot of people who must've gone through that, and when she told me I thought wow that's mad, do you know, on the outside it looks like everything's rosy but really and truly you don't know what anybody's going through. Nobody knew what I was going through, and I was going through a lot, do you know, and it's not just me and my family, there'll be people that will have gone through the same but worse. There were no social workers, but I reckon if social workers got involved and says to my mum, your gonna lose your kids I reckon my mum would have left.'

Eric's story

Eric selected this first track as it reminds him of his birth mother, who died when he was very young in the refugee camp. His family came to the UK as refugees from Rwanda. Eric was brought up by his father and his stepmother, along with his younger sister who he was close to. Eric noted that he had not had a chance as a child to mourn his mother's death.

DMX (2002)
'I Miss You'
A hip-hop track about bereavement, loss, and grief.

'When my mum died we never really mourned her, and then when we grew up we grew up with a step mum who was getting beaten up every day so she never showed us some sort of love and there was never anyone to talk to. So literally whatever your gonna go through your gonna be fine it's gonna be OK [referring to the lyrics], so literally as sad as it may sound I play that to hear it's gonna be OK, you listen to it imagining someone is saying it to you, someone who cares for you, as a kid whatever you're going though, my whole life they themselves have so many issues, she's raising kids that are not her own whilst she's getting beaten up, it must be hard for her. DMX here is talking about his grand mum but literally in my head I always thought about my mum, so yeah, that's um, yeah for me definitely this was the song that would take me back and make me feel like you're gonna be fine you're gonna be OK.

I was scared of my dad but not that much, but I know he wouldn't be punching me he would get a wire and throw water at me and beat me. He would do some weird ... he's just weird man. He would tip hot water put it in a bucket and I would hold it there [above my head] for hours, or he would wait, I would practice for a play, and he would wait till the day I had to go for the play and I wouldn't get to go. It was like weird stuff, I was like you have too much time on your hands man. But like I say it was like all of us regardless, we were never allowed to disrespect. Yeah but on my side of the story like um my dad's domestic, um, yeah I guess he came here, he was, you know he was like an accountant and he was alright in life and now he has to start again, my mum is fine with cleaning and doing nursing and stuff, he's not, he's nothing no more, even in the [refugee] camp he was maybe something, and it's just hard for him to adjust and they just couldn't get on, she was my step mum, she was my mum's friend from the war and going around a bit together, and there was just so much violence between them two. And then, but then when they're not fighting each other, sounds wrong, but when they're not fighting each other I didn't like it because instead they inflicted the pain on us now ... So I literally, like, coz most guys their house they'd be like yeah if I see my mum getting hit I would get involved, I swear to God I never got involved I just always left it. My sister would be unhappy but it didn't bother me in the sense that they were fighting for me to stop it, because once they stopped it would definitely change now it was me, and because of how, I don't know my dad used to say it was African ways or whatever, so he would just inflict pain on you as a way to teach you a lesson.

I used to say I won't get married because I grew up literally not having a family, I was in a house but their actions didn't ... when I saw what my step-mum would do to my dad, and then what he would do to us and then she would do to us, I was like I was clever enough to understand that's not love, and that made me realize that I don't have a family, because my family don't do that. I have my English friends and what I see [makes me] sad. When you see yourself, when you're young it's very apparent ... it's in your face because at the end of the day at school, whose picking you up? Some kids in high school they'd still get their parents picking them up, my Dad showed us where the school was from the first day. I mean that's self-sufficient cool, I like it, whatever, but then school, I was doing running, but your parents wouldn't come, and any parents knew who [name] was and want [name] to come to their house, I've always been OK, you know I would sit down and talk to people and they would invite me to come and see their house, that would be a mistake to me, I shouldn't have, because when you go to their house you know how different you are living. And I think what kills it, you can't invite, you don't want to invite them to your house, never, you'd be scared, I never wanted any of my English friends, I was afraid, for my sixteenth [birthday] that's when they came to my house and that's when it was my step mum and she was doing nights, because it was like she might get angry, their definitely gonna jump up this is not normal. I know the violence part, you never know what the next day people are going to say, so you don't want them in your house. It went on until I was 16 and I think, they go through the whole divorce because my dad one day literally went bad one day, and it was like man you beat her every day. And one day they fought, and she had enough and it's like you can keep on beating on somebody eventually they're gonna gain that strength.'

Dave's story

Dave selected the music track 'Runaway Love', which is accompanied by a music video showing a young girl being sexually abused. Dave did not explicitly disclose that he had personally been a victim of sexual abuse; however, he referred to these issues more generally and then alluded to his own experience of victimization through noting that he had been 'affected'.

Ludacris ft Mary J. Blige (2007)
'Runaway Love'
This hip-hop track and accompanying music video tells the story of a nine-year-old girl who is experiencing sexual abuse and physical violence by her mother's partners. The mother is unaware and using drugs. It also describes domestic abuse in the house. The accompanying video shows the young girl growing older, getting pregnant, and running away from home.

'I was torn with songs coz there's a few others that I had in mind … I know it [the song] has helped some people in that like it gives other people's perspective, so it might help make them think shit yeah it would affect anyone, it's like perspective, the little sister and all that I'm passionate about and I think they cover suicide, knife crime and then this like domestic [violence] and like paedophilia as well because that's something that I've been affected by. My mum's boyfriend was just bad. Like alcoholic, drugs and abusive and that. But like yeah he drank himself to death. I saw how he was with my mum, so got a bit of experience with everything unfortunately. What I went through with stuff I saw at home has made me like I am now, that's how I think like… the bad bullying where I couldn't leave the house sometimes because it was like terrorized but then when I was older because I was a victim for years but then now that's creating angry men do you know what I mean …I don't know it's hard to explain but you know what I mean it's like I went from being bullied and seeing all this mad stuff at home with my mum's boyfriend not being able to defend my mum and there was a lot of men walking around who are now super angry and full of like rage and quick to snap on someone and punch someone because of they felt for years that they couldn't do anything, so that's what happened with me anyway. I can't speak on behalf of everyone but for myself it's like I got sick of being a victim so I remember my mum's boyfriend hearing them downstairs fighting and whatever and I got to probably about thirteen [years old] and I confronted him the one time, he came round after he moved out, I don't know exactly how old I was but he was moved out at that point and they were like on and off and I heard from friends that they'd seen my mum and [name] down at the park and he had put a knife at my mum's throat and I was pissed off and I couldn't, I didn't know what to do, I remember one time picking up a Heinz ketchup bottle like a glass bottle and I remember walking out to him and saying fuck off, leave my mum alone and if he would have physically attacked me he probably would have battered me, but he walked past and other people got involved, neighbours like, and he got in the car and went off and yeah I just feel like I'm such a angry person now like not with everyone but just if someone's being a bully I'm like always looking out and I get involved in stuff and I like I feel I have to tell people like shut the hell up you know what I mean and I think that's from being bullied and from seeing all the mad stuff from my mum and everyone.

It's not your parents' fault because they didn't choose for everything to go tits up you know, I don't resent my mum either because if I tell people certain things I saw like when she had her breakdown and stuff, they could think badly of her, but that was her mental health, she didn't choose to, she felt bad when she was older, sometimes we used to use it as a teenager, I would say, I'm fucked up because of stuff I saw mum, you chose him over us, I shouldn't have seen you cutting yourself, I didn't see her cutting her wrists but I remember hiding razor blades and seeing them with blood on and crying to my mum saying don't cut yourself and I saw her ripping her hair out and whacking herself and everything and it is bad that I saw all of that but at the same time I know she did love us but she just went through a bad phase and she needed medication and whatnot.

The school were good I guess, but I didn't really get counselling or anything I remember. I remember one teacher coming out and she, I don't even call him my step dad but my mum's boyfriend, he had ganga [Marijuana] plants in the window and she saw them and didn't grass, at the time I thought that was good, it happened that at the time she, of all the teachers, she was the one you saw in the pub, so she probably had a smoke herself so she probably thought it's not worth grassing and that, so at the time I thought wicked, she's cool, but yeah like really they could have done more I guess to like take me to one side and say what's going on, but I think I've got a lot of issues with like from being a victim coz I got bullied bad when I was little by local kids to the point when I've had piss thrown on me, made to crawl around and stuff. I've had my windows smashed. I didn't feel safe at home.'

Discussion

Experiencing domestic violence and abuse

When talking about experiences of childhood DVA there were several interrelated thematic areas that arose in many of the narratives. These were that DVA was hidden, incomprehensible, and unpredictable. All of these dimensions of DVA point to a wider experience of powerlessness, which

I explore throughout this chapter. The participants discussed the wider ranging effects this had both on internal and external coping strategies. The first aspect of power relations that arose in the narratives was the way in which DVA was a partly hidden issue in childhood. In several cases this meant that the knowledge of the extent of the DVA has been revealed to the participants in retrospect as they got older. However, as is shown in Dylan's story, his mother used to make 'excuses' for her injuries. This raises the issue that both he and his mum were trying to hide the DVA in parallel, highlighted by Dylan saying no one was aware what he was going through (neither school nor social workers) and so both he and his mother were hiding the DVA from the outside world. But what was also striking about Dylan's passage is that his mother was trying to hide the DVA from him when they were living together. Travis also focused on the DVA that his sister experienced when he was a child. Travis noted that he blamed himself for not recognizing the extent of the DVA, as well as co-occurring child abuse against his nephew, which tragically resulted in the latter's death as an infant:

> 'You kinda like blame yourself, coz he [my sister's ex-partner] was like violent towards her as well and I regret not [crying] I regret not noticing it coz I could have been able to do something and now I can't [crying] … looking back there was things I didn't realize.' (Travis)

Travis's sense of regret was palpable in the interview and this passage shows the despair that he conveyed about not realizing that DVA was happening. This links back to Dylan's story where he discussed excuses that his mother used to make. DVA is an issue often hidden by those who are experiencing it. Compounding the hidden nature of the DVA in some of the narratives was, at times, the lack of classification of violence between adults as a form of DVA. This was pertinent in Lester's case; his mother was murdered by her ex-partner when he was very young:

> 'My mother got murdered when I was two [years old] … it was her ex-partner and what happened, he made her got drunk and strangled her … Basically she wanted to leave him and he didn't want her to and he said just come out one more time with me, that's what's a bad signal straight away, why are you coming out one more time with me for? What for? If I and you is done why do we need to come out one more time for? But some people are gullible. No one coulda told me that coz it's the first thing I'm gonna ask them and they are not gonna have an answer for that so that's what happened.' (Lester)

In this passage it is clear that Lester views the tragic incident of his mother's murder more through an understanding of violence informed by the 'code of the street' (Anderson, 1999), rather than violence in an DVA context. By this I mean that he focuses on his mother's lack of streetwise knowledge to interpret the violence, as outlined in suggesting she was 'gullible', rather than focusing on the abusive nature of the violence. Viewing the violence in this way enables Lester to strategize about how he would avoid the same fate, as a protection strategy. This resonates with Sandberg's (2009) work on the dialogic nature of victim and gangster discourses. He noted the way in which, by emphasizing street knowledge and kudos, the bravado detracts from the vulnerable realities of men's lives on-road. Lester related how the untimely and violent death of his mother had negative repercussions on his life: 'it sends you on the wrong trajectory'. Lester located this early experience as being influential on his later involvement on-road and in gangs.

DVA was at times a hidden issue. Yet when the participants (as boys) were aware of DVA occurring, it was clear in some of the narratives that due to their young age they did not understand the full dynamics and reasoning behind it. Some participants described hearing the various forms of violence and abuse but said they were not aware of the full extent of what was going on, as Sam noted;

'At a young age you don't know how to decipher what's going on around you.' (Sam)

The notion of DVA being difficult to 'decipher' is important here, as this word itself means to 'decode' (Collins, 1988). Sam's comment thus suggests that there is an unknowable code to the DVA (in contrast to the 'code of the street'). For the participants, living with DVA was defined by its unintelligibility. The inability to explain or make sense of the circumstances was also spoken about by Dylan, who described hearing his mother being beaten in the bath yet not being able to make sense of the violence. This example is an important illustration of the bizarre ways that violence in the DVA context was carried out. This shows how the code of DVA both unknowable and unpredictable, something which amplifies children's sense of powerlessness. It also conveys the alarming ways that Dylan was experiencing DVA in childhood. This was similar to the abusive techniques Eric's father used against him, which he described as deliberately surprising and hard to predict.

In DVA situations, it is not always the case that physical violence is ongoing, but rather is sporadic and thus can appear unpredictable to outsiders. Dylan associated his father's abusive behaviour with him being inebriated. The disjuncture between his father's persona when sober as 'the nicest man ever' is a complete contrast to him being the 'devil' when drunk. Framing the abusive behaviour served not only to add some degree of predictability to it (ie it happened only when the perpetrator was drunk), but also enabled

Dylan to place boundaries around the violence in order to identify some positive elements about his father. The unpredictability of DVA perpetration was also highlighted by Sam and Dave, who drew on the powerful imagery of terrorism as a way to describe their experiences of childhood violence. To terrorize is, according to the *Collins Reference English Dictionary*, to 'force, oppress by fear, violence'. A defining feature of terrorism is that it is unexpected and unavoidable. Sam noted that:

> 'You feel the way they are treating you and that's the way you explain it. It felt like terrorizing or bullying or control.' (Sam)

In this passage, he outlines that he experienced the DVA on an emotional level. This image, when coupled with the images of bullying and control, conveys a sense of the fear-induced domination that the perpetrator sought in the home. What these quotes show is the close relationship between experiencing DVA and feeling powerlessness, as well as a lack of knowledge about the whole picture. This was echoed in McGee's study, where she noted that 'hearing violence but not knowing what was actually happening, their own feelings of powerlessness increased' (McGee, 2000, p 64). For several of the participants in this study DVA was associated with a core sense of powerlessness. This sense of powerlessness was linked by Eric to the way that he then engaged with his peers at school, as he sought to regain a sense of power. DVA often occurs alongside other forms of child maltreatment. Jordan and Sam spoke about broader neglect. Sam and Eric discussed direct physical abuse from parents and carers. The link between DVA and child abuse has been explored in wider scholarship. Among children who witness child abuse, 40 per cent report domestic violence in the home (UNICEF, 2006). In a North American study it has been found that children who have experienced severe violence at home were 15 times more likely to be physically or sexually abused themselves than the national average (Volpe, 1996). This link has been found globally, with studies from a wide range of countries including 'China, South Africa, Colombia, India, Egypt, the Philippines, and Mexico' (UNICEF, 2006).

The experience the participants had as children, watching their mothers being victimized through DVA and not being in a position to stop it, presented them with conflicts and tensions they struggled to resolve. It conflicts with wider societal messages that take a paternal view of gender relations, which suggest the participants should protect women and, in turn, sons should protect their mothers. The participants understood this pressure in different ways. Some participants noted that it was not just the powerlessness of being in a home dominated by a DVA perpetrator, but more specifically the feeling of not being able to protect one's own mother in that situation that was so difficult. Dave described the feeling that he had in childhood that he 'couldn't do anything' about the DVA, which left him with an enduring sense of anger that he still carries around with him now. Dave recalled one occasion though when he was a teenager and did decide to act against the DVA perpetrator in an attempt to protect his mother from further abuse. Sam also mentioned experiencing the DVA and feeling that he was not able to prevent it or intervene:

> 'All you'd hear was big crashing and smashing and stuff and like sat listening to it and I'm so young and I can't do anything about it.' (Sam)

In this passage Sam is foregrounding the issue of his young age at the time as central to the ineptitude that he felt when faced with the DVA. Central to this is also the issue of fear, which is implied in the way that Sam mentions hearing the 'crashing and smashing', which must have been an unsettling experience. Eric, however, noted that he felt he should have wanted to do something, but actually developed a safety strategy for himself, which was to feel safer when the DVA was going on, as it meant he was not the primary target for abuse at those times. He discussed the pressure to protect – that 'most guys' would have 'got involved' – which signifies the pressure he felt to intervene. Instead Eric focused his role of protector towards his sister, as he talked about the lengths he would go to stop her being victimized herself, noting that he would even kill or 'go to prison' if someone abused her. Through this he is navigating the negated and now lost opportunities to protect his step-mother, an act which he now firmly feels would be part of his role as a patriarch in their family.

Dave's example of taking up the ketchup bottle to confront his mother's boyfriend was powerful. It expressed so much in the way of the tension that Dave felt between being afraid and feeling victimized, while trying to assert his power in young adolescence. There is an underlying thread in the passage of naivety and powerlessness, as Dave noted he 'didn't know what to do' and felt he 'couldn't do anything'. The poignant image of Dave clutching a glass ketchup bottle as a weapon to defend himself from a man who he was clearly afraid of presents the tension between a childhood naivety and a co-existing pressure to enact a tough persona. Dave acted at the point at which the DVA ceased to be purely a hidden and private phenomenon solely within the domestic sphere and instead became a public form of violence. Through Dave being told by peers and friends that his mother had been threatened by the perpetrator wielding a knife in the park, he then had an assumed responsibility to be seen to act. Indeed, in the situation Dave described, it was the public nature of the confrontation that made Dave act, yet was also protective, as the perpetrator decided not to react violently to Dave's provocation due to the presence of neighbours and passers-by. The shift between DVA in private to the public realm of the park completely changed the way the violence existed in the community; it became visible.

The varied responses to the DVA in childhood by some of the participants outline the tension between a sense of powerlessness, the pressure to protect, and the fear that they had to navigate in childhood. As shown in the analysis in the preceding sections, the way that participants experienced DVA, as well as their lack of resources to make it cease, was defined by their lack of power, both as children and as victims themselves. They were subordinated from the intimate partner relationship within which the DVA was centred. This left them trying to make sense of their experiences, which were often hidden and unpredictable and, overall, were incomprehensible when the participants were boys. As shown in the varied ways that they referred to experiencing and responding to DVA, it is clear that the presence of the DVA in their lives was far greater than them acting as *witnesses* or being *exposed* to it. Instead, they internalized DVA, manifesting it emotionally and relationally to the extent that it reshaped their relationships with family, school, and friends. If we accept that children experience DVA viscerally, then we have to acknowledge that it has the potential to be as damaging for them as for the intimate partner of the perpetrator.

Sexual violence

An unexpected theme in the narratives was that of being the children (or grandchildren) of rape victims. Both Dylan and Sam spoke to me about rape being in their family and the impact this had on their own identities. Viewed through dynamics of cathexis, this is complicated, as the men's relationships with their family members is tied up with this history of sexual (and sexualized) violence. The knowledge that they had been somehow involved in the sexual victimization affected their sense of masculine identity. This was pivotal for Dylan's view of his parents and how he felt about his own identity. In many ways Dylan conveyed the knowledge of his mother's rape as a more significant issue than the DVA, perhaps as he felt directly implicated in the act of sexual violence. Dylan later discussed the significance of rape and why he felt it is more damaging than the other violence. For him it centred on the act of power being taken from an individual through rape. The way that he asserted that rape takes people's power is notable here, as this is framed as distinct from other forms of more ubiquitous violence. Dylan had himself been involved in different kinds of violence during his time on-road. However, for him, the symbolism of rape, being about the ultimate robbery of a person's power, makes him feel it is 'worse than death'. Dylan noted that the instrumental act of rape is 'taking someone's power'. This conveys a sense both of masculinity and power relations that amounted from Dylan feeling that he was victimized through the rape of his mother. It is a degrading act, one which involves active physical humiliation demonstrated on the body; male power of the gender order enacted through the personal. Here he is referring to the complexities of the knowledge of rape being in a family lineage. This knowledge made Dylan think differently about his ethnic heritage, as noted, he referred to himself as mixed-race to distance himself from his 'rapist dad's heritage'. To be a product of both the victim and the perpetrator of a crime such as rape is an incredibly complex issue. It is where gender and race intersect, so that Dylan is grappling with his self as someone who is perceived as a Black man, which associates him more with his father. Dylan's identification as mixed-race detaches him somewhat from his father.

Sam also described the heritage of sexual violence within his family history. In his case it was his mother who was born as a result of his grandmother being raped. Again, it was not something that he was aware of until he was an adult. When Sam found this out it was a way through which he found some understanding for his own mother's life. Sam conveyed a sense of the knowledge of his wider family dynamics once he learned about the sexual violence history within his family. It enabled him to have a different understanding of his own mother's lack of emotional availability when he was younger, as being due to her working through her own rejection. Using Connell's analytic method of cathexis raises the issue of the way that the men's sense of gender identity was affected by the knowledge that they were born from a legacy of sexual violence (this is discussed further in Chapter 10). Dave did not directly talk about personal experience of sexual abuse, he went on to talk about an ex-girlfriend's experience, as well as the way that he had reported suspected paedophiles to the police. As shown, he directly referenced the way that the little sister was centred in the music video. As an adult Dave had responded to his past experiences by being hypervigilant to abuse around him. He recounted the ways in which he confronted people he considered acting abusively in public if he felt it was occurring.

Domestic abuse, race, and ethnicity

The experience of minority racial and ethnic identity was implicated in some of the participants' desire for acceptance and was reflected heavily in how they tried to understand their father's masculinity. As they enacted violence of their own, they framed it as a strategy both for coping with the anger and powerlessness they felt at home, as well as a way to harness masculine power and to claim the markers of masculinity that their fathers had shown at home: respect, power, and fear. The intersection of race was foregrounded by several of the participants in relation to their experience of DVA at home. Dylan emphasized that as far as he was concerned, it was normal for DVA to be present in the homes of Black families. Dylan then went on to explain how he felt violence had been passed down through the generations in his family (intergenerational transmission of violence), recalling that his grandmother was blinded by his grandfather. Dylan immediately racialized his family's wider historical experience of DVA, by noting that in the wider Black community in the past it has been seen as 'acceptable' for Black men to commit DVA. Although Dylan conveyed this sense of acceptance and normality about DVA and race, this was complicated within his own sense of self-identity as a mixed-race man. Dylan firmly located his identity as mixed-race, despite him being recognized within wider society as Black, as a political decision based on the way that he wishes to acknowledge his parents. Dylan was keen to note that he was a mixed-race man with a White mother; however, when he conceptualized the racial dynamics of DVA, he conceived it within an all-Black wider community. A key feature here though is that all of the perpetrators that Dylan described were Black men, and so he is distancing himself from that identity in the passage mentioned, which serves to distance himself from the DVA perpetration. For Dylan, this sense of a cultural normality stemmed both from the fact that most of his peer group were experiencing similar violence at home, but also because there was an intergenerational aspect of abuse present in his family. He observed the intergenerational aspect of DVA when he noted that his father had also experienced DVA at home, with a long-term injury being a visible example of the consequences of it.

The participants' experiences of their racial identities were often closely linked with their conceptions of their own masculinities. This was highlighted in Eric's comments on his own family experiences, where he was taught 'African ways' at home. Eric was managing the intersection of his African racial identity and his masculine identity, which were both embedded in the context of his identity as a refugee in the UK. Eric connected the ongoing DVA to the difficulties that his father had in adjusting to the loss of role and pride that he had in coming over to the UK to start a new life. Using cultural context as a way to justify abusive behaviour was also experienced by Eric, whose father had used his ethnic background (Rwandan refugee heritage) to explain his violence both to his partner (Eric's stepmother) and Eric himself. Eric then himself explained the DVA at home as very much related to his father's disempowerment through the refugee experience. He noted that whereas his stepmother was able to find domestic work in the UK easily, so took on work as a carer and a cleaner, his father, who had previously been an accountant, was not able to find work in that field. This caused a financial disparity and his father struggled to adjust to the loss of power and a sense of masculinity that he had before.

The 'trope of the black family' has been explored heavily by Gilroy (1993) in his book, *Small Acts*. He problematized the ways in which the 'symbolic projection of race as kinship' is a form of nationalism which is often externally defined for Black families (Gilroy, 1993, p 195). In saying this, Gilroy is problematizing the ways in which normal family conduct and management become heavily entwined with wider racial politics that seek to pathologize racial groups. Gilroy (1993, p 198) noted that 'Today we are told that the boys, and the girls, are "from the hood" – not from the race, and certainly not from the nation.' Through this discourse, community issues become separated from the wider structural and political issues that shape them. He asked, 'If the "hood" is the special urban space in which the essence of the new familial blackness can be now found, which "hood" are we talking about?' (Gilroy, 1993, p 198). Gilroy noted that to see race in this way, as an accumulation of families, is a response to the crisis of Black masculinity. Locating the problem of masculinity as a family issue means that it can 'be repaired by intervening in the family to compensate and rebuild the race by instituting appropriate forms of masculinity and male authority' (Gilroy, 1993, p 204). It personalizes the issue, viewing it on a micro level, keeping the issues behind closed doors. This is reflected in the ways in which the participants pathologized their family and community cultures as somehow maintaining and reproducing DVA, locating it as a Black cultural issue, rather than a wider issue of masculinities-in-crisis. This reflects a power structure constructed by White society/whiteness that has sought to denigrate Black masculinity and experience. This shows how the intersections of race, ethnicity, and societal norms all conflate to a wider acceptance of DVA as a normal part of society.

Boyhood powerlessness and subordinate masculinity

The narratives in this chapter portray a pervasive sense of powerlessness. This sense of powerlessness was linked by Eric to the way that he then engaged with his peers at school, as he sought to regain a sense of power. The following comments illustrate how lack of awareness of the underlying dynamics of DVA, alongside a lack of power to act, made home to be an undesirable place to be, while also illustrating the sense of powerlessness through being overlooked and not having distress acknowledged. While some participants (as boys) were aware of DVA occurring, it was clear in some of the narratives that the participants at a young age did not understand the full dynamics and reasoning behind it. Some participants described hearing the various forms of violence and abuse but said they were not aware of the full extent of what was going on.

The dominant power relation that was present when the participants lived with the DVA perpetrator was that of subordination, which resulted in the boys inhabiting a subordinate masculinity. This was more than just an issue of being younger and thus subordinate by age to the father or stepfather, who, in most cases in the present study, was also the DVA perpetrator.

But subordination in terms of masculinity was also expressed through the way in which the boys were positioned in relation to the male head of the household. While at home living with the DVA they described their sense of powerlessness in light of their mother's abuse, and in many cases, the direct child abuse they experienced as well. DVA perpetration can be seen as a form of protest masculinity on the part of the male perpetrator, as it relies on the exaggerations of male privilege and, in particular, grounds itself in the exploitation of unequal power relations between men and women. Ray (2018, p 123) noted, 'we should recognize that domestic violence is ubiquitous and a routine means of maintaining patriarchal power and authority'. This extended within the home over the primary victim (most often the mother in the participants' narratives) and the children within the house.

5

Learning How to Be a Man On-Road

Westside Gunn ft Tiona D (2014)
'Never Coming Homme'
This hip-hop track describes coming from an area that is defined by poverty and crime. The music video features the rapper looking smart (with an assistant holding an umbrella over him), which is set in contrast to the poor surroundings.

'So that song there I guess for me ... it's a song that I would say probably represented the early parts of my life in terms of growing up and the visuals, lots of kids in the house, single parent, kids looking like not really, not not being looked after but their environment that they're living in is a hard environment, the kids that they are going to school with, it's harder, maybe there's a lack of opportunities, there's not enough money, as a result you're just drawn, for me anyway, drawn to the streets, making bad choices, and drawn to trying to find a way out and in the process that comes with drug dealing, robberies, violence, respect ... it's more than just a song, I really relate to it.' (Jordan)

In this chapter I will explore the ways in which the participants talked about trying to achieve independence and gain a sense of their own emerging agency as young men. This will include analysis of violence in school as a way to gain peer kudos as well as a form of self-protection. There will also be a discussion of the ways the young men felt financial pressure to earn money and support themselves and sometimes their destitute mothers, which inspired an emerging involvement in drug dealing and running. These narratives will be explored using a gendered analysis, looking to the specific ways these pressures were related to the context of the participants' sense of subordinated masculinity at home and their attempts to redress this balance and become 'a man'. The participants indicated that they inhabited contradictory masculinity positions at a young age. They were living in a violent context where there was a male perpetrator who was performing protest masculinity, dominating the mother and the children in the house. Some participants indicated they had complex relationships with this violence and dominance, as they denounced it but simultaneously sought spaces (such as in school) in which they could enact violence. This was expressed as linked with a desire for power and respect among peers. This is distinctive, as both the fathers and the men themselves (as boys and young men) were marginalized and frozen out from traditional markers of hegemonic masculinity. This juxtaposition was spatially defined, as the participants inhabited a subordinate masculinity at home and then simultaneously enacted protest masculinity position outside of the home, in school, and on-road.

Violence was the constant thread in the narratives. What changed was the participants' relationship to the violence as they grew up. In early childhood they were victims of violence and abuse in the domestic sphere. At this time, they positioned themselves as both powerless and lacking the full knowledge of the violent dynamics around them. As they grew older, several of the participants framed school as being a site of their emerging perpetration of violence, where they started to enact violence against peers. This then escalated on-road, where the participants referred to experiencing violence (both as victims and perpetrators) on-road and/or in the gang context. As they described this evolving journey of adolescence around violence there was a sense of their relationship to the violence changing: moving from the position of experiencing violence as a victim to then taking opportunities to enact violence in a more agentic way themselves. Through this move on-road, as well as the shift to seeking ways to feel both a sense of developing protest masculinity and power, the ways in which they became involved with violence changed. They went from being victims to violence around them to more agentic in their involvement in violence as perpetrators.

Sam's story

DMX (1998)
'Slippin'
The format of this hip-hop track is an early life story of a boy who is neglected by his mother and who becomes increasingly involved in life on-road. At the end of the track the teenager was going in an ambulance to hospital.

'I chose that because it relates to me to a T literally everything … it [the lyrics] said at the start to live is to suffer and to survive is the ending of suffering and I think that's how it felt for a long time. Erm it just felt like the pain was eternal it was just never knew life without it. And there are so many bits in there that I can relate to, at home with my mum and she kept sending me to my dad's and my dad kept beating me and I kept telling my mum not to but she kept sending me there anyway. And I can relate to like obviously how he said he started to get angry and was an angry child and he was growing up and he just, he became feared by others, even the bigger boys like they was actually scared of me and I was always angry and then I remember like getting a dog and the dog was like my best friend but my dog was vicious as well at the same time. He'd protect me when I was out on the streets I remember coming home with the dog and the dog wasn't allowed in but the dog was my best friend and it was like sending me away at the same time. I remember my dad drinking alcohol and erm just abusing us, my brother and sister, but more me because I was the youngest and he just terrorize me in some ways, in like that's what it felt like, at a young age you don't know how to decipher what's going on around you, you just know that someone's treating you in that way and you feel it, you feel the way they are treating you and that's the way you explain it. It felt like terrorizing or bullying or control erm, and then I just became very violent, and violence became normal. As a child I suppressed my emotions and when I suppressed my emotions I, I then became desensitized and I was emotionally stunted and I never had a heart string to pull on, there was no "ah but if this happens" it was just action, there was no other remorse or other force that could stop me from doing what I was going to do.

If I was at my dad's I was getting beaten ... I remember like doors that had been smashed through like with his punch, I remember like all the doors always had a punch in it coz he's punching through it and stuff. I remember all you'd hear was big crashing and smashing and stuff and like sat listening to it and I'm so young and I can't do anything about it, even there for hours and hours even late it was late and I'm looking to see if his cars gone ... it was very hectic, it wasn't a normal upbringing that I had like. He sent me back to my mum's eventually and then coz she wasn't listening I left and that's what the songs saying, he said [in lyrics] he mum was on some fly, and then he chipped he left, then I was out on the streets and that's when I just grew into just a cold person like I didn't have anything left in me I was very empty and it just spiralled from there, um, even I relate to, how can you put a baby in a prison cell? I was [young] when I first went to prison.

So I had to grow up really fast, there's many nights when I was younger, selling drugs at the age of eight, like the older boys would come up to me, give me stuff and I would just go sell it, but I didn't know exactly what I was doing at that time either, so I was being groomed into a lifestyle that I wasn't aware of and my environment was training me and building me up … When I ran away from home I was in some hostel like sleeping on kitchen floors, wherever I could sleep really.

The first time I sold drugs was when the older boys they gave me this stuff, I was only eight [years old] and I walked down the road and … I had to give it to this guy and then they'd give me sweets and then fivers and it went up until one day I see the guy OD'ing [overdosing] on the floor and I realized what I gave to that man was drugs and I was scared and I didn't wanna be in that lifestyle so I kinda run away but I ran away from them but they lived on the estate so they was always there. But the things I seen … [redacted example] … I don't wanna see things like that, I didn't choose to see that, erm, and being around people that were threatening and scary they [were] carrying knives or they got guns, like the guys coming into the house with a gun and crack and brown all around you, you can't be a pussycat, when you're around these lines.

The first time I ever robbed something I was manipulated to rob by a woman that back in the day, to stay in these people's houses I had to do sexual acts with women to be able to stay in their house. So I didn't even know what sex was, didn't even know anything about that stuff, and I was brought into it at a very young age. I was asking for food coz I was hungry and I was always asking for food coz I never had food, never had money, and they'd call me a tramp, ponce [gay], all different names and then, then we'd like, go to the shop and steal some beans, some bacon and some eggs and I'll cook you some food, coz I can't even cook either, so the first time I ever robbed from a shop was because someone told me to so I could get some food, I didn't even know about robbing neither. See that is what Maslow [American psychologist who published a 1943 paper on humans' 'hierarchy of needs'] said, you go to get your basic needs, you'll go anywhere to find it and that's why we have sexual exploitation of women, they will be sexually being exploited by a guy that's beating them or treating them rubbish but coz they're getting their affection, their belonging, certain needs from that guy, they stay and I believe that's what I was doing for a lot of the time. Like all this stuff became new to me but it became my life, it became that's how you do it, I grew up like that. I had to do things I was in situations that I didn't wanna be in, doing things I didn't wanna do … I was growing up crazy but I didn't … I didn't … it started to become normal, the life that I was living when I was sleeping in kitchen floors over here and drugs was all here … it was becoming normal.'

Eric's story

> **R. Kelly (2002)**
> **'The World's Greatest'**
> *This R&B track is about overcoming obstacles. The music video features an actor representing Muhammad Ali, the world-famous boxer.*

Eric was introduced to music by a teacher at school, through becoming a member of the choir. Eric used the lyrics as conveying a voice of guidance. He noted that he would play music to be able to

> 'see beyond my situation … I needed it, this music I need, it literally was a part of my life because I needed something to make me think you're great, you can do this.' (Eric)

Using the lyrics as a way to garner advice from an alternative source is an element that was mentioned here by Eric. He used lyrics from R. Kelly's 'The Greatest' as an inspirational message. As shown here, the lyrics to this particular music track are centred upon empowerment and self-belief. Eric noted that he used this track as inspiration, to feel that he could also be great and could achieve things, even though his friends might think he 'made some crazy decisions'. The song was also significant in that he was introduced to it by the school music teacher, who he built a positive relationship with through his engagement in the school choir.

> 'It took me a long time to even realize I have a problem, there's something, before I was just normal there's nothing wrong with me, but if you literally, if you grew up in a house where you saw violence, I mean yeah like because when my mother used to beat me, I would go to school and I would stay and fight someone, they couldn't beat me in the way my dad beat me, because it's a man beating you, so a kid is gonna be come on man, so then, you end up in this violence thing with this kid or whatever, but how school works out is like ooh you're cool. So now it's working to your advantage in the weird way ever and that continues coz now there's this attention, so now you're looking more for this attention because so now you're picking fights for no reason.
>
>   Being feared is not something that I want now you know … The reason why I used to fight is like you couldn't fight a man you fight a woman, so for me any disrespect I saw with a guy I definitely would initiate a fight, I could lose the fight, there was times when I would get beaten up, I remember I would just go there and get beaten up by 10 guys coz it's like man, for me a man is not a person

who hits a woman, do you know what I mean, people who hits a woman don't hit men, they don't hit men, they don't fight men. But stupid me didn't realize they're all the same, it's just you're just doing the same thing. It's just you're doing it to a man, for me it was like I want to be a man, I wasn't man enough, because he was here having fights with woman, making woman get scared of him, for me no way, for me this was a big problem so it became a thing it was like, I would go up there trying to pick a fight with men, because it was a way to feel like a man, a lot of my friends we would grow up, because parents would beat you to put you in your place, he's the man of the house, he can get away with that, so now when you go outside there is no way I think there is no way you allow anyone to disrespect you, it's like you can't do that because it's been done to you at home, it's been done to you at home, you can't let another person.

So there was never any money, I never received any money growing up. I needed some sort of money to take to school, I was getting bullied for wearing the same clothes, for not making trips, I didn't have no money, my mum was like you make it to UK you know. So, I'm never really a money person, but my other friends on the other side, their parents were similar in a sense, so these guys were hungry for money because they didn't get it, they didn't get the little 20–30 pounds that over the weekend or £100, but you're growing up in an area where kids have some sort of money for the weekend.

She [my stepmother] didn't give us money, so the part me and my friends play is a role and obviously me I needed some sort of money to take to school, I was getting bullied for wearing the same clothes, for not making trips, I didn't have no phone, and my mum was like you make it to UK you know, But I get it but I was like I'm at school, you gave me the biggest gift I get it [by making it to the UK], but we are at school, but it's like, we gave you the biggest gift, and I get it, yes you gave me the gift but you're not understanding I'm a kid, I'm at school, you need certain things, we live in a very materialistic world, and my friends who are poor as well, for me I wanted bare minimum, so I started doing a paper round, then you start to buy stuff to invest, you start buying weed for your friends to sell and the elders they see you, the older guys they see you, that guys fight, coz I was fighting like guys 3 or 4 years older than me and I was this short guy so they would take interest in you, … I give you this money and then I'll buy my sister stuff but you know you're not realizing that what you're doing is like, if it continues now you're in that life, you're literally in that life for God knows how long.

Well that's what happened to me anyway, now I found myself just falling into it because it's like … people here they were soft, it's like, and that's like I was saying, there is the fact that you welcome someone in this country it's great, but if you don't socialize him or the kids or their parents, especially from a war zone, yeah it's like, I lived, coz I was in [location] and I grew up with guys from [location] who are mostly … from these war type of countries … when they come there I feel like they change everyone around coz the kids have to start acting, you know, a bit harder.'

Dylan's story

Bob Marley and the Wailers (1980)
'Three Little Birds'
This reggae track is centred upon a positive message that things will be alright in the end.

'I chose this because as a kid growing up my mum used to always play it and she always used to say we shouldn't be worrying about things. Do you know we shouldn't dwell on things, and things like that but that's where I'm different because I stress about everything. I overthink about everything. But my mum used to say you're not supposed to worry, you're supposed to live your life and be who you want to be and so on, and tomorrow's another day and to this day I stress about things. Like, I stress about what trainers what I wear tomorrow and it will stop me sleeping all night, do you know. That's why I picked that song.

I was taken out of school and put in a project because what was going on at an early age I had to see child psychologists from eight [years old] onwards because someone was arguing with me one day in primary school and I picked up a chair and whacked him around the head about five times with it, coz it was learnt behaviour, I thought it was alright to do that and then the next minute I was under child welfare and child psychology, but it was all because of what I seen from a young age that, I thought it was acceptable you know, even though it wasn't. What eight-year-old attacks somebody? And not only that, hits then around the head with a chair? Not on the legs or their arms but in the head? So, from then on I knew that I could do anything.

I was obviously, you know I come from a broken home and that's when I went onto the streets to escape, but what people don't know is that my dad was raping my mum as well, they know about domestic violence, but they don't know the ins and outs of it. So, when I used to hear my mum scream and I couldn't do nothing for her so I'd go onto the estate and someone and we started out as a group of friends and then to cut a long story, we went to all-out war, and it lasted forever basically. I started dealing drugs at thirteen [years old], and then I was selling heroin on the streets at fourteen and crack cocaine. I had obviously I wasn't mature as I thought I was, but I knew from the age eleven, twelve, that I could go out and kill somebody and not feel no way about it ... and that's how my life carried on.

Do you know, [dad] didn't provide for us, or anything. If we asked him for something he would get it, but he didn't just come and offer anything, because my mum left him but he didn't send money for us or whatever, my mum went and done what she had to do to bring us up. Where I lived it's like a council area, we lived in a housing association house, but we had better than most kids, we knew right from wrong, do you know what I mean, my mum worked three jobs to make sure we had everything ... you know I made a choice, I knew right from wrong I knew what I was doing and I still done it, and now I choose not to do those things. People can't say I was forced into it or groomed into it, because if anything I groomed myself into it coz I went there to escape what was happening in the house. A lot of my friends was going through the same thing and that's why we congregated and we kinda like a family on the streets, and we pledged allegiances and we, do you know, and that's how it stayed for years and years to come.'

Discussion

Poverty

Several participants linked a financial desire to their initial engagement on-road. They had all grown up in low-income houses, with some indicating they were living in relative poverty. Access to particular material possessions, such as clothes and money for social activities, was seen as necessary to gain acceptance from their wider peer group. For some participants there was an additional need to access resources from outside the home, which was also impacted by the domestic violence and abuse (DVA), in particular where the perpetrators of DVA were exerting economic abuse on the wider family. Economic abuse is an often hidden and invisible aspect of DVA, which has gained greater academic attention since the 2010s (Postmus et al, 2018; Portas and Sharp-Jeffs, 2021). Control over financial resources has been historically central to the sustenance of patriarchy and thus the construction of hegemonic masculinity itself (Messerschmidt, 2018). There is an enduring pressure put on men to be the breadwinners in their family (Martinez, 1995). Therefore, when the participants referred to seeking opportunities to make money in later childhood, this had connotations with also seeking increased power and markers of a type of successful manhood.

In the participants' narratives they described poverty and financial control over the family as part of the DVA, as well as the financial repercussions of the perpetrator leaving the family. The result of these different aspects was that the participants (as boys) were then not able to be provided with some basic provisions or money for luxuries such as fashion of a calibre that would allow them to keep up with their peers. For others, after the perpetrator had left and their mother was then a single parent, there was also limited access to money. These financial limitations were combined with the pressure that the participants felt to dress and act a certain way, in order to enhance their dominant status within their chosen peer group. Jordan's performance of on-road protest masculinity was embodied in his self-presentation through clothes. He stated that he was set apart from his peers because of his 'suave dress sense'. He also used his wish to present himself differently as a motivating factor in becoming gang-involved, as the criminal activities meant he could make money and afford better clothes. Jordan noted that buying clothes gave him a sense of self-esteem. He wanted his clothes to 'represent' him, as 'clothes say something about a person, especially in the culture where I'm coming from anyway'. Here Jordan is referring to on-road street culture in which he was becoming more involved. Financial motivations for gang involvement were common among the participants.

Eric mentioned money 30 times in his interview; for contrast, money was only mentioned by Travis once. Although numeric representations of the data are not central to this study, the contrast shows the emphasis that Eric placed on money in his narratives. Eric explicitly said that acquiring money was a strong motivation for increased gang involvement. He noted that he was being ostracized at school for not being able to keep up with his peers in material ways. As a refugee new to an area, Eric craved the acceptance of his peer group and felt he stood out. A tension is revealed here between his step-mother telling him to be grateful that he made it to the UK, which he is, and his attempt to carve out a sense of normality among his peers. This desire for relational belonging is typical for refugee children, who are in a continual process of constructing self-identity (Chen and Schweitzer, 2019).

Travis also recounted the pressure to provide financially for the necessities when you are being brought up by a single-parent family. The broad range of discussions around gendered financial pressures illustrates the way in which boys internalize the wider socio-cultural messages around hegemonic masculinity, which centralizes economic stability and the 'breadwinner' role. Inherent in this is also a reminder of the underlying gender order, which decrees that boys should take the dominant provider position over adult women, usurping hierarchies of age. However, hierarchy aside, being the breadwinner is a specific socially sanctioned way for men to provide care in the family, without risking their masculine status (Gough, 2018). When discussing these wider cultural messages, for instance to be the breadwinner, Dave became emotional as he outlined the pressure that this put him under.

> 'I feel like, even that kinda ties into road culture and stuff like that, coz a lot of that is being what you are expected to be kind of thing and not being able to cope with it. Like you're expected to be like the bread maker [sic] and look after your mum and that's why people end up on-road and stuff like that, and these are the pressures that can lead people to suicide, it's just like, what it is, it's like, trying a lot to live up to kinda thing and not being able to. Pushing yourself down into the dirt to try and be something you're not and being told not to speak about it and be strong and all that.' (Dave)

In this passage Dave is making a connection between the pressures that are placed upon men to be the 'bread maker' (breadwinner) and provide for his mother. This was in addition to the simultaneous pressures of having to be 'something you're not' as well as 'not speak about it' and 'be strong'. These are the markers of hegemonic masculinity outlined explicitly. Dave then referred directly to suicide as a route out of the masculine pressures. Male suicide rates have been high since the mid-1990s, however there was an incremental increase, peaking most recently in 2019, which was the highest rate since the year 2000 (ONS, 2019). This has resulted in high-profile campaigns urging men to talk about their feelings, alongside the wider discourse on toxic masculinity, both of which may have contributed to Dave speaking out (Gough, 2018).

Drug dealing, agency, and grooming

Following on from the prior discussion around poverty in childhood, for several of the participants poverty was a motivating factor in their initial involvement on-road, through drug dealing, which precipitated their increasing involvement in gangs. Street-based drug dealing was often the first business that the participants had with local gangs. This was framed by some participants as part of a grooming process (Sam), whereas others framed it as part of an agentic decision to become involved (Dylan, Lester), or as a combination of the two (Eric, Jordan). As drug dealing appeared to be so instrumental in the participants' pathways into going on-road and ultimately becoming gang-involved, it was impossible to separate the production relations involved in the trade of drugs with the power relations that were also at play. Dylan was clear on conveying that he went on-road and became gang-involved due to his own independent decision. He emphasized his own agency and rational choice in framing the alternative environment as a coping strategy to avoid his home, where DVA was being carried out. Dylan distanced himself from the concept of grooming, which implies your power and choice have been taken away. Instead, he focused on the way that he fled from his home as a rational response to the DVA. Dylan's point was emphasized when he said, 'I knew right from wrong', highlighting a sense of his agency and actively embracing what his perceived personal choice; taking power back through this interpretation of events. Paradoxically he says, though, he 'groomed' himself 'into it coz I went there to escape …'; this implies that really he did not have much of a choice as there were limited options to get away from home.

Sam firmly situated the beginning of his on-road life as a result of grooming, which started out by being asked to pass on packages to people in exchange for 'sweets, then fivers [five pounds]'. He noted that when he was being asked to sell things by the older boys, he hadn't realized at the time that he was engaging in illegal drug dealing. He then spoke of his shock when he first saw someone overdose and realized that it was because of the drugs that he had sold him. Sam conveyed how he felt 'scared', although it is less than clear whether that referred to being scared of being caught selling drugs or ending up overdosing himself; however, both were possible. Crucially, the futility of running away can be seen here, as he ran but they all still lived on the same estate, thus the expression 'kinda run away'. This emphasizes the ways in which living in a gang-affected area is a geographical constraint, as it results in limited options to reject the gang as a peer group. The basic fact is that Sam had nowhere else to go, at age eight, particularly when he was also feeling unsafe at home. Thus, grooming aside, his options were severely limited. Sam noted that these experiences meant that he needed to 'grow up really fast'. The idea of his environment *training and building him up* is a powerful image; grooming equating to training in part. He later told me that at the time he didn't know the concept or language of grooming. This is a concept of victimization that he has learnt later in life. This discussion of grooming presents a distinct form of power relations that were present in the participants' lives in childhood. Eric's narrative around going on-road and becoming increasingly gang-involved was more nuanced than the poles of victim/agency. Eric noted that he initially chose to start drug dealing as a way to gain money, to buy luxuries that enabled him to keep up with his peers. This then escalated as he became more involved with others who were gang-involved, until it was difficult to extrapolate himself. The complexity around grooming and the drug trade has been explored by Irwin-Rogers (2019, p 11), who looked at the way that the popular statutory approach has been to blame the 'violent and coercive gang leader' for young people's involvement in drug distribution. Irwin-Rogers argued that this keeps the blame on individuals, which is a distraction from the underlying structural factors that influence involvement, as displayed in the narratives given in this chapter.

Drug dealing was only one element that got Eric 'noticed' by gang elders. It is important to consider, as Eric indicated in this passage, that acceptance was a major motivation for his gang involvement, and so becoming noticed and appreciated would have been largely a positive outcome. The other was the fights that he was getting in at school. For several of the participants, Eric included, fighting was initially a way to offload residual anger from experiencing DVA, as well as inhabit a more emboldened masculinity performance. It is evident that Eric's narrative portrays more complexity between agency and grooming, which presents events and choices more like a slippery slope, which he didn't become fully aware of until it was too late. Like Eric, Jordan foregrounded the desire for money as a key motivator for his initial on-road involvement, as part of trying to 'find a way out'.

Sexual exploitation

In the interview with Sam, he discussed his experiences of exploitation, sexual and otherwise. He noted that he had had to exchange sexual acts with older women in order to be able to sleep in their houses. However, in talking about his experience of sexual exploitation, instead of saying initially outright he was a victim of this, he framed his experience as a 'women's issue', before later identifying himself as a victim of it. This suggests that he has an internalized perception of sexual exploitation as a gendered phenomenon, despite afterwards noting that he felt that it was happening to him. Sam's first shop theft was initiated by an older woman. She was exploiting him – if he stole food from a shop, she would cook it for him (as he was very young and didn't know how to cook). Referring to sexual exploitation as a 'women's issue' indicates Sam had a reluctance to identify his own victimization as a 'man's issue'. He associated victimization as something that generally happens to women. This is consistent with UK government policy, which frames sexual exploitation as 'violence against women and girls'. This indicates that, for Sam and most of the other men, vulnerability and victimization were at odds with the type of masculinity that they were seeking to perform at the time. Gender stereotypes have been identified as a factor that can conceal identification of sexual exploitation and abuse, as 'gendered perceptions of masculinity mean young males are unlikely to talk about having been sexually exploited due to shame, fear, and concerns about being labelled gay due to homophobic social attitudes' (McNaughton et al, 2014, p 14).

As shown in the participants' narratives, it was as if there was no language available through which to conceive themselves being direct victims of such emasculating and usually gendered (female-as-victim) issues. Existing research into male experiences of sexual exploitation indicate that boys and young men are a 'sizeable minority of CSE [child sexual exploitation] cases' (McNaughton et al, 2014). They found that boys were more likely to become victims of sexual exploitation at a younger age than girls and were more likely to have a criminal record (48 per cent of males they studied, versus 28 per cent of females) (McNaughton et al, 2014, p 7). This indicates that a story like Sam's is not unique, where he was in an already vulnerable and homeless position and was then compelled to carry out criminal acts (theft) by his abuser.

Managing anger, coping with abuse

The connection between DVA, internal pain, and committing violence was a common theme in the data. The emotion of anger is one which is relatively safe for men to express without damaging their masculine personas, as it is widely considered more 'masculine' (Gough, 2018). Eric described not knowing how to deal with the feelings that the DVA brought up. He described his response to these emotions, which included engaging in violence in school as a coping strategy to manage difficult feelings. Engagement in public violence was a way to react against the way that he had experienced 'invisible' violence in private at home. Engaging in public violence made him feel visible and provided an audience to the violence, which is the role that he had been placed in at home. An example of how the music elicitation method assisted the sharing of emotions and memories around coping with DVA and managing anger follows:

Cormega (2007)
'The Saga'
This hip-hop track describes the struggles of urban life in poverty, being surrounded by drug dealing, addiction, homelessness, murder, bereavement.

'The lyrics [of the song above] said, "the saga begins on a reflection of the drama within". And that's what you're seeing now in the streets, the knife crime, people being killed, it's an external thing, it's a reflection of the drama within and now you're seeing it poured out in this anger, in these killings.' (Sam)

As shown in this quote, Sam used the music track to help him talk about his feeling that issues generally labelled as related to youth violence were due to the outward expression of internal emotional issues. The sense of carrying around an internal anger was a theme that several participants referred to when describing the enduring effects of DVA experience. To talk about this, Sam quoted the lyrics in his first music choice. This example shows how music elicitation worked in practice, as other participants also drew on lyrics as a way to help them express their views. The way that the original song track refers to rap music as a 'mental narcotic' resonates with the way that several participants referred to using music as a cathartic and a coping mechanism in their past as well as in their current lives. Eric described not knowing how to deal with the feelings that the DVA brought up:

> 'You keep seeing it [DVA] at home, and you don't know how to deal with those emotions.' (Eric)

Eric then described his response to these emotions, which included engaging in violence in school as a coping strategy to manage difficult feelings. Engagement in public violence was a way to react against the way that he had experienced 'invisible' violence in private at home. Engaging in public violence made him feel visible, enabled him to take up space, and provided an audience to the violence, which is the role that he had been placed in at home.

In Dylan's narrative (earlier in the chapter) he describes hitting another child with a chair at school. Firstly, he directly relates carrying out the act of violence to the violence he had been experiencing at home. He notes that it was 'learnt behaviour' and he normalizes the violent response as a way to deal with someone he disagrees. Looking back in retrospect he asks, 'what eight-year-old attacks somebody?', highlighting his perception that this behaviour was not consistent with his peer group at that age. He stated, 'from then on I knew I could do anything'; he had crossed a boundary, or learned something he could use, both by gaining a sense of power from realizing he could be violent and also understanding that he didn't feel an emotional response to it, that he was desensitized from it. What is clear from Eric's and Dylan's stories of emerging school violence is that engaging in violence was perceived as an outlet for anger and as a way to seek markers of a type of masculinity that was denied to them at home, in particular, respect and power. Eric mentioned a similar experience to Dylan's: of perpetrating violence in school at a young age. He noted that he was both desensitized to violence due to experiencing it at home, as well as having an increased tolerance for violence when with peers. In this way Eric sought out people to fight at school as a way to reclaim the sense of power and dignity that he lost when he was being abused at home by his parents. Eric found himself searching for a place to let out the anger that he was carrying. For him, the place he found was the gang context, what he calls here in the initial stages a 'set', which he described as being an outlet for the underlying anger.

The concept of carrying around residual anger was a common theme that emerged from the narratives. The way in which it was spoken about was as if, through experiencing violence at home but not being able to act, due the protest masculinity position and dominance of the perpetrator, the participants then carried around vengeful anger that needed an outlet elsewhere. This anger then in turn transferred a sense of gaining the power and respect among peers that was not available at home. This is a type of protest masculinity transference, where the power relations that were vastly unequal at home were rebalanced among peers – the angry child finds that they are feared by others. A further aspect of Eric's juxtaposition of being victimized at home and perpetrating violence at school was that he also referred to how he had benefitted from being made 'hard' and 'tough' as a refugee from war, as well as the from violence that his father had inflicted on him, which his father had called 'African ways' (see Chapter 4). Eric was managing the intersection of his African racial identity and his masculine identity, both of which were embedded in the context of his identity as a refugee in the UK. There is a wider cultural tendency to gender the oppositional discourse of hard/soft. This was discussed by one academic who looked at the gendered use of these terms and found that hard was used to refer to masculinized qualities placed in opposition to soft, which functions to feminize (Hong, 2016). This language, which is used to demarcate different groups, was used by Eric to infantilize the soft people, whom he refers to as being 'babied', and as 'kids' that 'don't know nothing'. Eric mentioned he then became 'cool' due to his propensity for violence and the way he enacted a 'hard' persona. Allen Feldman (1991, p 28) defined 'hardness' as 'an interiorized quality extracted from risking the body in performance'. Jefferson extended this by including 'an indifference to the body's (often painful) fate', as well as 'courage or bravery, qualities of *mental* toughness which have nothing necessarily to do with muscle' (Jefferson, 1998, p 81; original emphasis). With this way of approaching it, it becomes clear that masculine embodiment cannot be centred on one element, physical or emotional, but is rather concentrated on the body as a whole. Jefferson notes that this idea is illustrated both in schoolboy sport or physical labour, that ideal masculinity incorporates embodies strength, skill, and competence.

Not all of the participants described a seamless journey into school and on-road that capitalized on being 'hard'. Dave had experienced extreme bullying in his younger years, noting that it got so bad that he was not able to go outside at times. After several years of this he finally reached 'breaking point' and decided not to be a 'victim' anymore:

> 'I was perfect for bullying, I was chubby erm, so I got terrorized but when I got older I went the opposite, no one can say anything to me and for years then no one would try and lay a finger on me coz I got to that point where I was like no one is fucking with me now, someone hits me I'm gonna knock them out. I just got to that breaking point and then I think people sensed that. They sense a victim don't they, if they look at you and your like head down, they'll think he's a pussy

I could bully him and when they know you're a bit dodgy [they leave you alone].' (Dave)

Dave transformed himself to enact a toughness that acted as a strategy for protection. He stated, 'I got sick of being a victim' and so started to act in a defensive way as a protective strategy. Through this redefinition of his own personal boundaries he emerged embracing the markers of protest masculinity, literally in protest against the conditions of his previous victimization. Sam talked about noticing that he gained a sense of power from realizing even the bigger boys were afraid of him. This was reflected in the way he spoke about his dog as being vicious as a mirroring of his own developing violent behaviour. The way he positioned his dog as being his best friend at the time could be seen as another type of metaphor. Sam shared the way in which his dog was rejected by his mother, which mirrored the way he also felt rejected by her, so together they went to live on the streets as homeless companions. Using Connell's analytic lens to focus on the way in which masculinity performance is implicated by power relations and the way in which the participants sought to enact violence in public highlights that they were seeking a sense of power that was unavailable to them at home.

School was shown to be a space where the dynamics of violence, agency, and resistance interacted. School offered an opportunity for the young men to find acceptance, a peer group, a way to be out of the house and thus away from the DVA. It was a space in which to regain a sense of lost power and test their masculinity through fighting. Fighting was noted by several participants as a way to cope with the anger that brewed within when faced with the DVA at home. None of the participants in the study mentioned disclosure, recognition, or support with regard to the DVA they suffered in childhood. Processing their feelings in a physically violent way led to them being labelled and often excluded for those problematic behaviours, furthering the push to another space: the life on-road. School was an in-between space that served to contextualize the participants' experiences as different to the norm through their comparison with their peers. For some of them, engagement in school was a coping strategy, both through full participation or as a space to enact violence, framed as a method of conveying and releasing anger. Gunter (2017) noted that school was often a site of contestation of masculinities for Black boys, who were also increasingly participating on-road, due partly to perceived mistreatment by mainly White teachers: these teachers 'disrespected' the young people, who then retaliated due to their engagement in the on-road 'code of the street'.

6

'a man'/'The Man'

In the narratives there were distinct ways in which participants described masculinity as something culturally achieved. This achievement was expressed through a discourse of being/becoming 'a man' and being/becoming 'The Man'. In the interviews, the process of becoming a man was mentioned in many different ways, focusing generally on the symbolic values and gains that the individuals associated with becoming a man. Alongside this was the discussion from some of the participants of their achievements of becoming 'The Man', which is capitalized here because it was conveyed as a title, rather than a description itself. In becoming 'The Man' there were even more layers of symbolic representation that conveyed what it is to become the ultimate man in the gang context. Discourses of perceived hegemonic masculinity were revealed in the interviews through the distinction between 'a man' and 'The Man'. Not all of the participants I interviewed had achieved this status, or at times were not certain if they had, but they all appeared to have an awareness and understanding of what 'The Man' was about. In the narratives, a distinction was often made between the qualities participants' attribute to an everyday masculinity ('a man'), which included independence, looking after one's responsibilities, a sense of being respected, and access to a type of power. As the participants referred to achieving the status of 'The Man', they then started talking about different elements of masculinity performance, including being feared, having power over others, enacting violence, and respect. As they then moved on to talk about being The Man from a retrospective position, several of the participants noted that, now looking back, they feel that they had conflated fear and respect at those times, which they now see as distinct.

In the interviews there were several references to the notion of 'The Man'. This title was most commonly used; however, other related terms included 'the boss', 'King', 'the guy', 'the man on the block', 'the man of the house', 'top man'. These all connote a sense of masculine hierarchies, with several terms also referring patriarchal norms. Some of the participants explained what this meant, and through this, what masculine status looked like in the gang context. Moving from 'a man' to 'The Man' was heavily based on the instrumentalization of violence and fear. Moving from subordinated masculinity to protest masculinity was based on the way in which the participants shifted from being in fear of the domestic violence and abuse (DVA) perpetrator at home, to mastering fear, and ultimately making others afraid of them. This was highlighted in the tension in the 'nutter' performance, which was performative violence as a protection strategy, outlining the way the participants discussed needing to make others fear them in order to lessen their own feelings of fear. In this chapter, the developments in the participants' masculine biographies are discussed in relation to their adolescence – this period represents their main on-road and gang-involved time. The participants revealed the various ways in which they adopted a protest masculinity defined by their marginalization and attempts to redress the powerlessness that they felt in younger childhood. When talking about his youth, Eric firmly centred his use of violence as a tool to 'be a man'. He clearly defines masculinity in relation to his experience of his father's dominance and violence at home, subordinate to his father, who was 'The Man of the house'. This left Eric wanting to search for his own sense of being 'a man' when outside of his home. For many of the participants the peak of their gang life was to become 'The Man'. Dylan plainly asserted:

'I was The Man, do you know.' (Dylan)

Several (Dylan, Sam, Lester, Jordan) mentioned being 'The Man' as if it was a self-explanatory concept:

'I was The Man, if you understand what it means … on one side I was the top guy and I had the pretty girls over here and they were all over me, and then I had all the mandem,[1] like the gang all respecting me, the streets respected me, I was The Guy.' (Sam)

It evoked a sense of being the ultimate masculine icon: *the alpha male*. Sam explained the concept to me as being 'the top guy', which came with access to women, and respect from the gang and the streets. 'Pretty girls' are clearly commodified in Sam's extract here, framed as a benefit of holding The Man status. In this way they are accessories, on the periphery. This was also mentioned by Dylan, who framed his increased status as including 'access to women', as if they were a type of profit in this enterprise. Sam also outlined that being feared by his peers was part of the process of becoming The Man. The idea of the boss represents being in control, and at the head of a company. This is a concept that has historically been associated with hegemonic masculinity. What became clear from the participants' narratives is that violence was of primary importance as they shifted to becoming gang-involved. It was ever present in the participants' lives in their younger years and as they got older their position in relation to it changed. They moved from straddling the distinction between victim at home and perpetrator on-road, to becoming both victim and perpetrator in the gang context.

Eric's story

2Pac (1998)
'Changes'
This hip-hop track discusses racism, police brutality, and drug policy, as well as the racialized perpetuation of poverty in North America.

'So then now you go to school and you you're good at school and yeah everything was good for me, everything except somehow, you want more. It's like you want a place to let out the anger and you don't know how. And once you find an avenue, you don't know it but you start going back, you know it's dangerous now, so then you're eight or nine [years old], every Fridays I would sneak out and go out with my friends, they would go and rob people, robbing people taking their stuff and doing a little robbing and then coz you're kids now you're in a little set and you realize there's another little sets and now you have a little problem, now the Fridays and the Saturdays are coming more, and before you know it now that's it, now that becomes normal, coz I feel like we owe a lot of these kids, they don't come out seven, eight, nine [years old], got gangs like no! no no, it's just you start off a certain way and now your started with those guys so if there was ten of us, all ten of us are stuck together. Now if you live on an estate and there's another estate, so that means you're growing up you're inheriting everything from ten years from then and if you're the weakest link you're gone, it's like, so that means that your gonna be a kid that's gonna be bullied and you're not gonna try to involve yourself, but regardless if that side knows that you live on this side that they have beef [conflict] with, they'll even kill you and you don't mean nothing to those guys, so for me I found myself that my friends were [area] based I was going to all their beefs, so now it was Saturdays and now it was growing even more now, and it was now we are gonna need to carry knives because punching wasn't enough.

I just started hanging out more now, coz now [mum's] working nights. I've got freedom, so if it's during school times I'll be safe. So in year ten or eleven we would always be setting ourselves up. So now my friends are being kicked out of school now because they are really bad, because that's an age when their little fighting is getting worse. Now so they're getting kicked out of school one by one, and

I'm still at school, Saturdays, Fridays now become every day, so now it's like, these beefs are getting worse and you know I think in year ten I get, I get yeah, someone bottled me and I'm like OK it's getting serious now I need to get myself a knife or something, so now I'm carrying a knife. My friend got stabbed in year eleven, carrying a knife, so now it's just intensifying, so now it's a normal thing, but I was lucky, like I said, you know I've came too far for me to just stop school, so I always kept that school thing going. But now my mum is finding out coz she's taking me to hospitals because people are coming after school, something that was a little Friday thing is just escalating, mate, every week she's taking me to hospital, now my hand is dislocated, then I got stabbed and my dad is like OK what is happening? He's scared? He, you know ... he was ... you know he was bad between them but he was still trying to be a father, you know. That day you know I was like I'm done with it, but you're not done your stuck with it for life, this beef now you inherited it, it's not inherited it but the game is intensifying people are dying now slowly and slowly.

Guys what you're doing on the weekend? I don't know. So now then you're going to rob someone's phone, trying to find to sell it, but now you've found an avenue to do something and coz you've done one you're doing two, you're doing three, now the elders are like you man I've got bigger moves for you, OK, let's go do bigger moves and then you go do bigger moves, so my friends were moving higher up. And I was like naahhh I've got college tomorrow I've got drama, I don't know if I really wanna go. By then my guys were actually bigger than me, I was like, that thing was like you guys don't change, you guys do that cool but I'm sticking with this. So they always respected that. So then, they will actually be trying to push me as well in a sense because it's like, I'm not about to go and sell drugs for you guys. And then when I was broke, I found a hostel, I had no money and I would jump barriers to go to college and you would sign on to get some sort of money but that just wasn't enough, it's literally nothing. So um my friend was like, "you wanna make the money?" cool, around these guys now, but that age all they talk about is money and how to make money and they've found an avenue, the little outcasts who can't fit in at school, but now they definitely fit in in the streets. And now they've grown they do bigger stuff and I'm like now what are you doing? Going to some countryside [cross county lines] to go and sell drugs. I go there one night and I'm like oh my God this is boring, this is boring I couldn't do this. It didn't sit well with me, nah guys this is not for me, I'm cool. I've got a robbery coming up, OK let's do robberies, it was post office cars back in the day, they are picking up money and um following them around the whole day, one or two, trying to get the money. So you're now doing bigger stuff that you could end up in prison and I'm just like … I'm just lonely in that hostel but then these guys they know, they know when to come when you're just lonely and there's just no one for you and they just wanna, it's like, when I came here I was young, I mean when I was in year seven, eight, nine [school years] when you don't have nothing as well you're not doing well in school, those guys are there to take you in and now you're in a hostel they're just, they're there to actually take you in again.'

Lester's story

Leroy Smart (1976)
'Ballistic Affair'
This track, by a Jamaican reggae artist, focuses on the senselessness of street violence, and preaches for unity.

'I'd be lying, if I said I just woke up and saw people older than me doing things, car, money, jewellery, this that, then they're robbing post office, robbing this and robbing that, then I started burgling like a lunatic and this old [local] man who used to drive a taxi, he heard what all the madness I was doing and he pulled me one day and he said listen don't shit on your own doorstep and he explained to me what that meant yeah, and from then on I just left and I was gone [to the suburbs], I saw some things I didn't even believe was possible, yeah like, swimming pool in your house and all that madness, this is how people are living yeah, I couldn't believe it. There's no pubs, no off-licenses nothing, just a little flower shop, little bank, and that's it. Every other road is private, and on another level, and that's what he meant yeah? Fine. And then from there it just continues until it spirals into what it spirals to where everything's just about money money money money and everyone professes to love you because you got money or because they're scared you and it's all fake coz they don't love you yeah and you just get caught up in it and if you rise to the top like I did you'll end up getting big money and then you'll have your gun with you every day and then everything will become normal and then you'll end up shooting people like it's normal and then it's obviously not normal and the more you do it the more casual it will become to do it, do you understand? Until you'll do it over anything and then you're in a bad place, you're not gonna come out of there unless you're dead or in jail and that's it. And that's what happened to me, that's sad.

I remember having times when things were hysterical when they weren't really funny when I look at it now, but at the time they just seemed dead funny. And I couldn't dream that I could ever go to jail. But all them things did happen.

First of all I was in [prison] yeah, they didn't want to move me to [transfer location] and I had to climb up on the roof inside the workshop just to get a move. So when I climbed up onto the roof in the workshop I'm telling you know, I got up on there yeah and there was just a little ledge space like this ... and these screws yeah were like massive and they were snarling and if they could have ever got me I would have been in bits "FUCKING GET DOWN HERE NOW", listen brother I'm not going anywhere innit and if you come any closer I'll jump. And this is the rest, get away from him and they started getting back down and away from me and then the governor come yeah and some speech ledge talker who could allegedly talk people out of things and I said listen to me carefully, you can't talk nothing out of me yeah, I'm gonna explain to you yeah. When I'm ready I'll come off here and we are going to the block and them I'm going to [area]. Your prison's racist, I'm not staying here anymore, and that's why I'm up here on the roof do you understand? So then the governor come and some screw come what I did trust and he said, it's me man there not gonna do you, I'm gonna stay here until you come down, I'm gonna put the cuffs on you and I'll take you to the block, and that's what happened. I sat down there for three months and started having to make some more complaints until I started making them out to the commissioner outside. The one thing about prisoners, they're resilient and they learn ways to get things done. Unorthodox but what works. So basically I got to [area] on the back of a bad ticket.'

Sam's story

Akon (2004)
'Ghetto'

This hip-hop track centres upon the cycles of poverty that are experiences in urban areas. It also discusses the physical and mental health impacts of living in poverty. It touches upon children drug dealing, upon hunger, police corruption, and the lack of help that exists.

'Both of these songs [DMX – Slippin, and Akon – Ghetto], literally word for word, just everything, that I lived, 100%. I went down a hard slope, sleeping in crack houses, taking crack cocaine from the age of 13 and then it [the song] goes onto saying he became a man and I became a man eventually and everyone loved me, well, they didn't but they feared me, I wanted respect ... but I didn't ... they feared me, and people showed me, like lifted me up, glorified everything that I did, erm, and I became the boss. I was a mess and I was becoming everything that people were saying about me. But underneath it all I was a king or I was even, not even underneath it, the way I was living, I was a king in a fairy tale, in my own world that I created and people saw me as a king in that world. Society has a world that they made as well, and there are kings in that world, well we've also make a world and there is kings in that world and I was one of them.

I've had fights with [dogs], like one on one ... and it's trying to bite me and I bottled it and hit it with a pole and I have to run away, and who wants to fight a [dog]. Someone who's not there really, who's gone empty. Warriors go into war, Spartans go into like 5000 people, they must've lost something, some connection to go in there and do that, to kill and that was me I was very disconnected, but very connected spiritually. Just sleeping on kitchen floors, talking whatever drugs that I could find, the drugs helped me to just come right from reality. And what I'm faced with, I made pacts that I'm going to be a certain way and there's nothing that's gonna stop me. I felt that from the very start of life to me. There was pain, and it was like I was being hurt from the start so now I'm here after all this hurt and now exploding and it's like why should I care about anything, what, or even how can I care about anything? When care was not given, wasn't an option for me. I've been to [many] prisons, been around gangs from all over, I seen people being stabbed, I've stabbed people, I've been bottled in my head, I've been bricked in my head, I've been run over. I've been thrown out of windows. I've just self-destructed myself that was how I was, it was self-harming basically. But when people punched me I felt good. Like I remember one day having a fight and this guy's on top of me and he's hitting me and I'm shouting "hit me", "hit me" and I've got my arms open and I'm letting him hit me, and then my boy runs over and kicks him off of me and we beat him up and my boys like "why are you doing this' like what's going on with you?" and I was like, "I don't care about life" and I was drinking and just like seeing all my friends die, my friend coming to meet me to come to a show and then he gets killed on his way to meet me. My other friend died on a bus we were all talking the next thing you know my boy's on the bus with a few of the guys and he gets stabbed on the bus and he dies. My other boy we were locked up together eventually after a few years ... it was really good to see him and stuff coz we was in the same prison and it was a nice experience to be with someone you know. Then you come out of prison and when he comes out boom he gets shot dead.

I was becoming desensitized and I was becoming more broken, and I just didn't have a care or, I couldn't care, when you're locked up in the jail or when you're out on the streets and you have nowhere to live and you have no food, no money, like you're living on the poverty line, your care levels [are] very low because you have to destroy it, I was locked up for years, say years you're in prison, you can't be caring because if you care then the whole time is gonna break you and then you'll probably commit suicide, that's why some of the people commit suicide because they've got so much care and they can't handle it and they're like, they get, it's too much for them. So what I had to do I had to suppress the caring, I had to do things that I didn't want to do.

I was The Man, if you understand what it means, I was the top guy and on one side I was the top guy and I had the pretty girls over here and they were all over me, and then I had all the mandem, like the gang all respecting me, the streets respected me, I was the guy, The Man on the block. I mean everything remember I'm the king pin over here and I just let go of all of that and people were shocked but at the same time I was The Man so even when I did it they couldn't really tell me anything because I was a nutter, they used to call me [nickname], they used to say he's [crazy] like, that's what he does, so no one could really say anything.

I disconnected from, erm, the world and the way that they do things and I decided I'm not doing it that way I'm doing it the way I wanted to do it, the way my life is going to go the way I say my life is going to go. I remember being with someone and they're telling me come home and I used to get really angry and I would say that's not my home, my home is on the block, that's like, I created my new home, my road mentality, I was a roadman, I was the biggest roadman you'd ever know in my life, literally I slept on the road, like, the road, like I had like, I got really angry if someone said something about the road or just the smallest things like, like when she said come home, that showed it, like what? I am home like, get really defensive about it. I couldn't leave it, it's just my life, erm, even when I was in prison like the Gov[erners] they get scared of me because I'm telling them when I argue, or not even argue when I shout or get aggressive I'm telling them this is my home I've been here longer than you, this is where I live, so they don't know what to do with me, most people want to get out and I'm like I'm home, and they are like what are you talking about, I was bad in jail, I was not, I was not right in my head, like, and then in the midst, so to show you how messed up and mixed up and how mad I actually was, they would get me out of my cell to beat someone up.'

Discussion
The nutter

A theme that emerged in the narratives around performative protest masculinity was the way in which the participants adopted a persona of being 'nuts'/'a nutter' as a protective strategy. Sam noted in the interview that one of the reasons that he was feared was because he was considered a 'nutter'. Sam had almost claimed nutter as a trademark at the height of his on-road and gang-involved life. He noted that he had a reputation of having fewer boundaries and not stopping when he got angry. This served to deter peers from being confrontational with him, as well as mitigating any responsibility for his actions when he did go further with violence than his peers. Acting crazy, or limitless, as a form of both protest masculinity but also a personal protection strategy was also described by Dave:

> 'I actually tried to look dodgy as well, I used to shave my head before it started receding and my mum said you look like a football hooligan and I said good, coz where I live, if they think I look nuts they are not gonna bother with me … but really I've liked it at times where people have said he's mad you know, he'll fuck you up or this or that, I used to have people who had this reputation or this idea of me that I was this nutter and really that is a shame isn't it.' (Dave)

Inherent in this passage from Dave is a contradiction between the need to seem like a nutter, which evokes the potential of volatile and extreme violence at short notice, with his own desire not to 'be a violent guy'. This was a strategy developed by Dave after his childhood experiences of severe and violent bullying by peers. He described the process he made between being a victim to defending himself, which was heavily tied up in his embodied performance of protest masculinity. Dave is reflecting on the past strategies he developed in order to reduce his changes of harm on-road. Looking back, he comments that it was a 'shame' that looking like that, and deliberately marginalizing himself in that way, was the preferable option. Dave entered life on-road after living in a gang-affected area and being badly bullied. As outlined in Chapter 5, Dave reached a point where he felt it was a choice of either starting to fight back or continue to be abused. This is reflected in his choice to look intimidating as a protection strategy. Looking like that will then have drawn reactions from others that would have positioned him even deeper within the protest masculinities discourse even if he personally did not identify with it. Jefferson (1998, p 93) noted that being considered 'the "headcase", or "nutter" is the extreme example of hardness because his willingness to risk the body in performance is apparently unfettered by any of the normal constraints, fears and calculations'.

Sam sought to convey the extent to which he was operating outside normal social boundaries. He was suggesting the prison guards' exploitation of his 'nutter' persona emphasizes how tough he was. However, this is also an example of the instrumentalization of his 'nutter' persona by the prison staff for their own means. As it happened in a prison, it is questionable whether Sam had much choice when asked to perform the 'nutter' on their behalf. This is therefore a complex power play between the prison guards and prisoner, as well as between ordinary and 'nutter' masculine performances. 'Going nuts' as a form of resistance has also been explored by Wilson (2003). In research in a young offenders' prison, he found that ' "Going nuts" was not something to be done lightly, but was instead strategy to be used sparingly and when other options had been exhausted' (Wilson, 2003, p 421). Lester alluded to 'going nuts' in prison in protest of the racism that he was experiencing perpetrated by the prison staff, after being transferred to a prison in a predominantly White area in the north of England. Phillips (2020, p 13) drew on similar themes of losing control due to the impact of being worn down by racism, referred to in her study as going '[incredible] Hulk'. The essence across all these experiences is the fundamentals of protest masculinity: violent and disruptive expressions of frustration, when all other recourses of redress are exhausted. In Lester's case he climbed up on a prison roof demanding to be transferred to a different prison, emphasizing his experiences of racism making his life unbearable.

In this story of Lester going nuts, he described negotiations of power throughout the incident. Initially he had power due to his behaviour, going up on a ledge and refusing to get down. However, he then mentioned his fear at that time, that if he did get down then the prison officers would have got to him and he would have 'been in bits'. Lester then agreed to come down not only after being heard by the governor but also from a prison officer whom he trusted to safeguard him when he did come down. Although he ended up having to spend a period of time 'on the block'[2] and it appeared that the initial protest didn't directly result in a move, when a move did occur Lester attributed this to his affirmative action. Acting out in order to be moved to segregation in prisons was constructed as an act of resistance by Maguire (2019, p 15), who researched prison masculinities and found that it was a both a 'high-risk and costly strategy for preserving main location masculine status and for dealing with the threat of serious violence'. This may also apply to Lester in his navigation of prison racism. Lester noted that this was an example of a strategy to be heard and to show resilience. Lester's story highlights the thin line between out-of-control nutter performance and an instrumental performance and perception of the nutter. This story is also about bravado, as Lester portrayed this incident as an example where he was both clever and determined, merely seeking his rights, even in the face of 'snarling screws'. Going nuts here was presented as a form of protest and of being heard.

Martial metaphors

In the interviews there were various examples where metaphors alluding to war were integrated into everyday speech. For instance, Eric referred to people as 'foot-soldiers', Dylan discussed the use of 'peace treaties' to resolve gang conflicts. One way that war language was used was to explain that the stakes were high – literally life or death. The notion of war conveys this grave reality. Sam also referenced war language to describe the mentality that is needed for someone to thrive while on-road, comparing it to the Spartans who went into battle with only 5,000 soldiers, evidence they must have 'gone empty'. In this passage Sam noted how he became someone who was internally lacking the connections needed to care. Sam likened this experience to historical warriors the Spartans, who engaged in win-or-die-style battles. This passage denotes a sense of fatalism and resignation, as if the choice to go to war was inevitable. The juxtaposition of war imagery and disconnection with a parallel sense of being 'very connected spiritually' echoes Deuchar (2018, p 177), who found that gang-involved men juxtaposed their journey as going from 'warriors to peacemakers'. Sam was conveying this message from a retrospective position, thus emphasizing the spirituality that was present in the years before he had a religious awakening.

A benefit from likening the experience to a war is that it can also explain how much time can pass within one extended disagreement. Dylan noted how he was engaged in several wars, which each lasted for several years. The language was used in different ways: to signify the high stakes, to portray the mentality of gang life, to explain the lengthy feuds. There is also a definite link to a traditional masculine imagery in the language of war: 'qualities such as aggression, rationality, or physical courage are identified both as an essential component of war and also of masculinity at a given place or time' (Hutchings, 2008, p 389). This taps into a very specific masculinity discourse, which conveys the notions of honour, of doing one's duty, of being part of a larger group. It also conveys the seriousness of the stakes, which people are fighting and willing to die for, however meaningless or incomprehensible this may look from the outside. Interestingly, Dylan states that the cause of gang feuds was on inherited issues from elders rather than drugs or territory.

Masculinity is often metaphorically linked to war because 'formal, relational properties of masculinity provide a framework through which war can be rendered both intelligible and acceptable as a social practice and institution' (Hutchings, 2008, p 389). In this way, the relationship between masculinity and war can be 'mutually constitutive and mutually reinforcing' (Hutchings, 2008, p 391). Kerig et al (2013) advocated looking at the parallels between gang research and literature on child soldiers. There seems to be some connection between the two experiences. They found that 'mirroring the literature on child soldiers, gang-involved youth are exposed to a range of violent experiences as both victims and perpetrators' (Kerig et al, 2013, p 775). War metaphors offered the participants a positive discourse to underpin the performance of masculinity. It alludes to a sense of loyalty with one's wider group or army, which includes within it the value of retribution on behalf of the group, without necessarily understanding why. It is violence in a societally acceptable context. It also explains the conditions in an apt way: you cannot choose to back out of a war, it is a long continuous battle which individuals play a bit-part.

Self-harming through victimization and perpetration of violence

Using Gilson's (2014) conceptualization of vulnerability, which emphasizes the close relationship between violence and insecurity, the pinnacle of this interrelationship is evidenced in self-harming. Self-harming in the narratives was discussed in a range of ways, both directly (harming oneself directly) and indirectly (harming oneself through engagement in fights). Self-harm in the form of alcohol abuse was mentioned by Dylan. He spoke about this as a way to convey the depth of his feelings and his vulnerabilities. The notion of engagement in violence as a form of self-harm was raised by Sam. Sam said that he lost the ability to care about himself or others. He noted that it was this lack of care and hurt that led him to the point of 'exploding'. He stated at several points in the interview that he got to the point of engaging in violence as a form of self-harming; finding solace in his own victimization. It should be noted that that is simplifying the issue, as the examples that he raised were often when he was engaged in violence himself (such as in a fight). He constructed fighting as an embodied coping mechanism at the intersection of victimization/perpetration. Sam's assertion he fought as a form of self-harm both distracts us from the plight of the people he victimized, but also emphasizes his own fragile mental state. Sam is emphasizing toughness and enduring violence and pain, which are highly valorized characteristics of masculinity, seeking invulnerability and omnipotence. However, at the same time he is also exposing his past vulnerability. To hear this type of narrative is a result of the retrospective nature of the interviews, as it is with hindsight that Sam has been able to group together these destructive behaviours as actually a form of self-harm. There is indeed a contradiction in these ideas, as he will have been engaging in violence himself in these exchanges; however, here he is framing himself as a passive party to illustrate his inner feelings of vulnerability. This theme is pertinent in the self-harm literature, which emphasizes the way that individuals' ideas of masculinity are implicated in their self-harming (Green et al, 2018).

White chavs, Black gangsters: race and status

The enhanced status within the gang of becoming 'The Man' was something that all the participants appeared to recognize as existing within the gang structure. However, there were many similarities with the way in which Connell described hegemonic masculinity in the mainstream; that it was a status of exaggerated masculinity that all men are aware of, but only few achieve. I interviewed an ethnically diverse group of participants, however of those, it was the three Black British men (Dylan, Lester, and Sam) who explicitly claimed that they had achieved being 'The Man' in the gang. In a complete contrast, the two White men firmly conveyed that they had been on the periphery and very much downplayed that they had a role in the inner workings of the gang they had been involved in. This could partly be due to the dynamics of what they chose to tell me, as a White interviewer. However, this alone does not explain the stark difference (even within such a small study). It could be to do with the subculture of on-road being grounded within a hypermasculine stereotype of Black masculinity. The White participants felt the presence of the 'chav' discourse, which is a specifically racialized form of class denigration that appears to refer mainly to White people. As Hayward and Yar (2006, p 24) note, chav subculture is tied up in 'cultural hybridity and racial bricolage' that 'reflect ongoing appropriations of black "ghetto" culture by white youth'. The term 'chav' is generally used to describe the White working class and has been often used in a derogatory way. Chavs are a social group in the cultural imagination who are characterized by negative class traits: 'dishonesty, laziness, fecundity, recklessness and ostentatious consumption practices' (Raisborough et al, 2013, p 253). This is a distinct stereotype from that of the Black working class and criminality, which tend to be more associated with US 'gangster' stereotypes, reinforced in music and fashion subcultures (Bengtsson, 2012). One has become elevated and notorious, the other degraded and abject in an unlikely but prevalent racialized inversion. This disparity could also be something to do with an internalization of the association with Black men and gang criminality, which the White participants I spoke to did not feel as keenly.

The two White participants referred to different markers of their societal marginalization, using the language of 'chav' to identify themselves and their presentation style. Dave referred to himself as being a 'chav' three times in his interview. In one case he was describing outspoken behaviour, as reverting to being a chav. Shaun noted that one of the biggest reasons that he wanted to engage in the research itself was to show people that he was not from a 'TV family'. This references the type of programme such as *The Jeremy Kyle Show*, which centred on the humiliation of White 'chav' families who led chaotic lives that were then exploited for television. Thus, what became clear in this contrast is that the stereotypes around marginalization and inner-city poverty, which are typified in chav discourse. Tyler (2013, p 162) framed 'chav' discourse as emerging from the 'new class of problem people', reframed in the New Labour years as being more about low expectations than just material poverty. Tyler framed this as the 'culturalization of poverty and disadvantage' (Tyler, 2018, p 162).

Both White men (Shaun and Dave) took a colour-blind perspective to gang activity and the people involved. Shaun, in particular, very much portrayed the gang as reflecting the racial dynamics of the wider community. He noted that he came from a multicultural area and the young people all spent time together; however, some of them happened to be in the gang, so they would all be spending time in the day 'playing FIFA'[3] and then go out to attend to on-road and gang-involved activities. Shaun emphasized racial and ethnic neutrality in terms of which young men in his local area became gang-involved. He downplayed the significance of ethnic and cultural differences in his neighbourhood, conveying a sense of an urban convivial multi-culture (Gilroy, 2004). To conceptualize whiteness in the book I have drawn on Frankenberg's (1993) work. She carried out life–history research with White women to look at how they conceptualized race. She found evidence of individuals using 'colour-evasive and power-evasive discursive repertoire … partly in response to essentialist racism' (Frankenberg, 1993, p 139). Thus, by claiming to be unaware of the racial dynamics, they are revealing a knowledge of the structural inequalities that exist. Frankenberg (1993, p 142) noted that using a colour-blind perspective on race is 'a mode of thinking about race organized around an effort to not "see", or at any rate not to acknowledge, race differences', which she calls the 'polite' language of race.

Despite talking about being personally unaware and unaffected by racism, Shaun in particular framed an association of Black hegemonic masculinity with gangs in his community. This was revealed as he had been criticized for enacting a pastiche of blackness. Shaun was the only White member of the gang he was involved with and insisted that this was non-political. Shaun found the biggest stereotyping that he faced while gang-involved was from his White peers in the wider community. Shaun noted that he would be criticized by people within his community for 'speaking like a Black guy':

'There is quite a few white kids [in the gang], more than you think … but in terms of my generation there was me, maybe one or two others … but the one or two others weren't in it like me. So if they did something I'd get the blame for it, coz they wasn't really known, it was the white one and my phone would ring. They'd think "he's the only white one"! but people would be like, he's not the only white one. It's funny when I think back. It is a bit mad, do you know what's mad like, it weren't being white weren't an issue being in a gang, you'd get a lot of people that would say I was … they'd pick up on the way you spoke, do you know what I mean, say "you're speaking like a black guy", I'd be like "how am I speaking like a black guy", I'm a white guy so I speak like me, I speak like the area that I come from, and it just so happens the area that I come from the majority are black folk. And if you really want to get technical it's not, speak like a black guy, because when you say black rap, you get like an African, if you've got someone with Jamaican or African roots and you get them where they are actually from I don't sound like them, do you know what you mean, and you'll get a black guy from [area] and he don't sound like them either. So if he don't sound like them and I don't sound like them, do you know what I mean? It's an area thing, coz you are into it, it's like there's so many white people. So many Asian people. So many black people. It probably is majority black people but I could easily string together 20 white, 20 black, 20 Asian and they'd all sound the same, so it's not like, it's just a, I don't know that will always be something that will be said.'

Shaun responded with claiming he spoke like someone from his area, rather than through racial codes. All of this puts into focus the extent to which on-road is considered by society as a Black space, despite there being multicultural engagement in on-road and in gangs. This could be do with the development of protest masculinity in the gang context being a space where Black males can claim a hegemonic position in a way that is less accessible in the wider society due to the effects of racism. However, it could also be because of the racism of gang labelling itself, via tools such as the London Gangs Matrix, that the wider society more easily situates Black men as claiming the ultimate position of gang leadership (Williams, 2015).

The trap

There was a definite theme of financial gain that also ran through the participants' narratives. In Chapter 5, I analysed narratives that focused on the ways in which the participants described their initial involvement on-road, which most often centred on seeking financial gain through involvement in drug dealing as a catalyst. Several of the participants then indicated their involvement in gangs spiralled from that point, escalating to a situation where they felt involved in 'bigger moves' (Eric) than they had originally planned or expected, such as robbery, county-lines drug trafficking ('going country'), and firearm activity. As the retrospective narratives developed the participants often reflected on the way in which money served as the initial driver for gang involvement but then things spiralled out of control.

Lester noted the way in which a desire to make money quickly evolved into carrying a firearm and normalizing extreme violence. Lester noted that as he accumulated more wealth it was directly linked with gaining power. However, in retrospect, Lester questioned that power, as he noted (a sentiment that was also echoed by Sam), that he wanted love but instead people were scared of him. This has a notable similarity with the role of a DVA perpetrator, whose masculine domination results in power gained through fear rather than love. Arguably, the patterns that the participants learned in their childhood, through the experience of DVA, are then repeated in their own pursuit of power at all costs.

Shaun had a similar story, which took the same trajectory from an initial desire to make money, and then escalated as he became increasingly gang-involved. In parallel to Eric's reference of things spiralling, Shaun said things 'switched up':

> 'I wanted to make money, but I wouldn't make it like get a job [laughs] probably like smash someone's window and take their satnav [laughs] do you know what I mean? Which is bad, but you're a kid, everyone's done some stupid shit when they're a kid … I don't know what happened, just all of a sudden it just switched up and yeah I was just involved, but then when I was involved. I was very very, very involved.' (Shaun)

In this passage Shaun was initially laughing and conveying his involvement in crime as an alternative to a regular job. He sought to downplay the effects of this, in actions such as theft of a satnav and damage of a car, by framing it as childish behaviour. By repeating the term 'kid', Shaun is emphasizing naivety and innocence as the context of the crimes. However, then he then referred to it 'switching up', which resulted in him becoming 'involved'. The repetition of 'involved' seems to serve as a euphemism for the way in which Shaun became more inextricably linked to the gang and involved with associated criminality (which was pertinent as Shaun ended up serving a long prison sentence). In the passage, Shaun also refers to the fear that he felt at the time, so he was able to convey the vulnerable masculinity that he felt at the time in which he was also exhibiting protest masculinity. This shows how the participants shared their past insecurities through retrospective narratives.

This same narrative theme, which involved the evolution from seeking money to escalating gang involvement, was outlined by Travis, who made a word play by referring to it as a 'trap'. This is both a reference to 'trap-house', the urban slang name of a drug factory, as well as the conventional meaning of 'snare':

> 'It starts off with the money but once you kinda get involved to that culture there's a lot of people out there who are probably making

enough money to get by now but they are still doing it anyway and a reputation and they fall in love with that kind of lifestyle, like the people that could just stop now and be happy are probably gonna carry on for a few years and either end up dead or in prison … that's why it's called the trap innit.' (Travis)

In this passage Travis sought to highlight the futility of 'the culture' of on-road and gang-involved young people. Mirroring the other passages explored in this chapter, he began by talking about the way in which the desire for money escalated to an increased involvement on-road.

Overall, the masculine pressures of financial independence and success cannot be underestimated in a capitalist patriarchy. This transition to develop an emerging protest masculinity on the road, in contrast to a subordinated masculinity at home, was also characterized by a shift in production relations. Participants experienced a range of economic backgrounds, from living in low-income households to living in relative poverty. There were various motivators to making money at a young age, from trying to keep up with peers in terms of clothes and pocket money, to the pressure to provide for their single mother. These reasons, as well as being approached by older peers from the local area and offered the opportunity to sell drugs, acted as push factors to engage in drug dealing to make some money. The money that the participants gained by this means supported them in their move from a subordinated masculinity to an emerging protest masculinity. Power was gained through both the change in power relations as well as production relations, which were altered as they moved between the private and the public spheres.

7

Love and Fear

Cathexis, in Connell's (1987, 2005) conceptualization, referred to the ways in which intimate relationships with women are framed in relation to the wider gender order. Connell focused on these interpersonal elements as a means to focus on the ways that men's protest masculinity became incorporated in their private relations. In this chapter I will focus on the ways in which the participants conveyed their personal connections and relationships, both within and outside of life on-road. This is because the 'ties' developed to the gang at times functioned as replacements for other intimate relations at the time, despite being perceived as based on fear rather than friendship. When talking about their time being gang-involved, all the men in the study described there being a bond or 'ties' between the men in the gang. Jordan spoke frequently about being 'tied' to the gang, which conveyed loyalties, as well as resulting in him not being able to freely walk away and leave the gang. Jordan conveyed his affiliation to the gang during his time involved, likening them to 'blood family' who you are 'willing to die for'. Dylan talked about how the gang was 'like a family on the streets'. Shaun described the strength of feeling that he had for the gang as akin to 'love'.

What was also revealed in the participants' descriptions of close relationships, was the gendered hierarchy of relations. The participants' reflections of domestic violence and abuse (DVA) perpetration presented a contradictory set of values. There was a disconnect between the espousal of anti-violence against women, as well as respect-for-women rhetoric, which was part of the narrative of the men's victimhood in childhood as they were denigrating their own fathers' behaviour, with a disclosure from Eric of explicitly perpetrating violence against women, as well as an indication from Lester that he was at least coercively controlling the women he lived with, and they accused him of imprisoning them. Lester framed DVA as an instrumental form of power that he did not have to use, whereas Eric shifted the blame onto the women for still hanging around with the gang despite being abused. Neither Lester nor Eric indicated that they had premeditated abuse against women, but rather that it occurred during their pursuit of a protest masculinity within the gang. The women were collateral damage in their pursuit of dominance and power. This fits with the hegemonic masculinity ideal, which inherently rests on gender inequality and masculine domination of women.

A mother's son

Devlin (2013)
'Mother's Son'

This hip-hop track talks about the value of boys' lives, as they all have in common that they are their mothers' sons. It focuses on the impact of gun violence on the women who are left bereaved.

The music track that Travis brought to the interview had a section that centralized the lives of on-road and gang-involved men as being important as they are their 'mothers' sons'. This is revealing about cathexis, which focuses on the emotional charge within relationships. Several of the participants framed their own value as contingent on if they were important to someone else. It was as if they were so inured to violence, criminality, and death that the personal effect of these on them ceased to be important. Instead, they focused on the consequences of these issues on the women closest to them. This is revealing about the wider gender order, as men conveying a lack of care for themselves is a typical display of masculine strength and invulnerability. By showing vulnerability through the lens of their mothers' worry and pain, they are reinforcing the feminization of both emotions and vulnerability and detaching themselves from it. This echoes the discussion in Chapter 5 about some of the participants' experience of sexual exploitation, where they constructed their victimization through framing it as a female issue. This trend shows the ways that the participants maintained a sense of masculinity by distancing themselves from feminized traits.

Positioning themselves as protectors of family members was the main motivation for change. It seemed to be easier for participants to frame their own vulnerabilities through identification with women's victimization rather than their own. It allowed them to avoid reducing themselves to being vulnerable. Lester explicitly referred to this in his narrative:

'Women, aunties, sisters, mothers for underprivileged people and especially Black women whose children are gonna be more likely to be the ones what are the victims to this, one's dead ones in prison yeah, that's always the scenario yeah, they got, you's have got the most to lose.' (Lester)

Here Lester is framing the female relatives of gang-involved men as the primary victims. By using the term 'you's', he is projecting onto me the representation of wider womanhood/motherhood, which reveals the underlying awareness of our gender differences in the interview dynamic. It is striking that he conveys that they/we have the 'most to lose', more than the men who end up dead or in prison. It is as if the value of gang-involved men relies on their relationships with others, that they aren't intrinsically worthy themselves. There are also racialized implications of Lester's statement, being that Black women in particular are the ones to suffer the most collateral damage from youth violence.

Dylan also framed his mother's concern with his wellbeing as a central issue, which he framed as more significant than the worry that he had for himself;

> 'My mum could only sleep easy when I was in jail for the simple reason that she wouldn't get a knock on the door saying I've been shot, knock on the door saying I've been arrested, knock on the door saying I've been charged with murder, knock on the door saying I've been shot again, knock on the door saying I've been stabbed, knock on the door saying I've been shot again. So, the only time she would sleep was when I was in jail.' (Dylan)

In this passage Dylan is sharing some of his own most troubling times that occurred at the peak of his on-road and gang-involved time. However, he used his own mother's worry and lack of sleep as a way to talk about times when he has gone through adversity such as being arrested, being stabbed, and being shot. This reinforces the underlying themes of cathexis as discussed throughout this section, as Dylan frames his own fears and concerns through the way they affected his mother. In doing this, Dylan maintains his own sense of invulnerable masculinity, while also sharing the situations that have indeed made him vulnerable.

> 'If me and you were boyfriend and girlfriend and were in a gang and you go out and get killed because you're in my understanding, you chose to do that, but you're not gonna, you're not gonna feel that pain, it's the pain that we leave behind, the ripple effect, the indirect victims, so I try and educate kids on how indirect victims come about, through our choices and our actions.' (Dylan)

When Sam discussed his intimate relations with women on-road and gang-involved they were heavily tied up with his simultaneously expressed desire for a mother figure:

> 'I was now forever searching for a mother figure in women, girls, and I would just go from girl to girl to girl to girl to girl, like I wouldn't

stay around, I'd always I wouldn't stay around because I was expecting them to leave me to do something, I'm expecting them, I'm waiting for it.' (Sam)

He firstly said that he was in a lot of relationships ('going from girl to girl to girl') due to his search for a mother figure. He mentioned one woman that he had a relationship with who lived at home with her wider family into which he was integrated quickly. Sam said through moving in with his girlfriend's family

'I got a mum, I got an aunty, I got a sister and a little brother, and I became a father figure to the baby that was in the house and a girlfriend all at once, I found a family and they all, and we grew, and we loved each other.' (Sam)

Sam's peers couldn't understand why he sought the domestic life in the way that he did, but he later noted 'to me it made perfect sense, it was my heart I was searching for a family, I was searching for love'. However, unfortunately the family themselves were also on the margins, dealing drugs from the house. As much as he sought the connection of family, Sam also noted that he didn't feel able to stay with women for long, as he would always be expecting them to leave. What this revealed was the vulnerabilities that Sam felt during his time on-road. As much as he appeared to have rejected the home environment and sought a space where he could enact a protest masculinity, he was still searching for a way to enact the traditional male role within a conventional family.

Gang love, gang ties

Shaun outlined the process of how one starts to inherit gang issues from older peers. He notes how the gang issues had always been 'in his head' from his wider upbringing on his estate. However, it was when he experienced perceived injustices himself, like peers getting killed, that he was able to relate directly to the feeling of anger and revenge. It is this process that personalized the wider gang issues to him. Here he conveys the power of those feelings, the cathexis evident in the emotive terminology:

'It's mad how you feel like what's in your heart. I remember how I felt, and that stuff got so strong in my heart, how I felt for them other kids that I didn't get along with, it was like a proper strong feeling to want to hurt them, do you know what I mean? The way you feel for the opposite side it's just, you wanna make money and not wanna get a job, it's like it's so strong, you're in a gang and your feelings for that gang is like mad, it's like love. It's mad, it is mad, you just love it. And it's like in your head and in your heart, you think you just want it to be strong and you don't want it to go weak, so you just want to be in the thick of it, coz you think you're not letting this shit go. Even now to this day I think sometimes something happens, it's always gonna be there in these things. But when you're older you know what's right and what's wrong. As much as things bother me you have to let things go.' (Shaun)

To emphasize the depth of his feelings for the gang, Shaun refers to 'my heart'. He repeats 'heart' three times here. Shaun is using this to convey the depth of feeling on a deep level. An intriguing factor in Shaun's discussion about the depth of his emotional connection to the gang is that he was not claiming to be seeking alternative relationships away from his family, but rather additional ones. He emphasizes the way in which the collective hate that the gang shared was a vehicle for experiencing the collective love of the group. It is another way in which protest masculinity and vulnerable masculinity are so closely aligned. The violence allowed Shaun to feel love and express it.

The narratives often focused on the way the participants grew apart from their families and became disaffiliated, then conveyed yearning for new connections. This often signified an emotional shift from loyalties moving from home to the gang. This was a form of cathexis, resolving or at least responding to their unmet emotional needs. This understanding, informed by Connell's (1987, 2005) theorizations, offers to deepen the scope of research activity looking at gang and gang-related activity as an alternative quasi-family space that addresses men's emotional desires. This trend for marginalized men to disassociate with their families and instead replace their primary ties with their peer group was noted by Collier (1998) in his study of men, masculinities, and crime. He noted that this shift often occurs as a tenet of achieved hegemonic masculinity and is signified by true independence of family or ties. Eric talked explicitly about a sense of realization and loss when he started to break away from his family and he later noted that he then started to detach from family and feel emotional connections with the gang instead. He noted:

'When I saw what my step-mum would do to my dad, and then what he would do to us and then she would do to us, I was like I was clever enough to understand that's not love, and that made me realize that I don't have a family, because my family don't do that.' (Eric)

In this excerpt Eric is conveying how he disaffiliated from his family, once he conceptualized them as not constituting a family at all because of the violence and abuse. By framing it that way he is evidencing his disaffiliation with his blood family, opening up himself for reaffiliation with the gang. This idea was also explored by Sam, who referenced his constant search for a mother figure in the women that he met when gang-involved. He noted that in his 'heart I was searching for a family, I was searching for love'. Sam repeated throughout his narrative his yearning for a family and a mother figure, in particular.

Eric's narrative outlined how he navigated a need for peer acceptance. As a refugee arriving in the UK in mid-childhood, as well as living with child abuse and DVA, he was incredibly vulnerable. Eric conflated acceptance and love by noting that 'the gang loves you … then you feel accepted'. Eric frames himself as naive in this exchange, by stating that he wasn't aware of the extent of what he was getting himself into initially – his motivation was framed as driven by the desire for acceptance above all else. He framed his acceptance in the gang as intertwined with his refugee experience. He noted that he was tougher than his peers because of his life experiences. These experiences are also conflated with cultural notions of masculinity, through learning from his father about how an African man 'should' behave. To understand how these elements of identity interact, it is important to frame Eric's intersectional identity in relation to his gang involvement.

Gang ties were specifically related to all-male peer groups. Even when women were discussed as involved, they were presented as outside of the intimate group. Also revealing in terms of cathexis was the way in which women were situated as separate, reified, and almost objectified, as a separate group who were at times victimized and then held responsible for this victimization. The participants appeared to talk about women as performing a function in their expression of heroic masculinity. In terms of cathexis, the participants detailed the ways their lives became entwined with the gang as their priority relationship. The primacy of this relationship was expressed by the repetition of 'tie/tied/tied' and similar sentiments. These gave images of a physical connection to the gang, as well as connotations of being restricted. Jordan emphasized this through his comment that 'it's not a matter of walking away', as he did not feel he could freely leave the gang as he wished:

> 'On the streets it's awkward being in it and when you're trying to get out of it it's difficult … you get a lot of hate as I was saying from the previous song, but that hate's now because you're gonna change, people feel loyalties, due ties, as people feel you're tied in almost it's not a matter of walking away it's like a family you just can't walk away from your blood family, even if you do walk away you're still gonna be tied because you've spent so much time and that's what it literally is, your friends on the street at the time can be closer than your actual blood family, where you're willing to die for them the same and you'd

die for your brother or sister or your mum or uncle, dad, or brother, or whatever brother or cousin.' (Jordan)

Jordan compared this commitment to the ties formed to family, which is a metaphor that helps him explain the way that you can physically move away from the gang, but, 'even if you walk away, you're still gonna be tied'. This conveys the complexities when someone tries to extricate themselves from a gang, comparing the invisible ties to those caused by blood. In some ways the gang is described as operating as a form of replacement family, as Jordan noted that 'at the time' the friends on the street can feel closer than related family. To really illustrate this point Jordan referenced the lengths that he would go to for this surrogate family, even die for them.

Bereavement

Depzman (2013)
'Reality'

This music track was selected by Travis, who used it to talk about his own experiences of street violence within his peer group. The track focuses on bereavement and pain after a peer of the rapper was killed. Travis wanted to convey the how ubiquitous fatal violence is within the on-road context from his perspective. He also shared the background of his track choice, which was written by the artist Depzman, and performed at a memorial concert for his own friend who had been killed by peer violence. In the lyrics Depzman shared his own grief for his lost friend. However, tragically, the artist himself was a victim of knife crime and was murdered at that very memorial concert.

It is essential to consider the vulnerabilities alluded to by the participants. As noted in Chapter 6, on the discussion about preferring to act like a 'nutter' as a form of protection, gang involvement can be a scary and lonely situation for young men. All of the participants had lost a friend to violence while on-road and gang-involved, and most had experienced the incident first-hand. These examples of the men's most vulnerable moments were tied up with experiences of violence. As Gilson (2014, p 48) noted, 'we discover in acts of violence an extreme form of the most fundamental dynamic: the way in which we are always vulnerable in relation to one another'. The way that vulnerability became visible through violence was emphasized in the narratives, through the illustrations of how the participants coped with the violence (both DVA and gang violence) in various ways. Almost coming full circle, they had gone from experiencing DVA as children to experiencing violence on-road as adults. This experience served different functions in the participants' life histories, but it was the most common aspect of all the narratives. Some of the participants mentioned being present at a friend's murder, others just heard such event had happened and attended funerals. Either way, these experiences, when compounded by the historic experiences of DVA, can be constructed as a form of revictimization. Add to that the complexity that gang-involved men who experience extreme forms of violence are often complicit and there is even less available empathy from society and services. All of the participants mentioned the death of a friend as part of their time while gang-involved. A picture emerges of men who are traumatized in multiple ways but have little access to support or sense of wanting to access it:

'I lost [dozens of] friends and family, in [a year] – my best mate was killed in front of me, shot in his head.' (Dylan)

'Seeing all my friends die, my friend coming to meet me to come to a show and then he gets killed on his way to meet me. My other friend died on a bus we were all talking the next thing you know my boy's on the bus with a few of the guys and he gets stabbed on the bus and he dies.' (Sam)

'My friend got stabbed in front of me, he's got his stomach got opened in front of me and then, it's just too, too, it's just, it was this summer ... just so many kids were getting stabbed, my friends were just getting stabbed up.' (Eric)

'When I went to do that talk in [area] when the boy died it hurt me so much. A boy was stabbed, and his guts had been exposed out on the pavement.' (Lester)

'Funerals and you know burying friends to good friends getting jail, that was all part of that experience which was negative.' (Jordan)

'My friend who's dead ... he got killed, he was only sixteen. He was in a car and some [gang] kids and some girl rang them and said these lot are here, so these kids ran on to the car and only he got shot and he got shot through his head.' (Shaun)

'I've had more than one mate be killed over the years erm and other mates being stabbed.' (Dave)

'Someone that I chilled with got stabbed to death recently and not long after another person who I used to chill with actually got arrested for the murder, so it puts you in the middle of some really weird situations.' (Travis)

The sheer ubiquity of the experiences of death and murder at a young age is a shocking indictment of the levels of violence that exist on-road and in gangs. Ongoing violent incidents were framed as part of a wider system of vengeance. Having a quick response rate between violent victimization and vengeance means that an individual does not stay a victim for long before changing the dynamics. It is a constant cycle of violent victimization and perpetration. This never-ending cycle was spoken about by both Dylan and Shaun. Shaun discussed how the awareness of murders within his peer group played a role in his increasing sense of loyalty to the gang he was involved with, which led him to become involved in the ongoing retribution:

> 'When you're a kid, you get a bit of "oh I love this older guy, he's cool" then you see him killed and then it's a bit of a, "why did he get killed", then another one will get killed and another one would get locked up and you just see things and you hear things and you don't like it.' (Shaun)

More explicitly for Dylan, his experience of his friend's murder was a key factor in him pledging revenge, which then led to a period of gang conflict. He noted that this was

> 'a pivotal moment because I vowed never to stop avenging for the sake of him.' (Dylan)

An important consideration here is that these experiences, in the context of the participants' experience of DVA at home, would have been very traumatic turning points. So, despite them talking about engagement in violence on-road and in the gang, it is important to consider the wider implications of their continuous involvement in traumatic events that they also experienced at the same time, highlighting the dual victim/perpetrator tension for gang-involved men. This dichotomy between victim/perpetrator has previously been explored by Gadd et al (2015, p 151), who noted how easy it is for young men who perpetrate violence to be constructed as the 'ideal offenders'.

The young people who are tied up with violence on-road that is associated with their peers' murders will not be looked at as victims of adversity in their own lives, but rather will be blamed for the dangers they present to wider society (Gadd et al, 2015). Renzetti (1999) looked at women who are both victimized and engage in violence. She proposed that we look at victimization through a strengths model, whereby both victimization and perpetration are viewed on a continuum of survival. She urges us to set aside the stigma and instead focus on the 'full humanity of an individual' (Renzetti, 1999, p 52).

Popcaan (2013)
'Unruly Prayer'
This track is by a Jamaican dancehall reggae fusion artist, who in this track laments on the number of incarcerated young people, as well as how many young people are killing each other on the streets.
Music track selected by Lester.

Fight men, not women

Some participants spoke about women, in particular their female family members, with a huge sense of reverence and value. However, at times they leaned towards reifying these women in an almost dehumanized way – they were placed on an ideological pedestal. This was extended in their retrospective narratives of adolescence, where some of the participants recounted their experiences of both protecting women and perpetrating abuse against them. In both of these cases, women were positioned in a way that framed them as objects against which the men constructed their masculinities, either as protectors or perpetrators. As such, this framing is consistent with Connell's (1987, 2005) account of cathexis, as the way in which personal relationships are constructed through personal feeling and what they reveal about the wider gender order. The positioning of women on the periphery, outside of the mainstream system of respect on-road was conveyed in a music track chosen by Jordan:

Young Dolph (2017)
'100 Shots'
Young Dolph is a North American rapper. The track title references the '100 shots' that were fired at the artist in a drive-by incident. He escaped unharmed. The track also talks about women as playing their part in drug smuggling, and being financially supported, but not being loved, rather functioning as accessories.

Several participants talked about their own views of DVA perpetration from their perspectives as adults. Dylan and Eric conveyed a broad disapproval of DVA. Dylan talked about the boundary of violence that excluded violence against women that he constructed from a young age. Dylan explained about how, from a young age, his personal boundaries precluded any violence against women. He stated that:

> '[I] knew from the age eleven, twelve, that I could go out and kill somebody and not feel no way about it, just so as long as it wasn't a woman.' (Dylan)

He asserted that he had never 'raised his hand to women' due to seeing what his mother experienced. He categorized people as either in one of two camps around DVA perpetration: those who are 'proper against it' and those who do 'hit women'. However, in the same passage Dylan explained that he 'shot and stabbed people' but that he always respected his mother (and by implication, other women too). He emphasized the strong boundaries that his mother placed on violence against her: 'my mum said if you ever raise a hand to a parent that's when you get disowned, so my mum never disowned me'. Dylan conveyed a sense of the hierarchy of violence in his view, framing his perspective of violence against women as being somehow more inherently wrong than violence in general.

The way that Dylan both normalized violence as well as disdained violence against women reveals the way in which he perceived wider gender dynamics. As a child he framed his mother as a victim, but his father as someone who was able to fight. In a similar vein, Eric talked about how when he first went to school he sought out fights with other boys:

'The reason why I used to fight is like you could fight a man, [but] you couldn't fight a woman, so for me any disrespect I saw with a guy I definitely would initiate a fight. I could lose the fight, there was times when I would get beaten up ... I would just go there and get beaten up by 10 guys coz it's like for me a man is not a person who hits a woman, do you know what I mean? People who hits a woman don't hit men, they don't hit men, they don't fight men. But stupid me didn't realize they're all the same.' (Eric)

However, this gendered approach to violence perpetration was not quite as simple, as he later disclosed he had in fact perpetrated violence against women. The conflict between gendered principles and gendered practice reveals something about how the code of the street works.

Violence against women

When I prompted Lester to talk about his experiences of DVA he initially thought I was enquiring about his own perpetration as he answered from the outset, 'I've not had the domestic part of violence. I'm not a domestic violence person.' To distinguish the 'domestic part' matches the wider finding in the research that gang-related violence is firmly situated within public rather than private space. Lester is acknowledging this spatial boundary of violence. This is because in the context of the wider narrative Lester disclosed various other types of public violence that he had engaged in, including gun crime. This suggests that Lester somehow differentiates people who engage in violence outside of the domestic space (public) as different from those who engage in violence within it (domestic). Lester then went on to describe a domestic situation where he lived with multiple partners, outlining that he didn't engage in DVA because he didn't 'need to'. However, the context he described appeared to be a controlling one, not least because one of the women accused him of false imprisonment when she escaped. Thus, there is potential that Lester carried out coercive control over the women, albeit without the physical violence usually associated with DVA. For Lester, if he was managing to exert power and control over his domestic situation without the use of violence then DVA was not necessary. Lester described how he displayed his power in that situation by conveying his expectations to the women, which worked because 'they didn't say no to nothing'. This revealed a functional attitude towards violence. Lester outlined that as long as 'they're getting what they want, you're getting what you want' then violence was not necessary. In contrast to Dylan, who asserted a more blanket negative attitude against DVA perpetration, Lester was instead acknowledging its uses for domestic control and saying it was not necessary in his context.

Eric discussed DVA perpetration in a different way. Eric recounted it from two perspectives, split by what I call a narrative break. He told one version of his story, then corrected himself and told a different version. This is significant as not only does it present the messy contradictions of the perspectives of a survivor of DVA himself, who then engages in the hyperviolent gang context. It also shows the effectiveness of the unstructured narrative interview technique, which gave space for self-exploration over structured questioning. Eric began talking about DVA by framing his sister as a potential victim and himself as the protector brother. Eric framed this part of the narrative as a hypothetical talk with a potential boyfriend of his sister. He laid down his boundaries, which is that 'you can break her heart … but what you can never do is hit her'. He then framed his stepmother as being a victim of domestic abuse because she didn't have a brother, the implication being that it is a male family member's role to protect women. Eric conveyed a hypothetical threat to an abuser of his sister, by stating, 'my guy, I do not do that stuff, but for you I'd go to prison'. Here Eric is emphasizing that this would be an extreme consequence for him, but one he would freely take – he would 'call the police and the ambulance and walk into prison'. This is a powerful image: that he would be acting with such clarity that, firstly, he would have no fear of the police or prison, but also have enough of a sense of humanity to call the ambulance the victim would certainly need. This is constructing a compassionate discipliner role. Eric notes his concerns that his sister could be especially vulnerable to DVA because of her experiences at home, which he is constructing as a gender issue that does not apply to him as a male who has experienced the same. Eric began discussing this with a monologue about how wrong it is to be violent to a woman. However, in a fascinating turn, after being so passionate about not being violent, he then admitted that he had actually 'hit girls' in past relationships. This was a stark juxtaposition between viewpoints, where Eric changed from presenting me with a sanitized account of himself, to presenting himself more honestly. The moment that of disclosure follows:

> 'For me a man is not a person who hits a woman, do you know what I mean, people who hits a woman don't hit men, they don't hit men, they don't fight men. Maybe it's just me but I couldn't do it [perpetrate DVA], that's the worst thing I could even do.
> Nah [pause]. Growing up though I have to admit I did hit girls [pause]. I did hit girls growing up [pause]. It's sad [pause].
> It was during the girls getting angry, it was never the girls that I knew it was always like, when you hang around the same crowd there's always people that always want to show off in front of people, and when those girls hang around with gangs, this is what's crazy, that you'd slap her and beat her and nobody ended it.' (Eric)

This was a significant disclosure as he had been talking extensively about the damage of DVA to himself in the past, as well as the threats to his sister. Eric framed the girls as having some responsibility for the violence. He noted that he was only violent 'during the girls getting angry'. He conveyed a wider tolerance for this as it was a way to 'show off in front of people … what's crazy, that you'd slap her and beat her, and nobody ended it'. Eric placed responsibility more on the girls for continuing to spend time with the gang despite being beaten, rather than on the perpetrators for carrying out the violence. He begged the question, 'my God, what kind of people were you … what was happening at home for you to feel that's fine?' Also inherent in this part of Eric's narrative was the way that he distinguished between boundaries of those who were gang-involved, and those who were not. For these two parties the rules were different. Eric noted that the girls who were victims of DVA were those who 'hang around with gangs'. He asked why they didn't call the police, because

> 'Snitching that don't apply to you, that applies to us on the street maybe, it does not apply to you, call the police, what's worse why are you still gonna be around?' (Eric)

Through this, 'the street' is defined as a male domain, one in which the women take a marginal position. There is also an inherent contradiction here, when Eric asked why the women – the victims of male violence in the gang – did not call the police, he downplayed any sense of fear they may have had of future violence. This is alluding to the 'code of the street', where a distinct set of etiquette outlines boundaries of violence, including a penalty for reporting incidents to the police. Research by Havard et al (2021) found that women are often subject to abusive tactics akin to coercive control within DVA in the gang context.

What these stories about DVA convey are distinct masculinity performances, or distinct positions in relation to the notion of DVA perpetration. Dylan positioned himself in a way that conveyed a sense of chivalry, whereby it was acceptable to engage in violence with men, but there was a boundary around the perpetration of violence by men against women. Lester viewed the issue differently, as instead of conveying a sense of disapproval about DVA, he framed it as functional, with him not needing to engage in it. In Eric's talk about DVA perpetration, his positioning shifted throughout the narrative. Initially he conveyed a heroic masculinity, framing himself as the noble protector who could/would be violent, but only if necessary, to safeguard his sister. He then disclosed his previous violence against women, which he framed as a fault of the women for tolerating it and not leaving. What these distinct positions reveal is the complex way that masculinity is navigated in the light of violence performance on the street. All of the participants referred to women being somehow different, or outside the usual code of the street, signalling the gender exclusion of women as well as the way that experiencing DVA does not necessarily make a person anti-violence.

DVA perpetration, on the surface, indicates a sense of masculine power and domination, expressed through violence. In the Duluth model, DVA is framed as an instrumental violence which is centred on the perpetrators' desire for power and control in the domestic setting (Shepard and Pence, 1999). However, the need for violence as a way to both express this control, as well as gain power over close intimate partners, has been framed as an expression of 'threatened masculinity' and 'resented dependence' (Ray, 2018, p 125). Gelles (1997) asserted that DVA perpetrators often have low self-esteem and have a deep sense of vulnerability and powerlessness. Framed in this way, DVA perpetration can be seen to have similarities with Connell's (2005) notion of protest masculinity, which has been threaded through this book in partnership with my assertion that vulnerable masculinity is an essential partner of protest masculinity. I propose that these two aspects of identity are in a symbiotic relation with one another.

Love and fear

Fear played an instrumental role throughout the men's lives as revealed in the narratives. Fear was present in childhood, as the men were scared of the actions and reactions of the perpetrator. The participants alluded to the way that they discovered could inspire fear themselves using their own violence. As the participants described the height of their time on-road and gang-involved, the existence of fear was a common theme in the narratives. This was largely due to the fact that these were retrospective accounts; they were allowing themselves to share their stories of vulnerable masculinity as well as stories of protest masculinity. This resulted in a unique snapshot of the internal emotional lives of the men as they dealt with these past fears. Shaun noted:

> 'I was very very, very [gang-]involved. But it's mad because when I look back now it scared me so much.' (Shaun)

This quote by Shaun is revealing. He noted that the fear was a powerful catalyst to violence, but he must have had to work very hard to suppress it in order to continue his activities. This is an example of cathexis at work, as he managed the contradictory feelings of power and fear. At times this was about the participants themselves being afraid, but also inspiring fear in others, which several mentioned, often citing the following conundrum:

> 'I wanted respect but I got fear.' (Sam)

> 'Everyone professes to love you because you got money or because they're scared of you and it's all fake coz, they don't love you yeah and you just get caught up in it.' (Lester)

> 'Growing up you realize that you don't know how to have good friendship with people and the people that you hang about with a lot, they're not your friends they're there for common goal maybe. Yeah we might be from the same area, we're boys we're bros, but it is not a friendship. Or they're your friend because they're scared of you, usually they're friends with you coz it's like I'd rather be friends with that guy than be his enemy, or his friends or the other group of friends because I have protection, there's kids that come out and like I got some sort of protection. And him he doesn't know what he's getting himself into. And when you see stuff like that you don't, coz it's like you're seeing it how they are, the love the affection they have that you don't, so know it's like, you're seeing films, you're seeing what love is. Yeah it starts making you feel like you're living a different life.' (Eric)

In this passage Eric is tussling with the emotional contradictions of gang involvement. In the preceding sections I have analysed both gang ties and gang love, yet here Eric problematizes them both as functional responses to ultimate fear. Eric is calling into question the very fundamentals of friendship with his peers, noting that perhaps it was only ever about fear, protection, and a 'common goal'. The way in which Eric distinguishes between being 'boys' and 'bros' but not friends shows the way in which the gang was tied together, in the same way a family is tied without a choice, which is quite distinct from a friendship. The close relationship between love and fear is emotionally charged.

In the participants' narratives about love fear always appeared to be mentioned alongside it. As mentioned, both Sam and Lester looked back in hindsight and now realize that they were not actually respected or loved but feared. This suggests being respected in the gang is to be feared. This close connection between fear and love mirrors their early relationships with their fathers, who they feared and loved, due to the existence of DVA. Their fathers related to them only through instilling fear and thus being 'respected' to a point. This analysis of fear and love links back to the prior analysis around gang ties and a sense of love within the gang. Eric's narrative goes further into the inherent contradiction of seeking love and getting fear that Sam and Lester allude to. There is a significant mirroring here of the relationships the participants had with their own fathers in the early years, where again, they yearned for love yet got fear and abuse. It is pertinent that both Sam and Eric who discussed this also experienced physical child abuse in their early years.

8

The Road Ahead

2Pac ft Danny Boy (1996)
'I Ain't Mad At Cha'
This track is by American hip-hop star 2Pac. In this track he refers to his youth before he became famous and the friends who left him after he became successful. It relays his journey from the 'ghetto' to becoming famous and the process of change.
Music track selected by Jordan.

For the men that I spoke to, life on-road did not last forever. All of those who participated in the study talked retrospectively about their lives. In that sense they were survivors – they had managed to live through and beyond their childhood lives, and their on-road and gang-involved time. In terms of a process of moving on from this stage in their lives, the participants were all at different points. This is not least because they were from a broad range of ages, from some in their early twenties, with others in their early fifties. However, they all talked about their process of desistance from criminality and how they disentwined themselves from their gang involvement. For some (Dylan, Lester, Shaun), this separation from a gang and on-road-focused life was prompted by long prison sentences, which served as a motivating feature of desistance. For others (Sam, Dave), enduring mental health problems initiated a search for help. Jordan and Eric completed a university education and sought to remove themselves from on-road life by seeking new employment opportunities. They spoke about getting tired of living on the run, on high alert. In reality, it was probably a combination of a range of factors that made them feel, I've had enough. This is typified in Sam's words:

'My life had just been a crazy riot and I just wanted change, I couldn't, I couldn't do it no more, and I'd gone too far. Too much on my brain, too much on my heart, just enough is enough kind of thing. I was in denial and there was a few points that said to me, no this isn't right, you need to listen to this, but I was always in denial, no need, don't care.' (Sam)

Shaun's story

'I think I just grew out of it. It's heavy, it's your family, you look at your family when you've gone to jail, and having to go on visits and see your mum stressed out and sad and my sister. And sometimes they'll be crying, and things and, you know what I mean, I missed my nieces being born, my sister started to need me and I missed them both. And them things are important to me and I missed out a lot of the years when they was tiny. I'm very close to them now, do you know what I mean. I didn't miss them years when they get to an age when they like, they were still babies when I got out. But all that beginning stuff, you want to see it don't you, missed so many Christmases, birthdays. I was in jail for the best part of my life and so I got out on the first time when I was 17, so up until I was 16, 17, and then onwards from that, 16, 17 I was either on tag or in jail all the way up until about 23, 24. So them years, they're like, I got some of my good years, but they was my good years in terms of playing out, but then you get your good years in terms of going out, I'm legal to go out, teenage years and having fun and those years I've missed all of them. 18 I was on tag, I remember I got early purposely to go on the estate, it was summer, I was getting a bit of a sun then, we weren't getting the [weather] we usually get it was very sunny. I was flying around on my quad on the estate all day, drinking, being stupid, I had a pretty good birthday. But then 7 o'clock came and I was home to bed.

So it's like, now it's finished, everyone's gone. It's just about lifestyle, how my lifestyle was then, so it was selling drugs for gangs, stuff like that, just not living very good. I enjoyed it at the time though, I loved it. I'm not gonna lie I look back and I just think, it's changed so much when I look at the estate and I look at my friends now how we have all grown up, some of us have become things no way I would have ever thought you would have become the person I have today. It's a good thing to be honest, it's just like so mad. So basically the idea behind this was, it's quite easy to explain, how many. How many more friends will I lose? So, how many of us will go to jail, how many times will we be locked up, it's just anything negative, how many times of it? It's just basically that, do you know what I mean.

When someone goes [to] jail for so long it just feels like one of the ones that have died coz you're not seeing them they've gone, do you know what I mean? It's mad. And that's what gets me mad as well, when

I see all these kids doing it, and they think it's smart I get so wound up, coz I think all that you're doing now eventually it all spirals out, it's a domino effect and all your friends gonna start disappearing on you, getting killed and getting locked up. Sounds bad to say but you'll be lucky if you're there to witness it all. It's mad really. But I suppose they'll just grow out of that, like I grew out of it. They've just set the bar for a new group of gangs and as the younger ones grow up they'll just know that that's all they know growing up, so it's just a cycle really. So all I'm moaning about it's just about being young and getting older and wiser it just irritates you. It just gets you mad.'

Dylan's story

Bob Marley and the Wailers (1977b)
'One Love/People Get Ready'
This reggae track talks about love, mercy, and unity.

'The one love. That's the way I feel right about now. I feel like everyone should spread love and positivity and everybody can live together. Because coming from the background that I come from I've done a lot of bad and a lot of bad has been done to me and if I can forgive and forget people can forgive and forget. [In my charity work] we spread love and positivity and we try and empower kids because the way we see it is, if you get two kids from different estates, nine of their ten hobbies or things they like the other one would like. They're so similar yet they're fighting and arguing over things that have no bearing on them. I take my hat off to people who work and do things the right way because the easy way is criminal, to be a criminal, that's the easy way to live in life, yeah you have occupation hazards you might go to prison and so on, but it's easier, you're always going to make money, but the hard way to live, and I respect everybody who goes out and works, it's the legitimate way, coz it's hard out there. When you go out and buy something you appreciate it when you work for it. When you're on the road like I was, coz I was major according to the police, so I didn't appreciate nothing, do you know, the girls, the money, the cars, the jewellery, I didn't appreciate nothing, but now, I take my hat off to people who have worked all their life. So that's where the turning point come. And now I just try to spread positivity everywhere do you know. [Most] of my work I do for free, I really struggle at times, but it's not gonna make me go back to the road, coz I made a promise to my daughter and my mum, do you know, thank God my mum lived long enough to see me turn my life around. She died in [year] but she seen me nominated for awards and that before she died and do you know it took her years to really say was proud of me.

My understanding is that I don't think there is such a things as a bad kid, people think there is bad kids, but kids are kids, and kids make bad choices, do you know, and take bad options, I don't believe there is any bad in any kid, do you know, because I've done more probably, most of the bad, more bad than anybody in this country, I'm not saying that being flippant with it, I know that I must have done a lot of bad, as much as the next person, but I know I've also done more good than anybody in my community, there's nobody that has worked with [many] kids over the years. And I don't do it for awards or rewards, I do it to help them to make the right choices and to live a peaceful life.

[Talking about his children] I wouldn't let them go down the road I went down I would die before that happened. Back in the day, because I used to be well off financially, I used to think it was all about throwing money at them and possessions, and now where I can't afford it, do you know they love it that I'm just here to spend time with them and not in jail. They appreciate it more, and nowadays they don't have to say thanks for possessions now they say thanks for being with us and they are proud of the work that I do. And they know that I struggle but as long as I'm helping people I'll pay it back at some point. You know, that's all what I do, make the world a safer place.'

Eric's story

'One thing I kept regardless of how stupid I was, I've always went to school. I'm turning eighteen [years old] I go to college and my step mum, I think she'd just had enough of me so she kicked me out and then, I think that's when I realized … I literally had no one there. So all these guys I had been stabbed for, been beaten how many times, none of them were there, and I think that was partly one of the best things for me. So I would take a train and sleep on it, go and sleep on a friend's house and wake up and still go to college, coz like I say the one thing I always had was school … I was like I made it to this country and now I'm homeless and it's like, I feel like I failed myself as well and but then there's no one. There's no family … I never had enough money.

I was always good in school, the grades were there, so when I done my UCAS and I went to uni[versity] and I met normal people. And it was like when you're always an outcast, even when I was doing all this good stuff, you go to school I'd do poetry, I'd do campaigns but then when you'd come home the people you'd talk to are kids that don't live at home or gang type of related people, outcasty types of people.

Homeless hostel people. And you go to uni and you realize that people have the same mind-set as you, you know and then it's like oh this is great, but then what happened is that at uni in the first week I was robbing people's laptops and one girl took me on the side and I took a laptop and I tried to sell it to her it was her friend's and instead of telling people she took me aside and said you actually don't have to do that, your money's coming in, I didn't know how to do the student finance, it came in November by then and it was like ah, I don't have to do that, I feel like that touched me, for me it's always been about people touching your life, there's always been people touching me that has changed my thing, it's not been the money or nothing like that, and I'm like yeah I'm really gonna calm down.

I ended up praying I was just like, I I I had enough, it's not I had enough I was just like, well I was homeless, and you guys have a lot of money and nobody helped me but nah, my school is cool I want to be creative, I want to make something of myself, but what happened actually, no that story sounds too good. What really happened is my friend got stabbed in front of me, he's got his stomach got opened in front of me and then, it's just too, too, it's just, it was this summer in [year], just so many kids were getting stabbed, my friends were just getting stabbed up. And then we done a gang robbery in a shop and then they and then they gonna, and then nine of us got caught, they all got caught, coz me and my friend were discussing it, and we just was like "this is just way out, this is just beyond us", so the camera was looking that way and then my friends were like you guys were like "you guys just pushers anyway you stay here and we're gonna go do it" and they went to prison now.

After that … each year of uni I went to hospital, so you're down with that life, but there's still something I haven't, there's demons that I haven't, your parents, what your dad was doing to you, what your dad was doing to your mum, I'm always fighting, so is the whole I'm done I'm in school I'm doing, but you're angry, it's like any person disrespects you I end up in a fight especially when you drink and that whole life comes back, everything you thought you left behind comes back. But that thing of anger is still there, even in [uni] I got arrested twice, and … you've seen a good life, I'm a good person in my heart but how's this keep on happening?

Obviously, I'm grown up, coz mine is weird it's like there's other refugee life but taking that away, growing up in [city] it's like, you're still having to come to terms with it as a man … I've got so far in my life I think to prove a point to these guys, to my friends or to myself. Oh, you can disrespect me if it makes you feel better … you're lucky I'm not at work or I'd call HR [human resources] I'll call HR on you … I think how I dress and how I walk they see you, I feel like guys who have been in gangs and whatever, they know each other, we know each other and how you look, coz you look at someone in the eye and you won't look away, someone I catch myself I'll look at him, guys are looking at me and they're like "bruv what you saying" and I'm like "I'm not your guy, I'm just coming from work are you alright?", and then he don't know what to say and he'll come like I'm not your guy, if you guys are about to come and beat me, you're probably about to do that, you're about to beat me you're definitely going to win, this is not me guys, I'm not a dickhead I'm not a prick like that, maybe you catch me when I'm drunk and boy you're gonna wish your didn't do that, or maybe you're gonna catch me with my boys, they're gonna wish you didn't do that, but my guy but that's past me cuz, that's not me.'

Discussion
Charity work

A common career trajectory in desistance was as an expert-by-experience in the field of gang prevention and/or anti-youth violence initiatives. In some cases, this was as a main role, whereas for others it was conveyed as a passion in addition to their other work. Making money from this type of gang consultant and campaigner roles was referred to as difficult by all the men concerned; however, they were clear that money was not a key motivator. Becoming a moral expert by drawing on their past experience was developed as a tool for their new sense of themselves as reformed men. It enabled them to retain some of the symbolic markers of their former gang lives, by emphasizing their former toughness and street credibility, while simultaneously constructing a superior achievement in that life through being a survivor, when so many others are not. This echoes the findings in Maruna's (2004, p 85) exploration of desistance narratives, where he found that the motivation of 'making good' or giving something back to society as a form of reparation was pertinent. As noted in Dylan's narrative, he framed the charity work that he does now as both giving back as well as mitigating against his former self. Similar to Lester, Dylan distinguishes young people who 'make bad choices' from being actually bad themselves. He then changes to refer to himself directly, where he outlines that, although he has done 'more bad than anyone in the country', this has been outweighed by his subsequent charity work. This reveals the way in which Dylan uses his current work to neutralize his past. In the interview, Dylan also clearly pointed out that there was not a financial incentive for him to do his charity work. He noted that he often worked for free, foregrounding a sense of selfless charity, rather than opportunism.

Lester recounted that he earned small amounts for his charity work, however, was more explicit about seeking future profit. He lamented the difficulties with making a success of a freelance-type organization without having the 'machine' (infrastructure) behind him. He held faith that the 'big money would come' and ultimately felt that young children who were at risk of being gang-involved would be 'ten times more likely to listen' if he had a Mercedes to jump into after they met him. Through this, Lester is navigating how to form a new non-violent masculinity via charity work, yet also recognizing that the younger men that he seeks to influence will be impressed by the markers of hegemonic masculinity as he was.

A large part of the motivation for this work is clearly to 'give something back' to society and help young men in a similar situation. However, it is also important to consider that a function of enduring structural inequality against marginalized, ethnic minority ex-gang members with a criminal record means that it is less than easy to shake off prejudice and seek employment in a conventional way after recovery. In a way, the participants who adopted the idea of experts-by-experience as ex-gang members were still capitalizing on their previous protest masculinity success, yet have inverted the marginalization of their criminal record and gang-involved pasts by reclaiming them as experiences that they draw on to inspire positive change and promote non-violence.

Dave found an alternative means of production as he had turned to blood donation as a way to exhibit a new type of masculinity. This masculine expression was centred on helping people, 'giving something back', and finding a resource that he could offer. At the point that we met Dave had completed dozens of blood donations and was donating platelets, so he could give more frequently. He described a new type of pride that he gained (in contrast to on-road pride) as he received certificates from the blood donation service thanking him. Dave noted that giving blood provided him with a good opportunity to feel a new positive sense of pride as he conveyed the impact of his donations.

> 'If you're like me and you're not feeling really proud of yourself do something good, there's no guilt in doing something positive … I know I've got people who hate me, so when I put out something positive, I'm like well look at him pretending he's a nice guy, but actually I will be honest, I'm giving something back … one donation could help 12 babies!' (Dave)

There is something beautiful in the simplicity of blood donation as a form of new pride. Dave searched resources literally from within himself and used this as a way to produce something he could be positively proud of. He planned to get to 100 donations and then give the certificate to a deceased friend's mother, in his friend's memory. This is another example of the ways in which prior on-road experience, such as seeing friends die through gang violence, can be inverted to look for the ways in which a positive can be now found in contrast.

Guilt, self-forgiveness, and self-acceptance

> 'Right, so then first you go through a process that, you first have to judge your own self, you have to go to yourself that certain things you were doing was wrong, and atone for that, genuinely.' (Lester)

Lester discusses the power of forgiveness as an important part in his recovery. He noted that he has judged himself and apologized for what his actions, which, he felt, was a powerful experience. In Lester's comments it seems significant that he talks about how he had to honestly judge himself and admit that some of his actions were wrong. Forgiving these transgressions would have been difficult, as he was entrenched in gang life for decades. Judging himself rather than referring to being judged externally from the police and courts was significant here. This refers to the importance for him of reintegrative, rather than disintegrative, shaming, deployed in restorative justice (Braithwaite, 1989, 1993). Judgement mattered most when it is from people valued and respected by the perpetrator, who can often be outside of the criminal justice framework. To explain his recovery and the formation of a new masculine identity, Lester noted, 'I used to be an idiot, but I've evolved that's the difference', ascribing his recovery to his own personal evolution rather than as a product of the external fact of being imprisoned. Evolution as a concept implies progress and advancement. Despite this sense of change, Lester highlighted the importance of authenticity:

> 'Deceit doesn't work, you can't keep that sham up forever coz it's not gonna happen, you've got to be yourself, consistent.' (Lester)

The notion of being yourself indicates that there is an inner essential self who endures through time. Lester showed a value-based constitution of the self, based on idealized notions of being a morally upstanding person in a way that now fits with wider society, rather than the 'code of the street' morality he spent his earlier years living by. This idea has been explored in depth by Maruna (2004, p 88), who found that the establishment of a 'true self' or 'real me' was an essential part to every desistance narrative. This sense of a true inner self who continues as the positive aspects of a person through desistance and recovery was reflected in the participants' narratives in this study. Mirroring Maruna's (2004) findings, the participants reached back to their past former selves in order to desist and recover, rather than discovering new selves. However, this idea of being their 'true self' is somewhat in conflict with the notion of stripping away previous masculinity performances. Instead, it could be seen as returning to the prior vulnerabilities that were previously hidden. In doing this, they stripped back the desire to perform a type of hegemonic masculinity and instead centred a more genuine and muted sense of masculine self, which foregrounded authenticity and vulnerability over exaggerated traits in protest masculinity.

Several participants mentioned the ways in which they had looked back on their pasts in order to understand themselves (Eric, Sam, Dylan, and Dave). There was a tendency for the participants to describe their past lives using popular psychology and self-help therapeutic discourse as a way to explain to themselves. For instance, Sam told me he had 'studied his life' to understand what had happened to him. At different points in the interview, participants referred to their own situations using phrases that have their origins in psychotherapy but have since become more mainstream. Examples include Dylan noting in the past his actions were 'learned behaviour'. Sam conveyed several points drawing on therapeutic language. He noted 'you become what you've been labelled', he had become 'desensitized', 'labelled', 'dehumanized'. Sam also drew heavily on Maslow's (1943) hierarchy of needs at several points in the interview as a way to explain his past behaviours, namely, 'he says when your basic needs aren't met you're likely to go elsewhere to find them', in particular he was looking for a 'mother figure'. These examples show how the participants had sought theories to explain the paths that their lives had taken, outside of the realms of structural inequality. Instead, these reasons are focused on individual and family deficiencies, which result in the personalization of the problems they faced.

When focusing on these narratives of self-acceptance and self-forgiveness, one that really stood out was Jordan's narrative thread of 'shining' through (despite) his past circumstances. Jordan made a strong case throughout that he was different, stood out from his peers, which is why he has succeeded in life. In different ways all three of his music choices explored this theme. The first track showed vulnerable children, with whom which he identified, but this then contrasted with a 'suave' rapper with whom he identified with as well. In the second track the rapper was talking about a lucky escape from a shooting. Jordan used this track to convey his own sense of feeling 'bulletproof' and 'blessed'. Lastly, he chose a 2Pac song. Jordan told me how much respect he had for him as a Black man who had been involved in street life but was also an entrepreneur.

In the following excerpt Jordan really delves into how he perceives his past and how he locates himself as someone who differs from his peers. His high self-esteem and confidence are clear here and he does embody it in his persona. As I listened, I wondered if his enthusiasm for life was something to do with his age (26 years), or whether he was just so pleased that he had survived his past and was a successful entrepreneur. I think it is also worth considering that, as branding himself as a role model, the consumer of his product is buying him, his story, his own persona. So, in that way he is embodying his message and product, which is a successful ex-gang member, a 'positive role model' like he says:

> 'I feel bulletproof you know physically mentally and spiritually I really do; I feel I'm blessed and that's one of the reasons why I made the transition from being on the streets into kind of not even kind of, getting a degree setting up a business, going into the other side of life, you know the other side of the fence, the reverse side of the coin … And that song as it says is 100 shots and I've had more than 100 shots at me and I'm still here, still excelling, still outshining myself, in every move that I make, I always surprise myself as the years progress. Every year more achievements, more goals are being accomplished. And that's what it's about. It's being a positive role model and that started to occur in that part of my life towards the end of my life the violence.' (Jordan)

When explaining this part of his life he again conveys a sense of standing out among his peer group. I think his comment here really conveys the sense that being positive and internalizing this survivor narrative has been an active choice by Jordan as a way to make sense both of his own physical survival when some of his peers did not, as well as a determination to survive the gang life and see his life turn into something different. Drawing on the symbolism of survival has been part of feminist domestic violence discourse, but in slightly different ways. I wonder if there is a similarity here, that concentrating on your own survival is more positive than wondering why the bad things happened to you.

Fatherhood and family

The element of cathexis surfaced in the participants' talk about their recovery and how it was centred not on intimate relationships with partners, but by a changing self as they became fathers. This was a contrast to the interpersonal relationships that were foregrounded at other points in their lives, representing a shift in the way that the participants perceived themselves in the nexus of their personal relationships. Starting to see themselves as important to dependants was a part of the development of a different identity, based on interrelatedness rather than independence. Forging a new sense of self around the prioritization of their role as fathers, brothers, and sons, was transformative for some of the participants. In this way they looked to the wider repercussions that their behaviour had on those around them. Fathering as an identity can provide opportunities for men to develop different masculinities and 'expand their repertoire of emotional communication, while distancing themselves from a mothering or feminised position' (Gough, 2018, p 42). Thus, fatherhood presents novel opportunities for men to enhance their 'caring masculinities' through nurturing (Gough, 2018, p 58). Some of the participants had shifted from being an uninvolved absent father during the height of their time involved in gangs and on-road, to, through their recovery, centralizing this role in their lives.

Dylan very much centred his current masculinity as being focused on his role as a father. On his past parenting, he noted that he used to 'throw money at them' whereas now he values the time he has to spend with them instead, particularly in contrast to the lengthy prison sentence that took him away from them. Dylan conceptualized a new sense of pride, which is distinct from the pride that he felt during his gang-involved time. As is seen in Dylan's comments, he is making a distinction between his role as a father at the height of his time on-road and gang-involved and his current identity. Grundetjern et al (2019) carried out an exploration into 'marginalised fatherhood', by looking at the ways that drug-dealing fathers assigned their identities as parents. They found that, in contemporary times, new paternal identities have come to the fore, where fathers are increasingly expected to play a more active role in their children's lives. However, despite this, there is still a tendency to focus on mothers rather than on fathers, which has left a less clear 'cultural content ascribed to fatherhood' (Grundetjern et al, 2019, p 2).

Shaun referred to the process of realizing how much he missed out on in regard to his family while he spent five years in prison. It seemed easier for him to appreciate the losses through looking at his family and in particular his mother's suffering during his time incarcerated. He conveyed a sense of remorse over the lost time, for himself as well as in relation to his family. Realizing that he was 'needed' by his sister indicates that he was forging different types of 'ties' than gang ties. It was a process of shifting the affiliation away from the gang and back to family that enabled him to achieve a different sense of belonging after his experience in prison.

Dave recounted an incident where he had been attacked publicly and then vowed to get revenge. However, not long after Dave became a father himself, he saw via social media that the perpetrator had also become a father. These shifts made Dave consider the issue differently, as if both their lives had become more important through their relation to others:

> 'I could see him one day and punch him and think that was deserved but I thought I could give him brain damage, I could get myself locked up, he's got a daughter to think of who yeah her dad in my eyes is a dickhead but that's not her fault.' (Dave)

As the stakes got higher once Dave had children, it has since caused him to fear bringing his children to where he lives, as it is still a gang-affected area. He noted that he was 'scared for my son, and for myself as well, because where I'm living'. He says the next generation of gang-involved young men spend time on the streets close to his house and he has been mugged and had a knife pulled on him since desisting from gang activity. Returning to be a 'civilian' in the area after being gang-involved caused a shift in his own perception of risk and safety. Jordan described being scared of becoming a father, as, if his relationship broke down, he would not want to be the 'weekend person', referring to a part-time parent with joint custody. He noted that, 'It must be quite heart-breaking … It sorts of puts me off having children.' He shared his desire to 'be [a] proper' father and the weight of it felt considerable to him.

Finding God

Joyner Lucas (2016)
'I'm Sorry'

This track, by a North American rapper, deals with depression and suicide. Music track selected by Travis.

Dave, Lester, and Sam all described religion playing a role in their lives and in their recovery, although in different ways. Sam was approached by a pastor who made it his business to reach out to him as well as listen and answer his questions. In Sam's narrative it became clear that he felt surprised that someone had been 'nice' to him, which Sam had not experienced before. This was coupled with a persistent offer to help, as well as patience to listen to the many 'why' questions that Sam asked. The kindness, alongside the listening, of a stranger was a powerful combination and it appeared to give Sam external validation of himself as an individual worth listening to, as well as a sense of belonging to something bigger, outside of the gang framework. Jordan emphasized the role of grace within the Christian faith. Grace is the concept of love and forgiveness provided unconditionally and regardless of past transgressions. He described how he had been carrying the 'condemnation' that he described as being 'clogged up in my heart, shame and guilt and so many things that I went through'. Religion offered him a way both to understand and to repent the past, which enabled him to understand his past in light of the adversity that he had experienced. Sam talked viscerally about his journey to religion as a catalyst for his exit from gang involvement:

> 'I looked up to heaven and I just prayed and prayed, and I believe from that day it's when my whole life completely changed and I became

a Christian and that's when I started pursuing a new life. I started pursuing and reading the Bible and so on and just renewing everything that I once learnt what once was and getting forgiveness in areas that I was carrying, there was like condemnation that I had that was just clogged up in my heart, shame and guilt and so much things that I went through and I, I took on as yeah this is me yeah this is me and that's something that I should never have done and I think through coming to Christ is how I've learnt how to release a lot of stuff that come and that I believe was my changing point but there was destiny helpers along the way like mentors that came in and helped me through different stages of my life so I can't, I can't take all the credit like, like that or, but I know it only happened when I turned to God.' (Sam)

A different way that some of the participants referred to shifting power relations in the formation of their new sense of self was through finding a place within a religious system. In this way, there was a relinquishing of power to an external God. This also gave an opportunity for a different type of understanding of their past behaviours, as well as the adoption of a new framework through which to construct both a self-forgiveness as well as an external forgiveness. Deuchar (2018) explored the function of religion and spirituality in the recovery of formerly gang-involved men. He found that engaging with spiritual endeavours offers ex-gang-involved men ways to develop alternative masculinities in the process of recovery. He noted that religion offers men the opportunity to move from 'masculine criminal distinction' to 'masculine spiritual distinction', meaning that through this shift men are able to avoid their ever-present fear of emasculation in the process of recovery (Deuchar, 2018, p 245). By adopting new identities through spiritual pursuits, ex-gang-involved men were able to find new means of achieving status and capital which offered a chance to adopt a new code, distinct from the code of the street.

Engagement in religion not only offered the opportunity for self-forgiveness and external forgiveness, but also presented a different moral code to the 'code of the street'. This was indicated by both Sam and Lester, who found comfort in the behavioural prescriptions of religion. Sam noted that since finding religion he just 'goes by the Bible', which clearly demarcates what are the 'right things' to do. Lester described the role of religion in his life being predominantly about the way that he constructed a morality that transcends judgements from his peers and is instead founded on a relationship with God. Lester noted that he is most afraid of people who say they don't have religion, because in his eyes they do not have a moral code to prevent them doing the most harm. Dave focused more on the practical support that he had received by engaging in the church. He discussed that he had been helped by the church in recent years. He had gone to a local church when he had been struggling financially and they had helped him and his children with a grant for essentials.

Marginalized masculinity and the struggles of earning money

Lester was insistent about foregrounding his racial identity in the interview. In many ways, Lester's interview was constructed on his political commentary about structural inequality. To describe his view of racism more clearly Lester used his song choice of Bob Marley's 'Natural Mystic' to describe the ways in which he experienced a feeling of being an outsider due to his racial identity.

Bob Marley and the Wailers (1977a)
'Natural Mystic'

Lester used the analogy of the 'natural mystic' to describe the ever-present element of both racism and racial awareness. He likened it to the feeling that his dog gets when he smells the air to 'pick up everything that is going on', then decides if he feels peaceful or uncomfortable. Through this analogy Lester is conveying a sense of race as a haunting presence that is part of the environment and atmosphere but is invisible. One becomes aware of it by sensing it. This notion of the natural mystic that Lester discusses is strongly reminiscent of Avery Gordon's (2008) sociological analysis of haunting. Gordon (2008, p xvi) denotes haunting as 'one way in which abusive systems of power make themselves known and their impacts felt in everyday life, especially when they are supposedly over and done with (slavery, for instance) or when their oppressive nature is denied'. This fits well with the racism that Lester is referring to as in the air. Gordon uses the term haunting not to refer in particular to the experience of being oppressed, exploited, or other forms of 'social violence', but rather it is the haunting that is produced by them (Gordon, 2008, p xvi). The imagery of haunting also conveys the way that discrimination is hard to grasp, talk about, or get rid of, as like a ghost, it is an experience few may believe or understand.

The main theme that ran throughout Lester's narrative was his concern with structural inequality in society. Throughout the interview he linked different types of societal inequalities, in particular those determined by race, money, and power. One of his key phrases was to say that everything is 'stacked', which refers to structural inequality and the way in which he regarded economic success as largely predetermined, by those who were 'born lucky' with fathers who were 'money men'. Lester focused on vast societal inequalities, which mean that

'Only a certain amount of people gets the good spots and the good jobs and the good money ... And all the people with all the good spots make sure all their cousins, their friends they get it.' (Lester)

Lester felt particular disdain for the superficial rhetoric of meritocracy: 'what about *best man for the job?*, all of it stinks, you understand?' He noted, 'everyone's battling for the same crumbs. And there should be no battle for crumbs, it should be all inclusive.' Lester's frustration refers to the barriers he has faced when finding work in his new capacity as a freelance gang consultant. He is network-poor due to a significant time spent in prison and so is unable to pull the strings that are needed to break into a new commercial industry. The entrepreneurial skills that he acquired on-road do not transition to recognized skills of the conventional workplace, so he seeks to financialize his gang experience.

The production relations about desistance and recovery that were revealed in the narratives were very much centred on the ways in which men attempted to reconfigure their means of production away from gang criminality. However, inherent in this process is the conundrum that protest masculinity is often formed due to a sense of marginalization and exclusion from mainstream means of production. At the time of interview most of the participants were facing not only the personal challenge of changing their lives but had to face the existing structural inequalities that excluded them in the first place. The production relations changed enormously when the participants described ending their gang involvement. For several of the participants, the process of leaving was more of a gradual process and one which was fraught with trying to find alternative ways of earning money and supporting themselves away from crime. Dylan, in particular, noted that 'the easy way [to make money] is criminal'; despite the 'occupational hazards' of the threat of prison or harm, it is easier because 'you're always going to make money'. Eric talked at length about his journey away from gang involvement as a long process where he lived in homeless hostels and committed crime in the evenings, but then also attended college or university during the day.

Complicit masculinity

Eric's story of his transformation was one centred in code switching (Auer, 2005): initially trying to navigate being a college student while living in a homeless hostel, jumping the train barriers as he couldn't afford the fare. When he made it to university, he didn't understand the student finance system and so stole laptops from fellow students until a peer explained the process and that he would be receiving financial support. Throughout his studies he was negotiating a balance between low-level criminality and being arrested for fighting, alongside an emerging other identity of an educated young person pursuing a career. He has now achieved this and was speaking to me as a professional in his sector; however, the tension he feels when he returns to his old area, or when he sees men on-road, is clear. There was a tension throughout the narrative between Eric identifying himself as someone who is inherently a gang-involved man or as professional man with little knowledge of violence. In the latter part of his narrative Eric positioned himself as an educated professional. Eric contrasted his current contemporary young professional identity with his historic gang identity by comparing a violent response to an issue with 'going to HR'. It is as if, once his professional identity developed, it was a second adolescence where he grew up in a different way, moving away from his old gang identity. In Eric's narrative, he switches from referring to other 'guys who have been in gangs' as 'they', then 'we'. This evokes the tension that exists between his identification as one of them, or as a member of the different group. A feature of this passage is the conflict between two distinct masculine codes of performance. On the one hand, there is the protest masculinity of the streets, which is defined by the codes of respect and power sought through violence. The reference to being 'seen' by other gang-involved men is also powerful, suggesting that even though Eric's clothes and demeanour have changed, he cannot shake the on-road-based protest masculinity within. The confrontational nature of that exchange is clear. Eric also made thinly veiled threats, that if the opposers caught him drunk, or with his 'boys', they would wish they hadn't. This protest masculinity performance is then contrasted with his complicit corporate masculinity, which he developed while working in a professional role. This also signifies living by a different set of mainstream/corporate rules as distinct to the 'code of the street'.

Learning to walk away

The issue surrounding power relations when desisting from the on-road life was largely about letting go of protest masculinity as the predominant expression of masculinity. In this section, the ways in which the participants described this initial process of separation is outlined. Some participants discussed a residual sense of anger after experiencing domestic violence and abuse (DVA) at home. In their narratives of later life this was still discussed as enduring after their exit from gang involvement. Eric spoke about how he experienced numerous setbacks after starting his new life at university, blaming these on his 'demons' that kept coming back. At this point in the narrative, Eric's frustration with himself was palpable. He referred to going to university and spending time with 'normal people' yet finding it difficult to disentangle himself from the 'code of the street', which prioritizes pride and respect as of utmost importance. This difficulty in changing the habitual responses to being challenged or disrespected was also discussed by Dave. Dave talked in his first interview about his current aim to promote a non-violent message to youths and to set up a campaign in his local area. He subsequently requested a second interview to focus on the way in which although this was his aspiration, he was struggling to let go of his anger as well as the tendency to exhibit confrontational behaviour, which would fit in with the 'code of the street' (Anderson, 1999) but not with civilian life. In particular, he had developed a habit of intervening in other people's conflicts if he considered their behaviour to be bad, for instance a man hitting a child, or a man acting inappropriately with a child. In these situations, he was able to justify himself as acting as a sort of social policeman, to call out the bad behaviour and challenge the perpetrator. Dave mentioned that it caused issues at work with managers, where he was expected to follow a different social code to that of the street. He noted that he could 'just flip with someone'.

Dave rooted his short-temperedness in his childhood experiences and, in particular, to the point in time when he decided not to 'be a victim' anymore, referring to this as a powerless position. He had developed a tendency to 'over-compensate' for his previous feelings of disempowerment:

'So pride is getting people killed isn't it, it's getting people feeling that they have to prove I'm not a little boy, I'm not some little idiot who you can talk to like that, and then if I hear about a pal of mine that has been stabbed or whatever when he didn't walk away I think ah you idiot you could have just walked away you have kids. But I know I need to practice what you preach, because I definitely am all about walking away, but at the same time I'm quick to snap and I'm not gonna blame everything on my childhood, but I can't ignore everything either.' (Dave)

As outlined by Dave, in his life recovering from gang involvement he has been straddling the tension between trying to move forward with a new sense of himself focused on 'walking away' from conflict but remaining caught up in 'pride' and the residual effects of his childhood trauma. Dave commented that his feelings of pride were 'macho bullshit'. This reference is revealing about the way that Dave felt masculine pressure to protect his own pride yet was also referencing it as 'bullshit'. This aspect may have come from the retrospect nature of the narrative, in that he was looking back over his life and the way that pride had been implicated over the years. Dylan had developed the protection strategy of talking to people about his stresses, rather than trying to 'bottle it up', as otherwise,

'When I'm frustrated it's gonna come out in a way where it might get me killed or send me back to jail so therefore, I'd rather discuss it with somebody.' (Dylan)

Travis also talked about the pressure on men 'not to speak out':

'Trying to live up to what society expects from you ... The expectations and stuff that you know you can't reach but you got to try and putting too much pressure on yourself and like the whole thing about recently it changed a lot with telling men not to speak out and all that, but all the stereotypes, strong male role models, bottling everything up deep in yourself.' (Travis)

In this passage Travis is referring to the markers of hegemonic masculinity, which are propped up by the 'strong male role models' who convey the ideal version of masculinity to younger men. He became very emotional when he spoke about the confines of masculinity on him, even talking about how he had felt driven to suicide at times due to the pressure these expectations placed on him. Both of the retrospective reflections by Travis and Dylan show the way that their perspectives on masculinity and vulnerability have changed from the protest masculinity performance that they had foregrounded when gang-involved, where there was little space for expressing vulnerability at the time. Gough (2018) noted that there has been a shift away from the traditional idealization of the unemotional man, due to wider recognition that stoicism is not positive or sustainable.

In the interview Dave focused on his recent discovery of the term 'toxic masculinity'. He noted that when he found out about this concept, 'it all makes sense'. The term 'toxic masculinity' has been popularized since the 1980s when there was an emerging focus on the ways in which aspects of masculinity affected men negatively. It is a notion that is then pitched against an idea of 'healthy masculinity' (Kimmel and Wade, 2018, p 237). Kimmel and Wade (2018, p 239) noted the experience of toxic masculinity among men being as if they are 'experiencing a conflict, inside them, between their own values and this homosocial performance'. It is the barren emotional territory of homosocial groups and their conflicts that Dave refers to, noting that,

'There's so much stuff with lads that are told you know if you're hanging round the wrong people it's all about being tough, it's all don't be a pussy, don't be gay.' (Dave)

The homophobic culture of gangs was discussed at length by Dave and was the focus of one of the music videos that he selected for the interview:

Logic ft Alessia Cara and Khalid (2017)
'1-800-273-8255'

This hip-hop track and lyrics are about feeling suicidal and the music video follows the persecution of a young man dealing with homosexuality and being ostracized for it. The double meaning of the song was revealed only in the video. Although Dave didn't disclose at any point that he was himself gay, he talked a lot about the negativity around homosexuality in the gang context and the general narrow-mindedness that on-road culture typified. In excerpts such as that just given, being gay is likened to being a 'pussy' (vagina), making a parallel between homosexuality and femininity, with both being devalued and the antithesis to masculinity. In this way, it is clear that gay masculinities are subordinated, and associated with femininity, in the gender hierarchy in gangs as in wider society (Connell, 2005). Reflecting back on their lives led some of the participants to reconceptualize their past situations, emphasizing the elements of disadvantage and looking at how they came to perform a protest masculinity. Lester commented on what he saw as 'the moral of the story', which was heavily tied up with an idea that performing a protest masculinity was in part predictable for young men in certain situations, hinting at the idea of protest masculinity as a rite of passage for young men:

> 'So, the moral of the story is … It's never the culprit or the persons who being painted as the bad guy who is really the bad guy … And that's the facts of life. These sixteen-year-olds full of testosterone and full of wild, come on, if you give him a gun you don't have to ask him twice to shoot it. It just fits into the narrative of everything.' (Lester)

By looking at the past through this lens, Lester was explaining the likelihood of young men committing to a protest masculinity as a likely scenario, relating it to their testosterone and them being 'full of wild'. Through this, Lester is referencing the inevitability of masculinity as having hegemonic markers, so that if a boy gets a gun, then the outcome is inevitable. This association of hegemonic masculinity with testosterone was also reiterated by Dave, who noted that 'it's just this toxic masculinity, alpha, too much testosterone'. By looking at hegemonic and protest masculinities as inherently linked with male biology, the participants were not only naturalizing their former behaviours but also suggesting a limited capacity to change.

PART III

Joining the Dots

9

Policy Links: Why Is 'Domestic Abuse' not 'Serious Violence'? A False Dichotomy

Since 2018, the UK government have adopted a national public health approach to 'serious violence' (SV), which focuses on youth violence, knife crime, and gang-associated exploitation activities such as 'county-lines' drug trafficking. In April 2018, Public Health England published a 'Serious Violence Strategy', which was specifically aimed at tackling the increased 'knife crime, gun crime and homicide across England' (Public Health England, 2019b). In this strategy they defined SV as:

> 'Specific types of crime such as homicide, knife crime, and gun crime and areas of criminality where serious violence or its threat is inherent, such as in gangs and county lines drug dealing.' It also includes emerging crime threats faced in some areas of the country such as the use of corrosive substances as a weapon. (Public Health England, 2019b, p 7)

It is clear from this definition that the core aim of the SV Strategy is to deal with street-based, gang-associated crime. This is reinforced by the associated funding for 'violence reduction units', which shared £35 million to create multi-agency hubs to deal with associated crimes (APCC, 2020). At the time of writing only half of the 18 new dedicated violence reduction units, set up using the SV prevention duty, have domestic violence and abuse (DVA) as part of their strategy (Y. Roberts, 2021). It appears violence that is considered serious is also aligned with that which is public, whereas private violence is hidden behind closed doors. This is despite available evidence that DVA takes up a significant amount of police time and resources (Oliver et al, 2019).

The Serious Violence Prevention Duty is part of the wider Police, Crime, and Sentencing Bill, which has been marred with controversy over concerns around its wider social implications. Human Rights watchdog, Liberty (2021), have lamented that it is 'One of the most serious threats to human rights and civil liberties in recent history', as it offers increased police and state powers in a range of areas aimed at public control. Within the bill is a brand-new legal duty for public service providers to collaborate in preventing SV (UK Parliament, 2019). As outlined in Chapter 2, there is an increasing body of evidence to suggest that a relatively high proportion of young people who are involved in what the UK government is terming 'serious violence' have experienced domestic abuse (DA) in childhood (either before or concurrently). Case review analysis from the Children's Commissioner estimate 37 per cent of children experience this overlap, although there is still room for more research into prevalence in this area. Children in this position occupy a complex position in relation to child protection, as they are simultaneously framed as child victims of DA (which is now enshrined in the new Domestic Abuse Bill, 2021), yet are also liable to be constructed as offenders in the context of SV, with the existing age of criminal responsibility being ten years old.

I take a critical view of the UK government's initial decision to silo out what they term SV as disparate from DA, which was formerly dealt with under the Violence Against Women and Girls (VAWG) Strategy but has now been separated off. Under the SV Strategy, violence is being steered by a public health approach to violence, which aims to take a broad-brush view of violence as a societal-wide issue. Separating this from forms of gender-based violence then appears to make little sense. Not only does this have a discursive impact (by calling one type 'serious' it implicates that the other is not serious), but it also separates a type of violence (DA) that is seen as gendered from violence is which is framed as gender-blind (SV). The distinct strategic approaches the UK government use to address societal violence are based on differing logics, and thus create artificial boundaries between them. Creating different cultural, operational, and theoretical planets by which to understand societal violence limits our ability to understand the interconnectedness of DA and SV and develop genuine public health solutions. Through focusing on the experiences of boy child survivors who experience life on each of the planets we can see how the separation of different forms of violence leaves gaps of understanding which limit young people's access to support.

The artificial and unnecessary differential between DV and DVA has also been reinforced by the Domestic Abuse Commissioner (2021a, 2021b), who noted that the proposed separation will create a statutory duty for local regions to work to prevent violence, which did not incorporate DA or VAWG. The commissioner noted that this not only failed to acknowledge the high levels of violent crime that are classified as DA, but also risks sending the message to the public that DA is not a priority in terms of violent crime reduction. At the time of writing this book, there has been a successful amendment to the Serious Violence Prevention Duty, part of the Bill, as it passed through the House of Lords. The cross-party campaign for this change has been led by Baroness Bertin and co-sponsored by Lord Polak, Lord Russell, and Lord Rosser, and was supported by the DA Commissioner (2021). In December 2021 the press reported that the Home Secretary Priti Patel would be bringing forward changes to the bill (Asthana, 2021) to include both DVA and sexual offences into the bill, however we have yet to see the reality of this on paper at the time of writing.

Despite the upcoming statutory changes which will put pressure on local areas to combine their resources for both SV and DVA, the lack of foresight on this across the UK is still questionable. To date there have been trials and successes of public health approaches to address physical violence in various UK cities including Glasgow, London, and Cardiff, but without explicitly including DA and other forms of VAWG (Chandan et al, 2020). The reluctance to connect masculinities and SV was highlighted by Walsh (2018), who argued for a 'gender conscious' approach which acknowledges that community SV is a 'male issue'.

Within SV discourse, the dominant 'perpetrator' is discussed as being in the ominous and opaque 'gangs'/'drug gangs'/organized crime groups. However, the complexity of this is clear even in the government's own strategy, as it notes young people can be both 'involved in' as well as 'exploited by' gangs (Home Office, 2018, p 54). Thus, the parameters between the role of exploiter vs. exploited are at times unclear (not least because the Home Office does not include definitions of these different gangs in its own strategy). It does note that there is 'evidence of considerable overlap between victims and offenders of serious violence' (Home Office, 2018, p 33). There is some acknowledgement (depending on which perspective is dominant) of some structural constraints that underpin childhood adversity, such as those that centre upon poverty, class, and race exclusion. However, within the dominant public health model the language of contagion is used to describe the way in which communities can experience high levels of violence. The public health approach frames violence as a disease, to be treated as an epidemic; a health issue that spreads via contagion. It looks at similarities between other diseases and the way that they spread and cluster, and have compared these with the way that violence does the same. The key seems to be a very responsive support team that mobilizes once an incident has occurred, paired with a negative community response every time there is violence.

One of the most significant differences between the SV and DA logics is that of victimization. In both planets, the majority of perpetrators are male; the divergence occurs in the understanding of who is targeted for victimization. The majority of victims of SV are also male (Home Office, 2018), whereas in the case of DA the majority of victims are female

(Hester, 2013). The extent to which gender is seen as an important factor in understanding the victimization from different forms of violence is interesting. On the SV planet, gender appears to only be considered in the case of looking at women's minority experience. In the SV Strategy the importance of 'gender sensitive responses' is only mentioned in relation to girls' support provision (Home Office UK, 2018, p 62). 'Masculinity/ies' are not discussed at all in the strategy as a factor for consideration. The extent to which the violence is seen as linked with wider criminality makes a big impact on the approach that is taken in national strategies. Due to the SV perceived links to organized crime 'gangs' and exploitation of young people through 'county-lines' networks, a dominant form of intervention in SV is the increased profiling and surveillance of gang-associated young people (Home Office, 2018). This is something that has been noted by contextual safeguarding scholars, who have raised concerns about the use of surveillance over support (Wroe and Lloyd, 2020). The SV planet has been characterized by a dual approach: both the enhanced use of surveillance of young people through techniques such as the Gangs Matrix, as well as the development of various multi-agency monitoring systems:

> In particular it needs the support of communities thinking about what they can themselves do to help prevent violent crime happening in the first place and how they can support measures to get young people and young adults involved in positive activities. (Home Office, 2018, p 9)

Both the SV Strategy and the DA Bill emphasize the importance of multi-agencies working with an increasing emphasis on the importance of non-criminal justice solutions to deal with violence perpetration. Cure Violence is an initiative that aims to reduce violence through street-based practitioners who 'interrupt' violence by working with those on the cusp of committing violence, as well as through the utilization of public messaging (Gebo, 2016, p 376).

What is required is closer joint work between DVA (and gender-based violence organizations) with youth offending/gang outreach organizations. The reason behind this study in the first place was a gap in professional practice and knowledge around the experiences of men who live with DVA in childhood and later go on-road and become gang-involved. The findings in this book show that there are threads in the life–history narratives around masculinity, vulnerability, and violence, which run through from the men's DVA experience to their on-road and gang experience. These findings could be useful for front-line agencies, which are, in the early 21st century, siloed into different 'planets' and are working on distinct constructions of victim/perpetrator, victim/offender, into which these men do not easily fit. This research could open up the conversation around the porous boundaries between these polarized labels and create empathy for on-road and gang-involved men, who (as shown in the literature) can be a highly labelled and stigmatized group. The broader question that this analysis has raised is why, if a public health approach to violence is supposed to be an all-encompassing take on community violence, have services from the grass-roots right up to Government policy making level, chosen to reinforce a distinction between SV and DVA? There are several false dichotomies between the two: private/public, female/male victimization. However, this is a false distinction as they are united by being different aspects of male violence in a patriarchal context. Both are gendered, often affect the same people and communities, and both can be more deeply understood through a lens of masculinity. Perhaps the logics of the two forms of violence are closer than they seem?

Gender-blind? The public health approach to violence prevention

The World Health Organization (WHO) has advocated for a public health approach to violence since 1996 (WHO, 2002). This centres upon the idea that diverse forms of violence are harmful on a population level and that a whole system response is most appropriate. A public health approach to violence has been advocated and explored by Public Health England (2019b) and the Local Government Association (2018). The public health approach focuses on '(1) preventing disease, (2) prolonging life, and (3) promoting health and efficiency through organised community efforts' (Public Health England, 2019b, p 14). The focus in public health approaches is utilitarian and aims to improve health and safety on a population scale. Fundamental to this is multi-agency and interdisciplinary collaboration, which aim to take a holistic view of community wellbeing. The first trace of a public health approach to violence was when Gordon (1949) called for injury prevention efforts to be broadly understood in a similar way to the prevention strategies for other diseases. WHO notes that 'almost all violence is predictable and therefore preventable' (WHO, cited in UK Faculty of Public Health, 2016). It uses the following definition of violence:

> The intentional use of physical force or power, threatened or actual, against oneself, or another person, or against a group or community, that either results in or has a high likelihood of resulting in injury, death, psychological harm, maldevelopment or deprivation. (Krug et al, 2002, p 1083)

In putting together a comprehensive definition of violence that incorporates both self-directed and interpersonal, as well as collective, violence, the WHO advocates for the use of the ecological model to understand how different forms of violence intersect. By likening the risk of later violence to risk of later illness, it frames the issues in the familiar discourse of health prevention. It is therefore argued that 'violence, like a range of other environment- and behaviour- related health problems – including HIV/AIDS, cardiovascular diseases, and diabetes – can largely be predicted and prevented' (Neville et al, 2015, p 323). In the same way as other public health campaigns, the public health approach is population-based and seeks to 'improve the health and safety of the population' (Neville et al, 2015, p 323). It is not just the actual incidences of violence that a public health approach seeks to address, but also the *fear* of violence, which can have a dramatic impact on individual and community wellbeing (Public Health England, 2019a). The impact of both fear and realities of violence in communities also intersects with other axis of inequality. Communities that experience the greatest levels of violence are also those which experience multiple axis of marginalization, 'the poorest fifth of our society suffering rates of hospital admissions for violence 5 times higher than those of the most affluent fifth' (Public Health England, 2019b, p 15).

The public health approach to SV was first conceptualized by Gilligan (1996), who started to apply the language of epidemic to societal violence. The collaboration between criminologists and public health specialists has continued and created important new insights to address SV in more holistic ways (Welsh et al, 2014). The public health approach to gangs and youth violence has been used in practice in Chicago Cure Violence model. Due to its success it has also been applied in the Scottish context, in Glasgow, and has also shown positive results in reducing youth violence and knife carrying among young people (Violence Reduction Unit, 2011; Williams et al, 2014). There are now calls for this approach to be adopted more widely across the UK where there are known gang issues (Youth Violence Commission, 2018). Although the public health model has been increasingly applied to gender-based violence as well, there have been dissenting voices which critique the way in which using health analogies can serve to depoliticize violence and abuse. Pease (2019) has spoken out critically against the transferability of epidemiological concepts to DVA:

> Violence is not an illness or a disease, but a behaviour and a social phenomenon. It is not something that goes into remission or something that someone has. When primary prevention is applied to violence against women, it removes reference to disease, although the language often remains, for example, in 'the epidemic of violence against women'. (Pease, 2019, p 18)

Public Health England has taken a focus in particular on violence that is perpetrated by children against children. They have created an approach that aims to deal specifically with this issue, the 'Collaborative approaches to preventing offending and re-offending by children' (CAPRICORN) framework (Public Health England, 2019a). This was created in response to an increase in knife crime and serious youth violence and a recognition from MPs that 'we can't just arrest our way out of this problem' (Public Health England, 2019a, p 5). In essence, it draws on the successes of the public health approach to SV in Glasgow, attempting to turn certain aspects into a transferable model. These are called the '5 Cs': Collaboration; Co-production; Cooperation; Counter-narrative; Community consensus approach (Fraser and Irwin-Rogers, 2021, p 11).

The public health approach frames violence as a disease, to be treated as an epidemic; a health issue that spreads via contagion. By likening the risk of later violence to risk of later illness, it frames the issues in the familiar discourse of health prevention. Unlike the individual-deficit focus of the adverse childhood experience (ACE) perspective, the public health model frames so-called 'gang violence' as situated within the wider community and as a concern of the whole community. By conceptualizing it this way it focuses more on collective responsibility than individual deficit. The results are impressive, with big reductions in violence in the areas that this approach has been trialled. In the first few years of its application in Glasgow, there was a 46 per cent reduction in violent offending by those gang members who engaged, as well as a 34 per cent reduction in all other types of crimes (Violence Reduction Unit, 2011). Research also suggests that this model has resulted in a reduction in weapon carrying by young people (Williams et al, 2014). In the UK there has been an increase in interest in the public health approach to violence, despite the fact it has been developed in a way that treats SV and DA as separate entities and through disparate strategies. This is notable, as it in some ways goes against a broader public health principle: that using a public health framework can prevent the development of fragmented violence prevention.

The conceptualization of violence as contagious removes the onus from the individual perpetrator-and-victim dyad and instead, through the metaphor of contagion, suggest involvement is somewhat choice-less. By framing youth violence as a health issue, proponents have found that the approach is more readily accepted by affected communities, as to use this framework rather than a punitive criminal justice approach emphasizes 'wellness rather than individual blame' (Gebo, 2016, p 376). One of the defining features of the public health approach to SV has been to focus more on the wider community than on the interpersonal dynamics between the victim and perpetrator of the violence. There are several reasons for this: firstly, there is an increasing awareness that for many types of SV there are porous boundaries between those who can be considered victims and perpetrators. Some police forces are now using the term 'alpha victim' to describe the way in which some former victims of exploitation become involved with organized crime and then go on to exploit others (MSPTU, 2018).

The main way that DVA is included in policy documents in the public health approach is in the existence of childhood DVA as a risk factor which impacts on young people's own propensity for violence. As noted by the Wales Violence Reduction Unit, 'The scourge of domestic violence and abuse is often in the background of street violence and vulnerability – sometimes feeding into organised crime. These issues are all connected, and so must be our response' (APCC, 2020, p 16). Likewise, the Hampshire Violence Reduction Unit Strategic Lead Karen Dawes discussed the high prevalence of childhood DVA among surveyed offenders of knife crime and found the markers of the *toxic trio* of mental health, DVA, and substance misuse in the majority of the family backgrounds of knife-crime offenders (APCC, 2020, p 31). In a 2021 UK report advocating for the use of the public health model to address 'violence reduction' (but again, this appears to be excluding gender-based violence), DVA is shown on an ecological framework diagram which outlines such risk factors as 'Exposure to domestic violence and abuse' at the community level and 'Victim/survivor of domestic abuse' at an individual level (Fraser and Irwin-Rogers, 2021, p 5). In this report the authors highlighted an example of a partnership in Essex where 'school readiness, preventing domestic abuse, and tackling gang activity and violence' were all tackled under the violence reduction umbrella (Fraser and Irwin-Rogers, 2021, p 16). However, upon exploration of the Essex data project, it is focused on data sharing and gathering across the county in order to inform local commissioning. The 'Violence and Vulnerability Unit', which developed from this work, includes DA as a risk factor alongside several other markers, including school exclusion, which identify a young person at a higher risk of involvement in 'county lines' crime. It notes that the funds gained through the data gathering will focus on 'opportunities for disruption and enforcement in the short term and produce evidence to plan for longer term prevention and early interventions' (Future of Essex, 2018). There was no explicit mention of the funding of direct interventions with child survivors of DVA. I hope this strategic partnership and others like it shape services that focus on DVA so DVA is seen as more than a 'risk factor' but rather a tangible issue that children need support to deal with, long after the risk ends.

The Cure Violence Programme has worked on training around DVA as interconnected with other forms of violence in the community.[1] It conceptualized DVA as part of the wider 'culture of violence' that it seeks to mitigate. It makes the link between DVA as a form of violence and wider gang violence, yet sees this transition more as a slippery slope. One worker testimony noted that DVA can 'turn into a shooting' in a relatively short space of time (Cure Violence, 2013). The risks with this approach are similar to the ACE discourse; those disparate forms of violence/abuse can have different dynamics and to view DVA as outside of the context of patriarchal gender inequality misses what we know about this form of abuse. Although violence is the common thread, it is essential to look at the fundamental dynamics of the violence in order to understand the way it is reproduced within communities. There is a fundamental tension between promoting a public health model to address violence and then separation of two of the most prevalent forms of violence into disparate strategic approaches. This is an issue because there is an explicit link between young men who may have experience of violence on both planets. However, this connection is only regarded as a risk factor, without any adjoining theorization about gender, the experience of male violence, or the link between gender inequality and the impact that this has on young men.

10

Understanding the Pathways from Domestic Abuse to Gang Involvement

As mentioned at the outset, this study has not been focused on deterministic pathways or proving causal outcomes after the experience of childhood domestic abuse (DA). It is imperative to always keep in mind that most child survivors do not end up following the life paths of the participants explored in this book. However, what we need to grapple with is the relatively high prevalence of childhood domestic violence and abuse (DVA) among young men who do find themselves on-road and gang-involved. When focusing on the life journeys of the participants, despite the individual differences, there appeared to be a common pathway in terms of masculinities, which is visualized in Figure 10.1. What was interesting in this study is that, although based on a small sample, there was a pattern emerging that matched those which professionals working in outreach had mentioned to me. In order to test this, I conducted a deep-dive of Serious Case Reviews (SCRs) that had similar case characteristics to the life stories shared. This is synthesized in Table 10.1.

Learning from cases involving child deaths

SCRs are carried out where abuse or neglect of a child is known, and the child has been seriously harmed or has died.[1] They obviously represent the tip of the iceberg, being mostly those children who experienced a tragic early death, they can tell us a lot about risk management and support of the most vulnerable in society. Out of an available 1,641 records on the National Society for the Prevention of Cruelty to Children (NSPCC) National Case Review Repository, I searched for those that mentioned 'family violence', 'youth offending', 'gangs', and 'county lines'. I initially identified 22 relevant cases, of which 13 showed both childhood DVA and youth offending, with a

Figure 10.1: Masculinities experienced by the participants

Common background context	Childhood Domestic Violence and Abuse	School-based Peer-on-peer Violence	On-Road
Violent masculinity from male at home	Subordinated masculinity	Emerging protest masculinity	Protest masculinity
Intersectional marginalization (class, race, poverty)	Powerlessness	Trying to harness power and agency through violence	Involvement in organized crime gangs/groups
Living in a gang-affected area	Desire to be out of the home	Rejecting victim status	School exclusion
	Male patriarchal violence		Drug dealing
			Exploitation

further three who were possible cases of DVA (mentions of multiple adverse childhood experiences and child protection plans but no details). Identifying relevant cases was made more difficult due to the disparate language and labels that were used both to refer to DVA and gangs: these terms were used in discretionary ways. DVA was coded in the NSPCC database as 'Family violence', which is an ambiguous term. Other phrases used in the report included: 'Domestic incident' (CHSCP, 2020, p 8); 'household violence' (ESCB, 2015, p 10); 'a family in which domestic abuse was a feature' (DSCB, 2014, p 13). Further, in several reports there was minimal mention of DVA and the impact or details were not examined. It was similarly difficult to make sense of the diverse language around youth violence. This has clearly changed over time, reflecting the emerging term 'county lines' as being synonymous with organized crime and exploitation. In some reports activities were framed as 'youth violence', 'youth offending', 'peer association'. Yet with the reports published in the last five years there were mentions of 'child criminal exploitation', 'county lines', 'gangs', 'serious organized crime'. Through this there was a shift in police surveillance and criminal justice involvement in case management. Where the 'gang' label was used there was seldom any external concrete definition offered in the report.

Of the 22 cases that were relevant, 13 met the criteria of explicit reference to childhood DVA and either gang involvement or youth offending. As can be seen from Table 10.1, there are several other similarities that resonate with the life histories explored in this book.

Although there is geographical diversity in this tragic sample, it is notable that the majority of children were from Black and Minority Ethnic (BME) groups. The cases cited spanned London, Southampton, Derbyshire, Oxfordshire, Manchester, Barnsley, and Stockport. The distance is perhaps less surprising taken in context of the move to 'county-lines' drug dealing, which is highlighting the ways in which organized crime groups operate around the country (Harding, 2020). The language that was used to refer to DVA was varied, but there was a consistent reluctance to name the DVA perpetrator as the source of harm. It was common to see DVA framed in ways that presented the issue as neutral, as something that was either a 'household' issue or an event that happens to the mother (with the perpetrator and/or father not mentioned). The perpetrator was seldom held to account in the reports, or through interventions. By way of example:

'history of domestic violence' (BSCB, 2016, p 6)

'Domestic abuse was known to be *a feature in this relationship*' (DSCB, 2014, p 12)

'allegations of *domestic violence in the family*' (HLSCB, 2015, p 95)

FROM DOMESTIC ABUSE TO GANG INVOLVEMENT

Table 10.1: Case features from Serious Case Reviews

		Date of review	Age of death	Cause of death	Childhood DVA	School violence	School exclusion (V=voluntary)	Exploitation	Drugs using/dealing (CL=county lines)	Youth offending	Gang label
Liam	White British	2021	17	Stabbed	Y	Y	Y	Y	Y (CL)	Y	Y
Sam	Undisclosed	2020	N/A	Arrested for murder	Y	Y	Y	Y – sexual	Y (CL)	Y	Y
Child C	'BME'	2020	15	Stabbed	Y	Y	Y	Y	Y (CL)	Y	Y
Archie	Afro-Caribbean	2020	15	Stabbed	Y	N	Y – V	Y	Y (CL)	Y	Y
Chris	Caribbean	2018	14	Shot	Y	Y	Y	Y	Y (CL)	Y	Y
Child AX	Afro-Caribbean	2016	17	Stabbed	Y – in refuge	Y	Y	N	Y (dealing)	Y	Y
Child M	Rwandan	2015	14	Stabbed	Y – in refuge	Unknown	Unknown	Y	Y	Y	Y
Child CH	Jamaican	2015	15	Stabbed	Y	Y	N	N	Y	Y	Y
Child R	Eastern European	2015	15	Drug overdose	Y	Y	Y	Y	Y	Y	Y

(continued)

147

Table 10.1: Case features from Serious Case Reviews (continued)

		Date of review	Age of death	Cause of death	Childhood DVA	School violence	School exclusion (V=voluntary)	Exploitation	Drugs using/ dealing (CL= county lines)	Youth offending	Gang label
Jaiden	White British	2016	15	Road traffic accident	Y	Y	Y	Y – sexual	Y	Y	N
ADS	White British	2014	17	Suicide	Y – in refuge	Y	Y	N	N	Y	N
Child D	Black Caribbean and White British	2018	17	Stabbed	Y	Y	Y – V	N	Y	Y	N
Child N	Unknown	2016	15	Drug overdose	Y	?	Y	Y – sexual	Y	Y	N

'a *domestic incident between* his mother and stepfather' (CHSCP, 2020, p 8)

'*incidents of domestic abuse in the home* involving his mother and her partners' (Unnamed Local Safeguarding Children Board, 2019, p 12)

'Liam witnessed *acts of violence on his mother* from an early age' (SSCP, 2021, p 20)[2]

What is notable in the phrasing here is that there appears to be a reticence to identify the primary perpetrator of abuse as well as the non-abusing parent/carer. Instead, DVA is framed as a household issue. The problem with this framing is that, by refusing to identify the abuser from the abused, the dynamics of power are obscured. There was evidence that in the case of Child M this view was taken by the police, who attended a call out to the house, but considered the first alleged incident a 'malicious report' by the mother. In response the police 'took no action but gave advice to both parties' (CSCB, 2015, p 12). As can be seen in the Table 10.1, three of the 13 cases (23 per cent) had become so severe the family resided in a DVA refuge. This indicates that the victim was considered at very high risk of harm.

In general, it appeared that where the DVA was between heterosexual couples there was a resistance to identify the dominant abuser. It is important to acknowledge, however, that at times disclosures of the details of DVA are difficult to obtain. In Child AD's case the report noted that the DVA was 'minimized' by his mother when communicating with professionals (DSCB, 2014, p 12). Not all of the cases, however, followed this traditional path. In the case of Child AX, his mother was assaulted by her brother-in-law, which instigated a move into a women's refuge for their protection (ESCB, 2016, p 5). In the case of Child CH, the report author noted that due to the DVA involving a same-sex couple (Child CH's mother and female partner) there were concerns that it was not recognized as DVA. The report author noted that there were 'extraordinary levels of violence' that were seen as 'less harrowing to the children than heterosexual partner violence' (ESCB, 2015, p 14). In this case the lack of recognition of the DVA resulted in a lack of appropriate safeguarding action being taken by the local authority. This has similarities to Liam's case, where the child protection case was closed once the perpetrator left.

> The Police had a lot of contact with LM due to four reports of domestic abuse perpetrated against her. On one occasion Liam who was aged 7, witnessed his mother being beaten around the head and face by her then partner. The partner also caused significant damage

to the flat within which they lived. Neighbours called the police on this occasion, as screaming could be heard from their house. As LM had separated from her abusive partner the case was closed. (SSCP, 2021, p 7)

This is a concerning but not unusual trend. In an analysis of identified harms and subsequent contacts sent for assessment, 82 per cent of domestic violence cases were assessed as 'no further action', with only 18 per cent progressing (Lloyd and Firmin, 2020, p 86). With referrals for 'gang-related behaviour' 100 per cent of cases were 'no further action' (Lloyd and Firmin, 2020, p 86). A further notable point about the DVA found in the SCRs is the co-existence of other safeguarding issues, including the 'toxic trio' and child maltreatment and neglect. Child N was placed on a child protection plan before he was born due to a 'history of domestic violence, parental drug misuse and neglect' (BSCB, 2016, p 6). Jaiden's report authors noted that there was a distinct lack of professional understanding about the impact mental health, substance abuse, and DA had on his 'internal world' (Stockport Safeguarding Children Board, 2016, p 88). As can be seen in Table 10.1, school violence and later school exclusion was common among the cohort. Examples varied from anti-social behaviour and disruption, to peer-on-peer violence. Liam, when aged ten, displayed several incidents of 'anti-social behaviour', including ' "waving" a knife at another pupil whilst he was in primary school, threatening to smash windows and threatening to stab people' (SSCP, 2021, p 8). When outlining the pathway from school exclusion to gang involvement one passage very much resonated with the narratives collected as part of my wider study (see Chapter 6), highlighting the relative powerlessness that childhood DVA caused and a desire to redress the power imbalance felt at home:

> Liam had witnessed significant domestic abuse towards his mother at home … Liam had explained to a professional that he had felt vulnerable and powerless to protect his mother, and that he would never allow himself to be in that position again. A professional told the practitioner event that they had asked Liam why he felt he always needed to be 'top dog', and he had explained that it was because of what had happened to LM. (SSCP, 2021, p 21)

The desire to seek an alternative place to reside as a reaction against a difficult home life was suggested as a motivator for Archie. The report authors noted that Archie would refer to his friends as 'FAM' (family), and had sought spaces to be outside of the family home as 'an indication that family dynamics were not working' (SSCB, 2020, p 15). They named the risk factor as 'lack of a stable home environment' (SSCB, 2020, p 14).

What appeared to unite the different cases was the initial involvement in gangs being through either drug use or dealing. However, this is where the parameters of what constitutes gang involvement, membership, or association become more problematic. As noted in Chapter 2, the foregrounding of terms such as 'gangs', 'county lines', and related exploitation has become more prevalent since the 2018 Serious Violence Strategy connected these dots and named the problem. All of the boys were involved in youth offending, yet what changed is the ways in which these acts were labelled. In fact, in several of the reports the labels of 'gangs' and 'county lines' were discussed as possibilities rather than backed up empirically. For example, in the case of Child C it was noted that he faced 'issues relating to gangs' (CHSCP, 2020, p 7). For Child AX, the connection between him and gangs was made due to his drug dealing, which professionals suspected would '*likely* would have brought him in contact potentially with older, more sophisticated criminals, from different, close-knit gangs and *rival ethnic groups*' (ESCB, 2016, p 30, emphasis added). The claim here about ethnic rivalries is another assumption that has no empirical grounding in the report. It is unclear as to the extent to which gangs around Child AX were constituted as 'rival ethnic groups', or how this can be externally verified. At a different point in the report it was noted that, despite the assumptions, his school did not consider him to be a 'member' of a gang, but rather 'on the fringes of gangs who had territory adjoining the areas where the school was located' (ESCB, 2016, p 12). As can be seen in the case of Child AX, although gangs are mentioned three times in the report, it appears he was not thought to be involved himself, but rather was associated with this label due to his involvement with drug dealing and assumptions from outsiders about his circumstances. Similar trends can be seen in other reviews, where professionals identified connections with gangs that were not always supported by evidence. It appeared that young people's gang involvement was based on a professional consensus.

In some cases, it was the child's family that had raised the possibility of gang with the authorities. In Archie's case his mother reported to the Youth Justice Service case manager that 'she was worried he was being drawn into gangs and that she could not keep him safe' (SSCB, 2020, p 24). Child CH's mother alerted the authorities she worried he 'was on a worrying trajectory of violence, offending, disengagement and rootlessness and he was seeking increasingly to identify with gang culture' (ESCB, 2015, p 18). Whereas, for others, the family disputed this label. Child Q's mother felt there was no evidence of her son's *gang membership* and it shouldn't be included in the SCR; however, his father disagreed (CSCB, 2019). The report author of Child M's SCR appeared sceptical of the gang label used by professionals in the gathering of the report and explicitly disputed the professionals' claims in that the child was involved in gangs. The report author noted:

> These ... issues as they are written in the terms of reference, suggest that they are based on facts about Child M's involvement in gangs. However, the view of the Overview Author and the SCRP is that they are unfounded. (CSCB, 2015, p 8)

Similarly, the report authors of the SCR of Child R also note that the level of the alleged gang involvement was unclear. The report notes that 'Different agency records give different accounts about this including gang activity with peers and acting as an accomplice to older criminals, some of whom may have been members of his community' (HLSCB, 2015, p 96). The concerns raised in these reports suggest that there is a distinct level of ambiguity in the labelling of some young people as gang-involved or affiliated. Agencies may bandy these terms around; however, without a clear criterion for the label to be applied it can be both opaque and contentious. When children are identified as being gang-involved it appears that this results in an increase in their surveillance rather than support. Children who display behaviours that are defined as high risk are increasingly managed via monitoring through multi-agency forums. In Croydon, for example, gangs are variously managed 'via a gangs' partnership, missing via a missing panel, and children at risk of sexual exploitation are managed via multi-agency sexual exploitation (MASE) meetings; offenders managed via YOS risk or compliance panels etc.' (CSCB, 2019, p 15).

The use of surveillance as a tool to 'support' young people who are identified as being involved in gangs has been highlighted by Wroe and Lloyd (2020), who noted that the use of surveillance can have a great impact on trusting relationships with young people, particularly with groups already marginalized through race and class and other axis of discrimination. Two of the children in the SCRs were included on the Gangs Matrix: Chris and Child Q. As can be seen from Chris's case, being on the matrix did not result in an increase of Children's Social Care support, but rather an increase of criminal justice services:

> Chris was added to the gangs' matrix as a green nominal ... Chris was discussed at the Gangs Tactical meeting ... Chris was then discussed at a Multi-agency Risk Vulnerability Panel (MRVP meeting) ... A crime report was created following the information Chris's mother provided to a social worker regarding Possession with Intent to Supply (PWITS) which resulted in no further action (NFA). (NLSCB, 2018, p 29)

One strategy that can be put in place when a young person is deemed to be a 'gang nominal' and at risk of harm is a managed move out of the area. This is what happened to Child Q, who was placed in foster care after being identified as a 'red rated gang nominal' (CSCB, 2019, p 17). A managed move out of his home area was also suggested for Child C. This was initiated by the social worker who contacted Child C's biological father to discuss the child moving to him. However, his mother rejected this plan due to her prior experience of DVA perpetrated by Child C's father (CHSCP, 2020, p 17). This is a good example of why prior DVA needs to be taken into account in the wider safety planning strategies, particularly considering the fact that the majority of young people will not have had active Children's Services support. Considering the difficulties both in external gang labelling and also the associated stigma can be a reason to look instead to the broader subcultures of being 'on-road'. In all of the cases discussed, the young people could have been considered as being 'on-road' (see Chapter 1 for definitions).

School violence, school exclusion

School is an important feature in young people's lives. As noted in the narratives in earlier chapters, the participants had differing experiences. Eric and Jordan found school a refuge from the chaos and violence of their lives outside the school gates. Notably, these are the only two participants who then later accessed university-level education and who did not serve substantial prison sentences. However, for most other participants school was a site to define their propensity for violence and gain respect among peers. For those men, several were excluded during their school career, which is a pattern reflected in the SCRs analysed in the previous section 'Learning from similar cases where children have died'. Unpicking the role of schools in the life trajectories of young people who experience childhood DVA and on-road and gang involvement is therefore a delicate task, yet it is clear that continued engagement in school is a protective factor for vulnerable young people who face adversity. The axis of school violence and school exclusion appears to be an important factor in child survivors' pathways to increased involvement in on-road life and later gang involvement.

Children's school experiences can be disrupted by the experience of DVA itself, from missed school days as well as frequent school moves to escape the abuse (Donovan et al, 2005). DA co-existing with poor mental health are two of the predominant experiences that impact on children at risk of school exclusion (Graham et al, 2019). School exclusion itself is a catalyst for poor mental health and exclusion increases the risk of mental illness (Specht, 2013). Students who become alienated from school communities are also more likely to experience depression and become involved in negative associations outside of school, including gang activity. Schools have a core role not only in primary prevention, but in 'raising awareness about domestic violence in school-aged children and challenging attitudes that blame the victim and/or condone violence' (Donovan et al, 2005, p

15). Schools are also 'on the frontline in dealing with the effects of children living with domestic violence' (Donovan et al, 2005, p 15).

In the life stories of several participants, as discussed earlier in the book, school violence was framed as a masculinity response to DVA at home, which was inverted to feeling agentic as it was admired by peers. This first aspect highlights whether the enactment of violence in school can be seen as an indicator of DVA at home and should prompt an investigation. In research with adult survivors, the behavioural problems that were being enacted by child survivors at school could provide an opportunity for initial recognition of the problem. In one example, 'Doris for instance had not talked to anybody about the violence she had been living with for over 10 years until her son's behavioural problems at school became serious' (Donovan et al, 2005, p 17). Spencer and Scott (2013) found that experience of DVA was extremely common among students who are excluded from school. They found 'students often brought their frustration and anger into school' (Spencer and Scott, 2013, p 32). Experience of DVA has been associated with school bullying and enactment of school violence (Baldry, 2003). Some studies have found that boys who have been exposed to DVA present more externalizing problems than girls (Wolfe et al, 1985, 1988, 2003). This is reflected in the school exclusion rate, as in 2016/17 boys were excluded over three times more than girls (0.15 per cent versus 0.04 per cent) and the fixed period exclusion rate was almost three times higher (6.91 per cent compared with 2.53 per cent) (Graham et al, 2019).

The extent to which increasing involvement on-road and in gangs impacts on school engagement is debatable. Research by Irwin-Rogers and Harding (2018) found that schools and gangs can co-exist as distinct social fields and young people can leave their gang identity at the school gates and positively engage with school. Interestingly, they also found that some school staff noted that gang-involved students were less violent in schools than their peers, despite it being more likely that they would carry a weapon to ensure their safety on the journey to school. No data on co-existing DVA was recorded in order for a comparison to be made between gang-involved young people with stable home lives as opposed to those also living with violence at home. The relationship between involvement on-road and school exclusion was also explored by Gunter (2010). He noted a core reason for issues at school among young people on-road was exclusions and bad reports, or conflicts ('beef') with peers that 'spilled over from road life into the classroom' (Gunter, 2010, p 138). However, he was also critical of the alienation that can occur with Black boys who feel misunderstood by their teachers. Gunter also explored co-existing family conflicts, which can result in a breakdown of relationships between the students and their parents. However he didn't offer an in-depth examination of what is meant by the 'conflictual situations' or 'family crisis' to which he refers (Gunter, 2010, pp 138–9). The lack of clarity on such terms makes it difficult to note whether he observed DVA as part of the family landscape.

The report from the Children's Commissioner recommended that schools should track school exclusions as they are 'a trigger for a significant escalation of risk for children' (Dempsey, 2021, p 3). Due to this, the point of exclusion can be a critical point for intervention. Based on the findings of this study I recommend that there is increased recognition of the importance of early identification of DVA occurring at home and suggest that violent behaviour at school is a potential DVA indicator. None of the participants that I spoke to had been offered specialized support by DVA organizations. In light of the data, I suspect this may be related to the difficulty of young men living in gang-affected areas to be recognized as anything other than emerging gang members and perpetrators of violence themselves. The need for agencies to identify DVA earlier in children is not in itself a new finding. However, what this book does shed light on is the way in which young men appeared to enact violence in the school and street context from an early age in reaction to the violence they were experiencing at home. Only by more fully understanding their agency in this complex and turbulent time of life can practitioners offer effective support and interventions that can get to the root of the ways in which the young men construct their masculine identities as shaped by their experiences of DVA.

There is also a need for the provision of safe spaces outside of school time, especially for young men who experience DVA at home and live in gang-affected areas, with a focus on understanding and accommodating vulnerable masculinities. The main theme that came out of the participants' narratives about experiencing DVA was that it meant that home became an uninhabitable space for them when it ceased to be safe as well as predictable. They often then described congregating on the streets with peers as a way to spend as little time at home as possible. For most of the participants, school became a contested space. However, it offered an outlet for Eric to stay out of his house for longer and thus he became involved in lots of extra-curricular activities. Nonetheless, school only offered refuge for him for a limited amount of time in the day. For the rest of the time the participants spent time in public space around their estates as there were no other options in the evenings and weekends. As noted in the literature, the policing of public space in urban areas has become a racialized issue, as Williams' (2015) research showed that the police, as made evident in the Gangs Matrix, monitor ethnic minority groups more heavily than others, which can initiate the cycle of criminalization. Thus, the use of public space is far from a neutral issue and can reinforce the stigmatization and marginalization of certain young men. This finding could be used to bolster the argument for the provision of safe spaces for young men, through, for example, the funding of youth groups, where they can safely go when home is no longer safe. This was highlighted by a report by the National Youth Agency (Aminata et al, 2020), who recommended that youth services provide an outreach service for young people who are avoiding being at home due to DA. The provision of safe spaces that also offer some protection from the grooming of young men by older gang-involved men is also of utmost importance. The participants referred to the pressure of having little money at home, as well as the lack of safety at home, as two key factors in their initial involvement with gangs. Negating these issues through free-to-access safe spaces such as youth groups is an intervention that may divert some young men from engaging with on-road life. This in itself is not a new concept by any means. However, within the period 2008 to 2018, which has been defined by the UK government's austerity programme, there has been a decimation of youth clubs for young people, with council funding for youth services being cut by almost two-thirds (62 per cent) (Mulholland, 2018). The Local Government Association stated that between 2012 and 2016, more than 600 youth centres and nearly 139,000 youth service places from across the UK have disappeared (Mulholland, 2018). The findings in this book suggest that the lack of provision of neutral spaces that are open outside of school hours could be instrumental in providing young men with a space outside of the gang environment. The provision of safe spaces with professionals within this environment who can recognize the signs of young people who experience DVA could also help early identification of children living with abuse. The concept of providing safe spaces for youths facing adversity is not a novel one, yet its importance has been highlighted in this study, as the men did not have another option to spend their time safely once school ended.

Hidden sexual violence

> 'I come from a broken home ... but what people don't know is that my dad was raping my mum as well, they know about domestic violence, but they don't know the ins and outs of it.' (Dylan)

When listening to the stories of survival shared by the participants of this study there was an unexpected theme of sexual violence that came to the foreground. Both Dylan and Sam shared the knowledge that there had been rapes that had resulted in births in their family histories. Dylan himself was conceived through rape, as was Sam's mother. Dave indirectly shared experiences of sexual violence and his informal activism on this issue later in life. Sam talked about his own experience of sexual exploitation by an older woman in a transactional exchange for food and lodgings. Although this is a small sample of stories, the range of experiences of sexual violence, as well as their non-promoted disclosures, suggest that sexual violence and exploitation, both vicariously – through attacks on mothers – as well as directly, are more common among young men than is widely understood. Testimonies of the impact of sexual violence among men and on men, and in particular ex-gang-involved men, are seldom heard. This was apparent from the men in this study who deflected reference to the impact on them of sexual or intimate partner violence as a 'woman's issue'. This did the work of both detracting from their own vulnerabilities but also emphasized that there was no readily available frame of reference through which they could 'see' or articulate their experiences in ways that would accommodate their victimization. In some ways this unsurprising as it is consistent with Connell's (1987, 2005) hierarchy of masculinities, in which sexual violence is associated with power and victimization with passivity and feminization. The theoretical frame of cathexis was useful to understand the ways in which the participants constructed the reconciliation of their traumatic experiences with their emerging identities of change and becoming another kind of man. Music elicitation offered a novel and significant mechanism for bringing these experiences at the border of articulation and coherence more firmly into view.

Powerful aspects of cathexis were evident in the memories the men shared and explored through the music elicitation process central to the data presented in this book. In particular, memories of rape and sexual violence in childhood and adolescence revealed cathexis. In the men's narratives of sexual violence, memories of trauma and confusion are a recurring theme. In Freudian terms, trauma is 'a wound inflicted not upon the body but upon the mind' (Caruth, 1996, p 3). Caruth explores the way in which traumatic experiences exist less as isolated intelligible events but in re-emerging and unassimilated experiences of pain. She notes that what keeps returning to 'haunt' trauma victims is not just the violent events themselves, but rather 'the reality of the way that its violence has not yet been fully known' (Caruth, 1996, p 6). For the men in this study, this was powerfully suggested in the way the interview and music elicitation process facilitated a retrospective 'taking-stock' of submerged emotional hinterlands. In some cases, these accounts were previously untold stories to which I was a bearable witness and facilitator. The nature of these unprompted disclosures indicate the 'endless impact on a life' (Caruth, 1996, p 7) that traumatic events have on the participants' sense of themselves. In all the narratives the men's sense of victimization was framed through accounts of female vulnerability; either through disclosing their mother's victimization, or, in Sam's case, framing it as a 'women's issue', or, in Dave's case, using a music track focusing on a female victim. This indicates that there is unresolved tension between the participants naming their own (vicarious or direct) victimization of sexual violence and the admission this gives of their own vulnerability and pain. The sexual violence trauma was hidden and unacknowledged, the vulnerability projected towards a female 'object' but, I argue, it provided fuel and motivation for a 'protest masculinity' in which a violent and tough persona was essential to life 'on-road' and while gang-involved. Acknowledging cathexis provides a more complete account of the mixture of rational, irrational, and contradictory motivations the men construct as intelligible narratives to carry them forward in life and away from the hurt of the past.

Men's experiences of rape and sexual violence as victims have tended to be overlooked amid the characterization of such crimes as gender based, with women as the main victims (Javaid, 2014). Rape and its association with masculinity have been driven by feminist discourse (Connell, 2005). Rape is seen as motivated by a desire to control and dominate the victim and sits within wider embodied tools of patriarchy for female domination. This can reinforce myths among men that frame rape as incompatible with a dominant masculine status (Ralston, 2020, pp 128–9). Although the typically gendered form of rape as perpetrated by men against women is salient, it has marginalized the various ways in which men are impacted from mainstream framing of sexual victimization (Walklate, 2004). Children who are born from rape are a group whose experiences are often hidden. The commonality of children born through rape has been highlighted since the inclusion of an amendment to the Child Benefit policy, which now will only provide financial support to two children per family, with one of the exceptions to this being when children have been born through rape. Since this policy was implemented in 2015 (enforced from 2017), records show 900 women disclosed their child was conceived through sexual violence (Butler, 2020). These claims come with a burden of proof, either of criminal proceedings or evidence of seeking help for trauma, so this number is likely to be the tip of the iceberg. There has been an increased awareness in the last year 2021 after the successful conviction of a man who had conceived a child with a 13-year-old girl whom he had raped. Although the offence occurred in the 1970s, it was the child who had been conceived through rape (now an adult) who led the campaign against him, proving through her DNA that he had fathered her. The brave campaigner, known as Daisy, spoke about finding out about her conception at the age of 18:

> 'To know that I am, for some, the embodiment of one of the worst things that could happen to someone ... I am more than evidence, I am more than a witness, I am more than a "product" of rape. I am not your shame and I will not carry the shame and horror of what you chose to do.' (Daisy, quoted in Baynes, 2021)

Being the child of rape is a complicated set of circumstances where there is a parallel victimization of the mother and the child. If there has been a dearth of research into male rape, then the consequences of children born of rape appears to be an even more conspicuous gap. One study has suggested that 5 per cent of UK adults suspect they were born through their mother's rape (Taylor and Shrive, 2021). This is a type of sexual violence victimization that still taboo. Gendered responses to the trauma of sexual violence has been explored by McGuffey (2005), who focused on the ways in which families create gender-reaffirming healing processes after sexual violence. The reassertion of traditional gender hierarchies post-sexual violence enables families to restore patriarchal norms, which are heavily influenced by the intersections of race, gender, and class. McGuffey found that marginalized men often respond to sexual violence by asserting their investment in traditional gender norms, through 'athleticism, emotional detachment, the promotion of hetero-sexuality, and the construction of male space' (McGuffey, 2008, p 217; see also Iantaffi, 2021).

Sam shared his experiences of child sexual exploitation (CSE) at the time he initially became involved in life on-road. When disclosing this experience, he framed it as an issue that women face as victims before then talking about his own experience. Research in 2020 found that 23 per cent of gang-associated children and young people have been identified as at risk of sexual exploitation, or had it recorded as a factor upon assessment (Aminata et al, 2020). Childhood DA also increases the risk. A study by McNaughton et al (2014) found that 54 per cent of boys in their sample who had experienced CSE had also lived with DVA at home. These statistics indicate boys who are in the position of having dual experiences of DVA and gang involvement are at a heightened risk of CSE. Living in a home where violence and abuse is present, as well a range of other issues, can 'push young people out of home/care and into environments that increase the risk of being targeted by exploitative peers or adults' (Shuker, 2013, p 127). Going missing from home is a key risk factor for CSE (Brodie, 2013). This fits with Sam's experience as his initial involvement in sexual exploitation was due to his dependence on the woman he was residing with: hungry and homeless as a child, he had few resources by which to refuse the conditions of his stay. This type of sexual exploitation – transactional or trading sex – was noted as more common among boys than girls in a study of sub-Saharan Africa (Adjei and Saewyc, 2017). Obviously that environment is quite different from the one in this study, but the issue is one that requires further exploration in the UK context. A large-scale UK-based study that examined 9,042 Barnardo's service users who had accessed CSE services was carried out by Cockbain et al (2017). They focused on gender differences between victims. They found that male service users were more likely to have a history of youth offending, with 10 per cent suspected of being involved in knife and gun crime. Boys were 1.7 times more likely to be referred to CSE support services via criminal justice agencies. Going missing was a referral trigger for boys double the rate of girls. Interestingly, there was a much higher rate of recorded disability among boy victims of CSE than girls. They concluded by highlighting that boys have been previously overlooked in this area and that gender should be factored into the design and delivery of support services. Lillywhite and Skidmore (2006) noted that among professionals who work with children there was a common perception that sexual exploitation did not affect boys, noting that this was particularly the case when they observed aggression and risk taking, which convey an air of invulnerability. Boys also have the masculinity pressures of portraying independence and strength, which limits their tendency to seek help. Pitts (2013), writing on gang sexual exploitation, noted that its presence is unsurprising given the inherently exploitative nature of gangs. However, the data he draws on presents it as a gendered issue whereby gang-involved boys abuse women as a way to enact masculinity.

Threaded throughout this book is a concern with masculinity as a fluid identity and it is important to consider the ways in which sexual violence is situated within masculine discourse: 'How a man perceives himself as a man and in what ways masculinities are formed within a social and cultural setting are vital to understanding male rape' (Javaid, 2014, p 283). Linking back to Connell's (1987, 2005) theorization of gender relations, experiences of rape and sexual violence are associated with feminization and subordination as an embodied practice of male dominance. This tends to preclude a wider understanding of more diverse and secondary impacts on men traumatized by various forms of proximity to their violent connotations and consequences. Our intention is not to suggest a more inclusive hierarchy of victimization but a wider sense of the reverberations of the violence. Connell (2000, p 13) prompts us to focus on men's 'contradictory desires and conduct' that render masculinities ever-changing, but far from random, aspects of the flux and flows of the gender order. Cathexis is the lens through which to focus on the sexual and emotional tension between men and in intra-gender relations. Frequently neglected, it both connects and underpins Connell's (1987, 2005) other widely acclaimed theoretical models. It anchors the analysis of gender relations in lived experience where desires, affection, and aspirations are rarely fully intelligible or coherent but are undeniably dynamic. The narratives, elicited with the help of co-listening to selected musical compositions and analysed through the lens of cathexis, revealed the ways in which the participants' masculine and racial identities were inflected by their experiences of direct and vicarious sexual violence. Both Dylan's and Sam's knowledge of rape in their maternal lineage was painful and conflicting. It established a troublesome connection with both the victim and perpetrator of the violence, which Dylan navigated by emphasizing his mixed-race heritage. Dave's and Sam's experiences of sexual abuse and exploitation was negotiated through the deflection of victimization as a 'women's issue', which was out of step with their masculine identities.

At the root of the tension between protest masculinity and vulnerable masculinity is the way in which the participants in this study always occupied an invisible space between victim and perpetrator/child-in-need and young offender discourse. They did not fit the 'ideal victim' typology and thus outlets for them to claim this identity have been limited. As noted in the literature discussed in Chapter 2, the concept of the ideal victim is often feminized and infantilized in a way that excludes young, marginalized men, especially those like the participants in this study, who were enacting violence, drug dealing, and becoming increasingly on-road and gang-involved from a young age. That is without mentioning the other intersectional aspects whereby the participants were structurally disadvantaged, such as race, ethnicity, class. All of this created a context where they, when experiencing DVA at home, were not able to find a space to be recognized as victims, or to even recognize themselves as such. This was indicated in the way that referring to their own experiences of victimization (through DVA, sexual abuse, or sexual exploitation) did not come easily to the men whom I spoke to. Sam referred to sexual exploitation as a 'women's issue', which was similar to the way Travis discussed child sexual abuse. These deflections suggest that the men did not have the language or external recognition of their issues to claim their experiences of victimization at the time (or since in some cases). This alludes to a lack of available language to conceptualize issues that are, as of the early 21st century, framed as forms of gender-based violence affecting boys. This can be linked to discourses on these issues in wider society, as highlighted in the government's language around the Violence Against Women and Girls Strategy (Home Office, 2016). This strategy includes work around childhood experiences of DVA, as well as sexual exploitation of children and sexual abuse. Despite numerous references to the phrase 'children' within the report, the overarching discursive framing is centred on female victimization. This is despite the fact that DVA at home as experienced by children isn't necessarily a gendered issue in the same ways as other forms of victimization. None of the men referred to their experience of DVA as centring their own victimization, nor had any been offered support to counter this perspective. Despite several talking about their transition to life on-road as influenced by the DVA that was ongoing at home, many rejected the idea that there was grooming involved. The ways in which they navigated this was to emphasize personal agency in the decisions, despite being children who were essentially fleeing violence. This is because the concept of grooming, by definition, situates the victim as vulnerable and as exploited, which was a position that the men were reluctant to adopt, despite being open to talking about their experiences in retrospect.

11

Masculinity, Vulnerability, and Violence

> 'Violence is the main language on the streets, violence is a way of communicating on the streets, it's the way we send messages, it's a way of getting respect, it's a way of getting paid, it's a way of surviving.' (Jordan)

Where there is protest masculinity – an exaggerated and aggressive form of masculinity performance expressed as a response to marginalization – there is also a vulnerable masculinity. They are two sides of the same coin. This was brought to the fore in the narratives throughout this book. Protest masculinity is constructed as a strategy to disguise insecurity, whereas vulnerable masculinity is the root of the discontent. Therefore, there can be no protest masculinity without vulnerable masculinity: they are in a symbiotic relationship. What became clear in the participants' narratives is that although protest masculinity could be used to conceptualize the main, externalizing parts of the participants' behaviour while gang-involved, it did not account for the co-existing vulnerable masculinities that the men discussed in retrospect. This is significant because, without looking at the emotional aspects of the men's inner worlds, protest masculinity alone can be seen to merely reinforce a marginalized pursuit of hegemonic masculinity: a toxic presentation of violence as an end of itself. However, this does not describe the complexities of how the invulnerable external presentation can be developed to mask complex underlying trauma. Violence was the means through which the men negotiated their position between these poles. Attempting to shift between subordinated childhood masculinity to agentic protest masculinity was a process of navigating the patriarchal world in which they resided. Violence victimization was an expression of vulnerability, which perpetration attempted to invert.

The narratives in this book convey an ongoing relationship throughout between vulnerability and violence, navigated within the pressures of masculinity. This began with participants' experiences of domestic violence and abuse (DVA), which I outline in what follows as itself an expression of the pursuit of power in marginalized circumstances (relying on the symbiotic relationship between protest masculinity and vulnerable masculinity). The participants inhabited subordinated masculinity in relation to the DVA perpetrator. In response, they sought spaces through which to seek power over vulnerability, through the use of their own violence in agentic ways, at school and on-road. Part of the attraction of these public engagements in violence was to portray perceived markers of successful masculinity – respect and pride – that were denied them in a home where DVA was being perpetrated. Experiencing DVA at home engendered a specific discourse on masculinity and violence, which the participants sought to redress by regaining respect outside of the home. As they became further gang-involved their violence increased, as did their vulnerabilities, although these were often expressed by looking tough and engaging in further violence (for protection as in Dave's case, or as self-harming in Sam's case for instance). Several of the participants alluded to a desire to engage in public violence from a young age, as a way of coping with the DVA as well as establishing a sense of dominant masculinity. They highlighted the way in which violence was used in an instrumental way and fights were engaged with as a strategy to regain a sense of personal power and individual masculine identity.

In childhood, the men (as boys) were residing in a patriarchal environment where the perpetrator of DVA was enacting a type of masculinity that drew on distorted markers of hegemonic masculinity. As the boys were living with DVA they had only this as a model for masculinity. For some participants there was a perception of DVA being commonplace within their communities or within their families, which conveyed a sense of normality about these behaviours as well as underlying gender inequality. The men conveyed a sense of experiencing DVA and being unable to stop it, akin to being rendered powerless. The pressure to protect and provide was all-pervasive. At this point a spatial split occurred, whereby the home was defined by fear and time outside the home became a time to cultivate fear from others. For several of the men this initial foray into seeking power was enacted through using violence and domination over peers within the school context, where the disempowerment and subordinated masculinity that they felt at home was inverted, as their desensitization to violence became a strength that made them appear 'tough' and 'hard' to peers. This opened doors to opportunities to capitalize on a propensity to violence through increasing involvement in the street hustle of on-road life. Several of the men started dealing drugs, some through a desire for material gain, or exploitation by neighbourhood elders, or most often a combination of the two. The money that they gained this way supported their move from a subordinated masculinity to an emerging protest masculinity. Power was gained through both the change in power and production relations, which were altered as the participants moved between the private and the public spheres.

Understanding the multiple masculinities that were at work reveals much about the way that the men both experienced this period in their lives at the time, as well as how they make sense of it in retrospect. It also helps us understand the competing pressures of masculinity: to be tough, yet protective; to be heroic and respected. Existing at all points of the men's journeys was also a shadow self of vulnerable masculinity. It would not have been clear at the time however, but in retrospect some participants described the ways they enacted toughness through personal presentation and engaged in violence as a form of protection. They referred to the emotional pain they were going through, as well as the anger that they carried from the experience of DVA. All of these elements should raise our awareness to the co-existence of protest masculinities and vulnerable masculinities. Utilizing Gilson's (2014) work was central to gaining this understanding, as she makes clear the ways that violence and vulnerability are so interconnected, that protest masculinity and vulnerable masculinity are two sides of the same coin. Vulnerable masculinities became more foregrounded in the process of desistance and recovery from the on-road/gang-involved lifestyle. In this part of the narratives, the participants referred to the strategies that they employed to recover from carrying the anger, trauma, and structural inequalities which hampered their pathway to desistance.

Using intersectionality as a lens, entwined with Connell's (1987, 2005) analytic framework, enabled a deeper exploration of the ways in which race, ethnicity, and class changed and shaped the men's experiences. Living in a White supremacist heteronormative capitalist patriarchy results in a specific web of structural constraints that young men have to navigate. It is important to understand the intersections of race and ethnicity, as they have great impact on the lives of men on-road and gang-involved. This is due to the highly racialized portrayal of gangs in the media and a targeted (and racially discriminate) police response (Williams, 2015). Thus, although the men in the study came from diverse racial and ethnic backgrounds, they were aware and influenced by the structural inequalities and interlocking oppressions that surround the association of Black men and criminality. The men prioritized their racial identities in different ways, as shown in the research findings. Using an intersectional lens showed how different aspects of identity affected the participants' performance of masculinities. Protest masculinity as enacted on-road and within the gang was heavily influenced by wider structural inequality as well as race and ethnicity. This was the case even for the White men who were gang-involved, as Shaun outlined in his experience of being accused of appropriating Black popular culture in his vernacular and dress. In this way, the expected gang-based protest masculinity was centred on a hegemonic Black masculinity, even for the White and mixed-race men involved. This was partly externally defined, as in Shaun's case, but was also described as a deliberate adoption of certain forms of dress and self-presentation. This is reinforced in UK society by the ways that popular culture has drawn on gang culture for capitalist consumption, reinforcing stereotypes of Black gangs in rap music and sportswear apparel, which draw heavily on the American context.

In the men's stories of childhood there was an enduring contrast of spatial power between the private and the public spheres. Violence in some form was a constant presence, but the dynamics of it shifted in subtle yet significant ways. Boyhood and manhood are social and contextual experiences. To view gender as performative, as something we 'do', is to see it as more than a sexed category from birth, but rather a social practice that is developed through the social worlds in which boys and men find themselves. Boyhood is shaped by a web of meanings from within homes, communities, and societies. In this way, every experience involving interactions is gendered, especially in the context of domestic violence (which is both a cause and consequence of gender inequality) and all-male social groups or 'gangs'. It is the juxtaposition of these two social spaces that is so intriguing from a gender perspective. Both the DVA household and the gang are patriarchal structures enforced by violence and regimes of fear. Listening to the men's life stories about their boyhood was about peeling back the layers of externalizing bravado. It enabled a more nuanced look at the ways in which violence was experienced in both contexts in both passive and agentic ways. To understand how boys and men are limited by performative gender roles enacted through masculinity pressures, re-centralizing patriarchy as the core power structure through which our society is organized is key.

Gendered understandings of child survivors

As a result of developing a gendered understanding of how children process DVA, I recommend future work involve the development of gender-specific and masculinity-aware interventions for male child survivors. This needs to be done in a way that does not convey an essentialist reproduction of those social learning theories that equate male children with future perpetration (as discussed in Chapter 2) yet do recognize that being a male watching a male role model enact protest masculinity ideals might affect the way in which boys instrumentalize violence themselves. There is existing research that promotes gender-specific work with adult men who have experienced trauma. One particular study by Mejía (2005) focused on the importance of developing gender-specific interventions for men in the counselling context. She noted that society is blind to the male experience of trauma as this conflicts with wider ideals of achieved masculinity.

The idealized qualities of hegemonic masculinity are 'toughness, fearlessness, and the denial of vulnerability', which create the context whereby not only are men not recognized as victims of suffering, but they themselves will not readily identify their vulnerabilities in therapeutic support contexts (Mejía, 2005, p 31). Thus, Mejia concluded that the trappings of masculinity affect how men cope with traumatic events in their lives. Mejia's recommendations are that treatment and support of male survivors of trauma should focus specifically on: redefining masculinity; and confronting the trauma and its gendered legacies (Mejía, 2005). Using the findings from this study, it is clear that a focus of the ways in which masculinities affect self-identity among men who experience DVA is important. As outlined in the literature, children who have experienced DVA have been historically overlooked and seen as add-ons to the non-abusing parent. Boys who experienced DVA have occupied a space of tension within feminist organizing around DVA. In the early days of the second-wave feminist movement, boys were seen as peripheral to the women-focused nature of the movement and its related interventions. This was reflected in the provision of women-only spaces as well as the enduring age limit on refuge provision for sons of DVA survivors. What these findings show concurs with the recommendations by Mejía (2005), who emphasized the ways in which dominant discourses around masculinity both limit men's ability to see themselves as vulnerable, but also limit services in recognizing their vulnerabilities. Mejía (2005, p 35) called this the 'burden of masculinity messages', which they carry into the therapeutic context with them. She noted that support services need to be attentive to the ways in which restrictive notions of masculinity inhibit men and may then impede therapeutic support. Such an approach has been trialled in South Africa, with the development of interventions which have focused on constructions of masculinity, navigating local traditions that have been associated with transitions from boyhood to manhood, such as circumcision rites (Mshweshwe, 2020). By challenging concepts of hegemonic masculinity among young men, the work has aimed to make connections between the 'complex relationship between domestic violence, culture and constructions of masculinity' (Mshweshwe, 2020). It has identified that the wider cultural norms of masculinity serve as 'enablers of domestic violence' (Mshweshwe, 2020). This is important not only because it connects wider societal gender norms and DVA prevalence, but it also deliberately focuses on masculinity messages in targeted interventions.

The task for front-line provision is to navigate the complexity of the apparent contradiction between protest/vulnerable masculinity and provide space for both. There are existing interventions, mostly for gang-involved men, who seek to work with residual anger. Boxing as a form of gang intervention has been explored in research by Deuchar et al (2015), who looked at how traditionally masculine-oriented sports have been used by organizations as a way to channel aggression in a safe and off-street environment. Deuchar et al (2015, p 733) noted that this is often one of the ways in which organizations attract gang-involved men to the programmes in the first place, as they use a 'strategic use of masculinity'; however, this leaves the question of how these interventions then use the opportunity to challenge hegemonic masculinities once they have the men engaged. In Deuchar et al's (2015, p 739) study, the authors recommended that organizations provide discussions that are offered in a safe context and that 'enable some aspects of local versions of reformed hegemonic masculinity to be promoted and upheld and will encourage young men to keep engaging and keep talking'. In light of my findings, I would add that there needs to be space for alternative vulnerable masculinities, in recognition that these are likely to exist as a shadow self in support settings.

Concluding remarks

In this book I have proposed that there is an ongoing relationship throughout the participants' narratives between vulnerability and violence, which was experienced by boys through the prism of masculinity. Childhood DVA is a relatively common experience for children around the world, due to its social ubiquity in all communities. Despite this, there is a real lack of understanding about how children's experiences of DVA, a form of gender-based violence, is *experienced in a gendered way* by children. This book has focused on a niche group of young men who lived with violence both at home, and on-road, in their adolescence. The men that I spoke to were the survivors. As the Serious Case Reviews indicate, many children do not get through their young lives blighted by violence. It is a national scandal. As I have reiterated throughout, adopting an understanding of patriarchy and gender inequality can aid a deeper understanding of why and how boys become embroiled in a pressure cooker of violence, pride, and prowess. The flip side of the tough 'hard' exteriors though is the symbiotic vulnerability. The inner fears which drive them both outside their homes, on-road, into the arms of gangs for a sense of protection which doesn't always materialize. These boys lived in fear, and violence was both the cause and the consequence.

The urgency for action is more pertinent than ever. This book has been written during the global COVID-19 pandemic. This has resulted in what the UN Women (2020) is calling a 'shadow pandemic' of increased rates of domestic violence and abuse (DVA). This means that many children who are living with DVA have been increasingly isolated and 'locked-down' in their home environments. National lockdowns were constructed on the premise that private homes were places of safety and sanctuary in the face of a deadly virus. The contradiction of this for victims of abuse was highlighted in the UK government's DVA campaign, 'At Home Shouldn't

Mean At Risk' (Home Office, 2020b). However, this campaign and associated awareness-raising had no mention of children who were living at home. National lockdowns have seen the widespread closure of schools and education settings, so young people have been in an unprecedented situation of having more time without structured supervision or their usual activities. Opportunities for welfare checks on children that happen informally by schools or health visitors were lost as group-based online teaching became normal. The connection between difficult home lives and risk of criminal exploitation during lockdowns have been made by front-line professionals in the media (Caluori, 2020; G. Roberts, 2021; Graham, 2021). They centre upon children who don't want to be at home due to conflict, and then faced being bored and lonely, and being approached and exploited. One youth service in Northumberland noted that both online and offline methods were being used to exploit young people who have faced a vacuum of support: 'over lockdown a chasm opened up between young people and the services that support them' (Graham, 2021). Support provision for children has never been more urgent.

This research, however, also highlights the plight of adults who were child survivors. The pain doesn't disappear at the age of 18. As was noted in Hague's (2012) ground-breaking book on this topic, this is a group who are *still forgotten, still hurting*. There is virtually no provision of support for adult child survivors outside of private therapy, which is limited to those with the resources to access it. As child survivors become adults and often parents themselves, we need to be alert to the ways in which past trauma can impact on their lives long after the objective 'risks' have diminished. We need to move beyond a crisis model of DVA support for both adults and children who have experienced the life-changing impact of abuse. In order to support child survivors of DVA we need to *see* them first. Not just as part of a Domestic Abuse Stalking and 'Honour'-Based Violence (DASH) risk assessment of the non-abusing parent, nor just as historical factor in an adverse childhood experience risk assessment. We need to prioritize offering recognition, help, and support at the earliest point of crisis in a child's life. This study has focused on the experience of boys; however, of course there is scope to explore the unique challenges that girls in this position also face. We need to move beyond reductive labelling of children, as well as the broad-brush approaches to the different categories of DVA as distinct from 'serious violence'. Children exist across these borders, and we need to find innovative responses which humanize them.

Their futures depend on it, as do ours, if we aim to live in a world free from violence.

Notes

Chapter 4
[1] Reproduced with the permission of Coleen McMahon.

Chapter 6
[1] Mandem describes an association to a group of friends/gang/family.
[2] Segregation unit.
[3] Football-based video game on Xbox.

Chapter 9
[1] https://cvg.org.

Chapter 10
[1] I have referenced the commissioning safeguarding partnership rather than the individual report author as I feel it is a fairer reflection of the collaborative nature of the reports that I am critiquing.
[2] Emphasis added by author.

References

2Pac (1998) 'Changes' [Song], USA: Amaru, Death Row, Interscope, Jive.

2Pac ft Danny Boy (1996) 'I Ain't Mad at Cha' [Song], USA: Death Row, Interscope.

Abrahams, C. (1994) *Hidden Victims: Children and Domestic Violence*, London: NCH Action for Children.

Adjei, J.K. and Saewyc, E.M. (2017) 'Boys are not exempt: sexual exploitation of adolescents in sub-Saharan Africa', *Child Abuse and Neglect*, 65: 14–23, Available from: https://doi.org/10.1016/j.chiabu.2017.01.001 [Accessed 20 January 2022].

Akon (2004) 'Ghetto' [Song], USA: SRC/Universal.

Alexander, C.E. (2000) *The Asian Gang: Ethnicity, Identity, Masculinity*, Oxford: Berg.

Allen, T.N. and Randolph, A. (2020) 'Listening for the interior in hip-hop and R&B music', *Sociology of Race and Ethnicity*, 6(1): 46–60, Available from: https://doi.org/10.1177/2332649219866470 [Accessed 20 January 2022].

Allett, N. (2010) 'Sounding out: using music elicitation in qualitative research', working paper, University of Manchester, Available from: http://eprints.ncrm.ac.uk/2871/1/0410_music_elicitation.pdf [Accessed 4 February 2022].

Aminata, D., Peart, D. and Turner, K. (2020) 'Hidden in plain sight: a youth work response to COVID-19', *NCTM*, 114: 486–7, Available from: https://doi.org/10.5951/mtlt.2020.0309 [Accessed 19 January 2022].

Amnesty International (2018) 'Trapped in the Matrix: secrecy, stigma, and bias in the Met's Gangs database', 23 November, Available from: www.amnesty.org.uk/gangs [Accessed 19 January 2022].

Andell, P. (2019) *Thinking Seriously about Gangs: Towards a Critical Realist Approach*, London: Palgrave Macmillan, Available from: https://doi.org/10.1007/978-3-030-12891-3 [Accessed 20 January 2022].

Anderson, E. (1999) *Code of the Street*, London: W.W. Norton.

APCC (Association of Police and Crime Commissioners) (2020) *PCCs Making a Difference: Violence Reduction Units (VRUs) in Focus* [Report], Available from: https://www.apccs.police.uk/campaigns/pccs-making-a-difference/ [Accessed 20 January 2022].

REFERENCES

Asthana, A. (2021) 'Home Secretary Priti Patel to change policing bill after pressure from domestic abuse campaigners', *ITV News*, Available from: https://news-assets.itv.com/news/2021-12-01/domestic-and-sexual-abuse-to-be-included-in-wording-of-policing-bill [Accessed 4 February 2022].

Auer, P. (2005) 'A postscript: code-switching and social identity', *Journal of Pragmatics*, special issue, 37(3): 403–10, Available from: https://doi.org/10.1016/j.pragma.2004.10.010 [Accessed 20 January 2022].

Back, L. (2015) 'How blue can you get? B.B. King, planetary humanism and the Blues behind bars', *Theory, Culture & Society*, 32(8): 274–85, Available from: https://doi.org/10.1177/0263276415605579 [Accessed 20 January 2022].

Baker, H. (2009) 'Potentially violent men? Teenage boys, access to refuges and the constructions of men, masculinity and violence', *Journal of Social Welfare and Family Law*, 59(3): 435–50.

Baldry, A.C. (2003) 'Bullying in schools and exposure to domestic violence', *Child Abuse and Neglect*, 27(7): 713–32, Available from: https://doi.org/10.1016/S0145-2134(03)00114-5 [Accessed 20 January 2022].

Barnish, M. (2004) *Domestic Violence: A Literature Review*, London: HM Inspectorate of Probation.

Baynes, M. (2021) 'Carvel Bennett: rapist jailed after victim's daughter wins justice decades later', *Sky News*, 3 August, Available from: https://news.sky.com/story/carvel-bennett-rapist-jailed-after-victims-daughter-wins-justice-decades-later-12371859 [Accessed 26 October 2021].

BBC News (2018) 'Rapper DMX played his own song to a judge in court', *Newsbeat*, 29 March, Available from: https://www.bbc.co.uk/news/newsbeat-43580650 [Accessed 30 September 2021].

Bellis, M.A., Lowey, H., Leckenby, N., Hughes, K. and Harrison, D. (2014) 'Adverse childhood experiences: retrospective study to determine their impact on adult health behaviours and health outcomes in a UK population', *Journal of Public Health*, 36(1): 81–91, Available from: https://doi.org/10.1093/pubmed/fdt038 [Accessed 20 January 2022].

Bengtsson, T.T. (2012) 'Learning to become a "gangster"?', *Journal of Youth Studies*, 15(6): 677–92, Available from: https://doi.org/10.1080/13676261.2012.671930 [Accessed 20 January 2022].

Bentley, H., Fellowes, A., Glenister, S., Mussen, N., Ruschen, H., Slater, B., Turnbull, M., Vine, T., Wilson, P. and Witcombe-Hayes, S. (2016) *How Safe Are Our Children? The Most Comprehensive Overview of Child Protection in the UK* [Report], NSPCC, Available from: https://www.nspcc.org.uk/globalassets/documents/research-reports/how-safe-children-2016-report.pdf [Accessed 19 January 2022].

Bernard, C. (2016). 'Black children's experience of living with domestic violence', in C. Bernard and P. Harris (eds) *Safeguarding Black Children: Good Practice in Child Protection*, London: Jessica Kingsley Publishers, pp 58–75.

Bob Marley and the Wailers (1977a) 'Natural Mystic' [Song], Jamaica: Island, Tuff Gong.

Bob Marley and the Wailers (1977b) 'One Love/People Get Ready' [Song], Jamaica: Tuff Gong.

Bob Marley and the Wailers (1980) 'Three Little Birds' [Song], Jamaica: Tuff Gong.

Bogat, G.A., DeJonghe, E., Levendosky, A.A., Davidson, W.S. and von Eye, A. (2006) 'Trauma symptoms among infants exposed to intimate partner violence', *Child Abuse and Neglect*, 30(2): 109–25, Available from: https://doi.org/10.1016/j.chiabu.2005.09.002 [Accessed 20 January 2022].

Boullier, M. and Blair, M. (2018) 'Adverse childhood experiences', *Paediatrics and Child Health*, 28(3): 132–7, Available from: https://doi.org/10.1016/j.paed.2017.12.008 [Accessed 20 January 2022].

Braithwaite, J. (1989) *Crime, Shame and Reintegration*, New York and Cambridge, UK: Cambridge University Press.

Braithwaite, J. (1993) 'Shame and modernity', *British Journal of Criminology*, 33(1): 1–18, Available from: https://doi.org/10.1093/oxfordjournals.bjc.a048257 [Accessed 20 January 2022].

Brodie, I. (2013) 'Young people, trafficking and sexual exploitation: a view from Scotland', in M. Melrose and J. Pearce (eds) *Critical Perspectives on Child Sexual Exploitation and Related Trafficking*, London: Palgrave Macmillan, pp 83–95.

BSCB (Barnsley Safeguarding Children Board) (2016) *Serious Case Review: Child N* [Report], LSCB.

Butler, J. (1988) 'Performative acts and gender constitution: an essay in phenomenology and feminist theory', *Theatre Journal*, 40(4): 519–31.

Butler, J. (2004) *Undoing Gender*, New York: Routledge.

Butler, N., Quigg, Z. and Bellis, M.A. (2020) 'Cycles of violence in England and Wales: the contribution of childhood abuse to risk of violence revictimisation in adulthood', *BMC Medicine*, 18(1): 1–13, Available from: https://doi.org/10.1186/s12916-020-01788-3 [Accessed 20 January 2022].

Butler, P. (2020) 'Data shows 900 women in UK affected by benefit cap "rape clause"', *The Guardian*, 17 July, Available from: https://www.theguardian.com/society/2020/jul/17/data-shows-900-women-in-uk-affected-by-tax-credit-clause [Accessed 26 October 2021].

Callaghan, J.E.M., Alexander, J.H., Sixsmith, J. and Fellin, L.C. (2015) 'Beyond "witnessing"', *Journal of Interpersonal Violence*, 33(10): 1551–81, Available from: https://doi.org/10.1177/0886260515618946 [Accessed 20 January 2022].

Callaghan, J.E.M., Fellin, L.C., Alexander, J.H., Mavrou, S. and Papathanasiou, M. (2017) 'Children and domestic violence: emotional competencies in embodied and relational contexts', *Psychology of Violence*, 7(3): 333–42, Available from: https://doi.org/10.1037/vio0000108 [Accessed 20 January 2022].

Caluori, J. (2020) 'County lines after COVID: a new threat?', *Crest Advisory*, 19 May, Available from: https://www.crestadvisory.com/post/county-lines-after-covid-a-new-threat [Accessed 4 November 2021].

Caruth, C. (1996) *Unclaimed Experience: Trauma, Narrative, and History*, Baltimore, MD and London: Johns Hopkins University Press.

Case, S. (2021) 'Challenging the reductionism of "evidence-based" youth justice', *Sustainability (Switzerland)*, 13(4): 1–18, Available from: https://doi.org/10.3390/su13041735 [Accessed 20 January 2022].

Centre for Social Justice (2009) *Dying to Belong: An In-depth Review of Street Gangs in Britain* [Report], Available from: https://www.centreforsocialjustice.org.uk/library/dying-to-belong-an-in-depth-review-of-street-gangs-in-britain [Accessed 3 March 2022].

Chan, Y.C. and Yeung, J.W.K. (2009) 'Children living with violence within the family and its sequel: a meta-analysis from 1995–2006', *Aggression and Violent Behavior*, 14(5): 313–22, Available from: https://doi.org/10.1016/j.avb.2009.04.001 [Accessed 20 January 2022].

Chandan, J.S., Taylor, J., Bradbury-Jones, C., Nirantharakumar, K., Kane, E. and Bandyopadhyay, S. (2020) 'COVID-19: a public health approach to manage domestic violence is needed', *The Lancet: Public Health*, 5(6): e309, Available from: https://doi.org/10.1016/S2468-2667(20)30112-2 [Accessed 20 January 2022].

Chard, A. (2021) *Punishing Abuse: Children in the West Midlands* [Report], West Midlands Combined Authority, Available from: https://www.wmca.org.uk/media/4678/punishing-abuse.pdf [Accessed 3 March 2022].

Chen, S. and Schweitzer, R.D. (2019) 'The experience of belonging in youth from refugee backgrounds: a narrative perspective', *Journal of Child and Family Studies*, 28(7): 1977–90, Available from: https://doi.org/10.1007/s10826-019-01425-5 [Accessed 20 January 2022].

Children's Commissioner (2019) *Keeping Kids Safe: Improving Safeguarding Approaches to Gang Violence* [Report], February, Available from: https://www.childrenscommissioner.gov.uk/report/keeping-kids-safe/ [Accessed 19 January 2022].

Christie, N. (1986) 'The ideal victim', in E.A. Fattah (ed.) *Crime Policy to Victim Policy*, London: Palgrave Macmillan, pp 17–30.

CHSCP (City and Hackney Safeguarding Children Partnership) (2020) *Serious Case Review: Child C* [Report], Available from: https://www.chscp.org.uk/wp-content/uploads/2020/12/CHSCP-SCR-Child-C-Report-PUBLISHED-FINAL.pdf [Accessed 3 March 2022].

Chu, C.M., Daffern, M., Thomas, S. and Lim, J.Y. (2012) 'Violence risk and gang affiliation in youth offenders: a recidivism study', *Psychology, Crime & Law*, 18, 299–315.

Cockbain, E., Ashby, M. and Brayley, H. (2017) 'Immaterial boys? A large-scale exploration of gender-based differences in child sexual exploitation service users', *Sexual Abuse: Journal of Research and Treatment*, 29(7): 658–84, Available from: https://doi.org/10.1177/1079063215616817 [Accessed 20 January 2022].

Coleen McMahon (2012) 'Beautiful Boy' [Song]. USA: Derek Nakamoto.

Collier, R. (1998) *Masculinities, Crime and Criminology*, London: SAGE.

Connell, R.W. (1987) *Gender and Power*, Stanford, CA: Stanford University Press.

Connell, R.W. (2000) *The Men and the Boys*, Sydney: Allen & Unwin.

Connell, R.W. (2002) 'The history of masculinity', in R. Adams and D. Savran (eds) *The Masculinity Studies Reader*, Oxford: Blackwell, pp 243–61.

Connell, R.W. (2005) *Masculinities* (2nd edn), Cambridge, UK: Polity Press.

Connell, R.W. and Messerschmidt, J.W. (2005) 'Hegemonic masculinity: rethinking the concept', *Gender & Society*, 19(6): 829–59, Available from: https://doi.org/10.1177/0891243205278639 [Accessed 20 January 2022].

Cormega (2007) 'The Saga (The Remix)' [Song]. USA: Stanley O.

Cottrell-Boyce, J. (2013) '*Ending Gang and Youth Violence*: a critique', *Youth Justice*, 13(3): 193–206, Available from: https://doi.org/10.1177/1473225413505382 [Accessed 20 January 2022].

Crenshaw, K.W. (1991) 'Mapping the margins: intersectionality, identity politics, and violence against women of colour', *Stanford Law Review*, 43(6): 1241–1299.

Crest Advisory (2021) *Violence and Vulnerability* [Report], February, London, Available from: https://b9cf6cd4-6aad-4419-a368-724e7d1352b9.usrfiles.com/ugd/b9cf6c_77c24c4c77d345b4b919ebf8df70a0c4.pdf [Accessed 19 January 2022].

CSCB (Croydon Safeguarding Children Board) (2015) *Overview Report in Respect of Child M: A 14-Year-Old Teenager*, LSCB.

CSCB (Croydon Safeguarding Children Board) (2019) *Serious Case Review Summary: Child Q: 'Where Were You When I Was Six?'* [Report], LSCB.

Cummings, E.M. (1998) 'Children exposed to marital conflict and violence: conceptual and theoretical directions', in G.W. Holden, R.A. Geffner and E.N. Jouriles (eds) *Children Exposed to Marital Violence: Theory, Research, and Applied Issues*, Washington, DC: American Psychological Association, pp 55–94.

REFERENCES

Cure Violence (2013) *Ceasefire Workers Receive Domestic Violence Training* [Report], Available from: http://cureviolence.org/post/ceasefire-workers-receive-domestic-violence-training/ [Accessed 1 September 2017].

Dave (2019) 'Lesley' [Song], UK: Neighbourhood.

Davis, J. and Marsh, N. (2020) 'Boys to men: the cost of "adultification" in safeguarding responses to Black boys', *Critical and Radical Social Work*, 8(2): 255–9, Available from: https://doi.org/10.1332/204986020X15945756023543 [Accessed 20 January 2022].

Dempsey, M. (2021) *Still Not Safe: The Public Health Approach to Youth Violence* [Report], February, London: Children's Commissioner, Available from: https://www.childrenscommissioner.gov.uk/wp-content/uploads/2021/02/cco-still-not-safe.pdf [Accessed 19 January 2022].

DeNora, T. (1999) 'Music as a technology of the self', *Poetics*, 27: 31–56, Available from: https://doi.org/10.1017/S1752196318000196 [Accessed 19 January 2022].

Densley, J.A. (2012) 'The organisation of London's street gangs', *Global Crime*, 13(1): 42–64, Available from: https://doi.org/10.1080/17440572.2011.632497 [Accessed 19 January 2022].

Densley, J.A., Deuchar, R. and Harding, S. (2020) 'An introduction to gangs and serious youth violence in the United Kingdom', *Youth Justice*, 20: 1–8, Available from: https://doi.org/10.1177/1473225420902848 [Accessed 19 January 2022].

Department for Education and Home Office (2010) *Safeguarding Children and Young People Affected by Gang Activity* [Report], London, Available from: https://assets.publishing.service.gov.uk/government/uploads/system/uploads/attachment_data/file/189392/DCSF-00064-2010.pdf.pdf [Accessed 3 March 2022].

Depzman (2013) 'Reality' [Song], UK: Independent.

Deuchar, R. (2018) *Gangs and Spirituality: A Global Perspective*, London: Palgrave Macmillan.

Deuchar, R., Harding, S., McLean, R. and Densley, J.A. (2018) 'Deficit or credit? A comparative, qualitative study of gender agency and female gang membership in Los Angeles and Glasgow', *Crime and Delinquency*, 66: 1–28, Available from: https://doi.org/10.1177/0011128718794192 [Accessed 19 January 2022].

Deuchar, R., Søgaard, T.F., Kolind, T., Birgitte, T. and Wells, L. (2015) 'When you're boxing you don't think so much': pugilism, transitional masculinities and criminal desistance among young ... pugilism, transitional masculinities and criminal desistance among young Danish gang members', *Journal of Youth Studies*, 19(6): 725–42. https://doi.org/10.1080/13676261.2015.1098770.

Devaney, J. (2015) 'Research review: the impact of domestic violence on children', *Irish Probation Journal*, 12: 79–94, Available from: http://www.probation.ie/website/probationservice/websitepublishingdec09.nsf/Content/Irish+Probation+Journal+2 015+Years [Accessed 28 March 2022].

Devlin (2013) 'Mother's Son' [Song], UK: Island, Universal.

DMX (1998) 'Slippin" [Song], USA: Ruff Riders, Def Jam.

DMX (2002) 'I Miss You' [Song], USA: Ruff Riders, Def Jam.

Dobash, R.E. and Dobash, R. (1979) *Violence against Wives: A Case against the Patriarchy*, New York: The Free Press.

Domestic Abuse Commissioner (2021a) 'Government amends Policing Bill to define domestic abuse and sexual violence as forms of serious violence', Available from: https://domesticabusecommissioner.uk/blogs/government-amends-policing-bill-to-define-domestic-abuse-and-sexual-violence-as-forms-of-serious-violence/ [Accessed 4 February 2022].

Domestic Abuse Commissioner (2021b) 'Violence against women and girls must be considered as serious, violent crime' [Blog], Available from: https://domesticabusecommissioner.uk/blogs/violence-against-women-and-girls-must-be-considered-as-serious-violent-crime/ [Accessed 23 June 2021].

Donovan, C., Gangoli, G., Hester, M. and Westmarland, M.N. (2005) *Service Provision and Needs: Children Living with Domestic Violence in South Tyneside*, South Tyneside Domestic Violence Forum, Bristol.

dos Santos, A. and Wagner, C. (2018) 'Musical elicitation methods: insights from a study with becoming-adolescents referred to group music therapy for aggression', *International Journal of Qualitative Methods*, 17(1): 1–9. https://doi.org/10.1177/1609406918797427.

DSCB (Derbyshire Safeguarding Children Board) (2014) *Derbyshire Safeguarding Children Board Serious Case Review Overview Report in Respect of ADS*, Available from: https://library.nspcc.org.uk/HeritageScripts/Hapi.dll/filetransfer/2014DerbyshireADSOverview.pdf?filename=AA58F75CEDE68892A73FB681FE246B8371684F102172D08A780A14959D3BCE5747137B3B2A935011CB8EC3068664FF481AA6D2524E357BABB6C006752CCD7567598D77BD1E189823A55CFAAE74B2EE64F46C611AD1724BE1AC50776135E7AAAFFECACF7BED2170E128B12C8E57F619CD5D14CD47D3BF2FE25DEB924DAF671B368AB8A64FE0B26102311267ADDF4831CE9484ED291E0B&DataSetName=LIVEDATA [Accessed 4 March 2021].

Dutton, D.G. (1999) 'Traumatic origins of intimate rage', *Aggression and Violent Behaviour*, 4(4): 431–48.

Ehrensaft, M.K., Cohen, P., Brown, J., Smailes, E., Chen, H. and Johnson, J.G. (2003) 'Intergenerational transmission of partner violence: a 20-year prospective study', *Journal of Consulting and Clinical Psychology*, 71(4): 741–53.

ESCB (Enfield Safeguarding Children Board) (2015) *Serious Case Review Overview Report: Child 'CH'*, LSCB.

ESCB (Enfield Safeguarding Children Board) (2016) *Serious Case Review: Child AX* [Report], LSCB.

Farrell, J. (2021) 'COVID-19: growing numbers of pupils at risk of exclusion and "falling off the radar" as schools return to normal', *Sky News*, 14 September, Available from: https://news.sky.com/story/covid-19-growing-numbers-of-pupils-at-risk-of-exclusion-and-falling-off-the-radar-as-schools-return-to-normal-12402634 [Accessed 3 November 2021].

Fatsis, L. (2019) 'Policing the beats: the criminalisation of UK drill and grime music by the London Metropolitan Police', *Sociological Review*, 58: 1–17, Available from: https://doi.org/10.1177/0038026119842480 [Accessed 19 January 2022].

Feldman, A. (1991) *Formations of Violence: The Narrative of the Body and Political Terror in Northern Ireland*, Chicago: University of Chicago Press.

Ferrell, J. (2018) *Drift: Illicit Mobility and Uncertain Knowledge*, Berkeley: University of California Press.

Firmin, C. (2020) *Contextual Safeguarding and Child Protection: Rewriting the Rules*, London: Routledge.

Fleetwood, J., Presser, L., Sandberg, S., and Ugelvik, T. (2019) *The Emerald Handbook of Narrative Criminology*, Bingley: Emerald Publishing.

Frankenberg, R. (1993) *White Women, Race Matters: The Social Construction of Whiteness*, Minneapolis: University of Minnesota Press.

Fraser, A. and Irwin-Rogers, K. (2021) *A Public Health Approach to Violence Reduction*, Dartington: Research in Practice.

Frosh, S., Phoenix, A., and Pattman, R. (2002) *Young Masculinities*, Basingstoke: Palgrave.

Future of Essex (2018) 'Violence and vulnerability', 10 December, Available from: https://www.essexfuture.org.uk/ecda/action/violence-and-vulnerability/ [Accessed 6 November 2021].

Gadd, D., Fox, C.L., Corr, M., Alger, S., and Butler, I. (2015) *Young Men and Domestic Abuse*, Abingdon: Routledge.

Gebo, E. (2016) 'An integrated public health and criminal justice approach to gangs: what can research tell us?', *Preventive Medicine Reports*, 4: 376–80, Available from: https://doi.org/10.1016/j.pmedr.2016.07.007 [Accessed 19 January 2022].

Gelles, R.J. (1997) *Intimate Violence in Families*, London: SAGE.

Gibbs, J.T. and Merighi, J.R. (1994) 'Young Black males', in T. Newburn and E.A. Stanko (eds) *Just Boys Doing Business?* London: Routledge, pp 64–80.

Gilligan, J. (1996) *Violence: Reflections on a National Epidemic*, New York: Penguin Random House.

Gilroy, P. (1993) *Small Acts: Thoughts on the Politics of Black Cultures*, London and New York: Serpent's Tail.

Gilroy, P. (2004) *After Empire: Melancholia or Convivial Culture?* Abingdon: Routledge.
Gilroy, P. (2011) *Darker than Blue: On the Moral Economies of Black Atlantic Culture*, Cambridge, MA: Harvard University Press.
Gilson, E.C. (2014) *The Ethics of Vulnerability: A Feminist Analysis of Social Life and Practice*, London: Routledge.
Glynn, M. (2014) *Black Men, Invisibility and Crime*, Abingdon: Routledge.
Gordon, A.F. (2008) *Ghostly Matters: Haunting and the Sociological Imagination*, Minneapolis: University of Minnesota Press.
Gordon, J.E. (1949) 'The epidemiology of accidents', *American Journal of Public Health*, 39: 504–15.
Gough, B. (2018) *Contemporary Masculinities: Embodiment, Emotion and Wellbeing*, Cham: Palgrave Macmillan.
Graham, B., White, C., Edwards, A., Potter, S., Street, C. (2019) School exclusion: a literature review on the continued disproportionate exclusion of certain children [Report]. Department for Education. Available from: https://assets.publishing.service.gov.uk/government/uploads/system/uploads/attachment_data/file/800028/Timpson_review_of_school_exclusion_literature_review.pdf [Accessed 3 March 2022].
Graham, H. (2021) 'Sexual predators and drug gangs used lockdown to target isolated teens, says Ashington charity head', *Chronicle Live*, 18 September, Available from: https://www.chroniclelive.co.uk/news/north-east-news/sexual-predators-drug-gangs-used-21575083 [Accessed 4 November 2021].
Green, J.D., Kearns, J.C., Ledoux, A.M., Addis, M.E. and Marx, B.P. (2018) 'The association between masculinity and nonsuicidal self-injury', *American Journal of Men's Health*, 12(1): 30–40, Available from: https://doi.org/10.1177/1557988315624508 [Accessed 19 January 2022].
Grundetjern, H., Copes, H. and Sveining, S. (2019) 'Dealing with fatherhood: paternal identities among men in the illegal drug economy', *European Journal of Criminology*, [online] 18(5), Available from: https://doi.org/10.1177/1477370819874429 [Accessed 19 January 2022].
Gunter, A. (2010) *Growing Up Bad: Black Youth, Road Culture and Badness in an East London Neighbourhood*, London: The Tufnell Press.
Gunter, A. (2017) *Race, Gangs and Youth Violence*, Bristol: Policy Press.
Haaken, J. and Yragui, N. (2003) 'Going underground: conflicting perspectives on domestic violence shelter practices', *Feminism and Psychology*, 13(1): 49–71.
Hague, G. (2012) *Understanding Adult Survivors of Domestic Violence in Childhood*, London: Jessica Kingsley Publishers.
Hague, G., Harvey, A. and Willis, K. (2012) *Understanding Adult Survivors of Domestic Violence in Childhood: Strategies for Recovery for Children and Adults*, London: Jessica Kingsley Publishers.

Hall, S., Roberts, B., Clarke, J., Jefferson, T. and Critcher, C. (2013) *Policing the Crisis: Mugging, the State, and Law and Order* (2nd edn), London: Macmillan.

Hallsworth, S. and Young, T. (2011) 'Young people, gangs and street-based violence', in C. Barter and D. Berridge (eds) *Children Behaving Badly?: Peer Violence between Children and Young People*, Chichester: Wiley-Blackwell.

Harding, S. (2014) *The Street Casino: Survival in Violent Street Gangs*, Bristol: Policy Press.

Harding, S. (2020) *County Lines: Exploitation and Drug Dealing among Urban Street Gangs*, Bristol: Bristol University Press.

Havard, T.E., Densley, J.A., Whittaker, A. and Wills, J. (2021) 'Street gangs and coercive control: the gendered exploitation of young women and girls in county lines', *Criminology and Criminal Justice*, [online], 1–17, Available from: https://doi.org/10.1177/17488958211051513 [Accessed 19 January 2022].

Hayward, K. and Yar, M. (2006) 'The "chav" phenomenon: consumption, media and the construction of a new underclass', *Crime, Media, Culture*, 2(1): 9–28, Available from: https://doi.org/10.1177/1741659006061708 [Accessed 19 January 2022].

Hester, M. (2011) 'The three planet model: towards an understanding of contradictions in approaches to women and children's safety in contexts of domestic violence', *British Journal of Social Work*, 41: 837–53, Available from: https://doi.org/10.1093/bjsw/bcr095 [Accessed 19 January 2022].

Hester, M. (2013) 'Who does what to whom? Gender and domestic violence perpetrators in English police records', *European Journal of Criminology*, 10(5): 623–37, Available from: https://doi.org/10.1177/1477370813479078 [Accessed 19 January 2022].

Hester, M. and Pearson, C. (1998) *From Periphery to Centre: Domestic Violence in Work with Abused Children*, Bristol: Polity Press.

Hester, M. and Westmarland, N. (2005) *Tackling Domestic Violence: Effective Interventions and Approaches*, London: Home Office.

Hester, M., Pearson, C., and Harwin, N., with Abrahams, H. (2007) *Making an Impact: Children and Domestic Violence* (2nd edn), London: Jessica Kingsley Publishers.

HLSCB (Harrow Local Safeguarding Children Board) (2015) *Serious Case Review: Overview Report and Executive Summary: Services Provided for Child R: October 2011– November 2013*, LSCB.

HM Government (2011) *Ending Gang and Youth Violence, Youth Justice*, Available from: https://assets.publishing.service.gov.uk/government/uploads/system/uploads/attachment_data/file/97862/gang-violence-detailreport.pdf [Accessed 2 March 2022].

Home Office (1999) *Report of the Stephen Lawrence Inquiry*, 24 February, Available from: https://www.gov.uk/government/publications/the-stephen-lawrence-inquiry [Accessed 19 January 2022].

Home Office (2016) 'Strategy to end violence against women and girls: 2016 to 2020', Available from: https://www.gov.uk/government/publications/strategy-to-end-violence-against-women-and-girls-2016-to-2020 [Accessed 19 January 2022].

Home Office (2018) 'Serious Violence Strategy' [Policy paper], 9 April, Available from: https://www.gov.uk/government/publications/serious-violence-strategy [Accessed 19 January 2022].

Home Office (2020a) 'Domestic Abuse Bill 2020: overarching factsheet' [Policy paper], 22 November, London, Available from: https://www.gov.uk/government/publications/domestic-abuse-bill-2020-factsheets/domestic-abuse-bill-2020-overarching-factsheet [Accessed 19 January 2022].

Home Office (2020b) 'Home Secretary announces support for domestic abuse victims', Gov.uk, 11 April, Available from: https://www.gov.uk/government/news/home-secretary-announces-support-for-domestic-abuse-victims [Accessed 4 November 2021].

Hong, R. (2016) 'Soft skills and hard numbers: gender discourse in human resources', *Big Data & Society*, 3(2): 1–13, Available from: https://doi.org/10.1177/2053951716674237 [Accessed 19 January 2022].

hooks, b. (1994) *Teaching to Transgress*, New York: Routledge.

hooks, b. (1997) *Cultural Criticism and Transformation*, Media Education Foundation Transcript [Online], Available from: https://www.mediaed.org/transcripts/Bell-Hooks-Transcript.pdf [Accessed 2 March 2022].

hooks, b. (2003) *We Real Cool: Black Men and Masculinity*, Abingdon: Routledge.

Hotaling, G. and Sugarman, D.B. (1986) 'An analysis of risk markers in husband-to-wife violence: the current state of knowledge', *Violence and Victims*, 1(2): 101–24.

Hughes, H. (1992) 'Impact of spouse abuse on children of battered women', *Violence Update*, August, 9–11.

Hutchings, K. (2008) 'Making sense of masculinity and war', *Men and Masculinities*, 10(4): 389–404. https://doi.org/10.1177/1097184X07306740.

Iantaffi, A. (2021) *Gender Trauma: Healing Cultural, Social and Historical Gendered Trauma*, London and Philadelphia: Jessica Kingsley Publishers.

Irwin-Rogers, K. (2018) 'Racism and racial discrimination in the criminal justice system: exploring the experiences and views of men serving sentences of imprisonment', *Justice, Power and Resistance*, 2(2): 243–66.

Irwin-Rogers, K. (2019) 'Illicit drug markets, consumer capitalism and the rise of social media: a toxic trap for young people', *Critical Criminology*, 27: 591–610, Available from: https://doi.org/10.1007/s10612-019-09476-2 [Accessed 19 January 2022].

REFERENCES

Irwin-Rogers, K. and Harding, S. (2018) 'Challenging the orthodoxy on pupil gang involvement: when two social fields collide', *British Educational Research Journal*, 44(3): 463–79, Available from: https://doi.org/10.1002/berj.3442 [Accessed 19 January 2022].

Iwamoto, D. (2003) 'Tupac Shakur: understanding the identity formation of hyper-masculinity of a popular hip-hop artist', *The Black Scholar*, 33(2): 44–9.

Jaffe, P.G., Wolfe, D.A. and Wilson, S. (1990) *Children of Battered Women*, London: SAGE Publications.

Jaffee, S.R., Moffitt, T.E., Caspi, A., Taylor, A. and Arseneault, L. (2002) 'Influence of adult domestic violence on children's internalizing and externalizing problems: an environmentally informed twin study', *Journal of the American Academy of Child and Adolescent Psychiatry*, 41(9): 1095–103.

Javaid, A. (2014) 'Feminism, masculinity and male rape: bringing male rape "out of the closet"', *Journal of Gender Studies*, 25(3): 283–93, Available from: https://doi.org/10.1080/09589236.2014.959479 [Accessed 19 January 2022].

Jefferson, T. (1998) 'Muscle, "hard men" and "Iron" Mike Tyson: reflections on desire, anxiety and the embodiment of masculinity', *Body and Society*, 4(1): 77–98.

Jewkes, R. (2002) 'Intimate partner violence: causes and prevention', *Lancet*, 359(9315): 1423–29.

Jones, S.K. (2016) *A Cry for Health: Why We Must Invest in Domestic Abuse Services in Hospitals* [Report], 16 November, Bristol, Available from: http://www.safelives.org.uk/node/945. [Accessed 19 January 2022]

Joseph, I., Gunter, A., Hallsworth, S., Young, T. and Adekunle, F. (2011) Gangs Revisited: What's a Gang and What's Race Got to Do with It?', [Report] Runnymede Perspectives, Available from: https://www.researchgate.net/profile/Ian-Joseph/publication/281620233_What%27s_a_gang_and_what%27s_race_got_to_do_with_it/links/55f0171c08aedecb68fde879/Whats-a-gang-and-whats-race-got-to-do-with-it.pdf [Accessed 2 March 2022].

Joseph, P.E. (2021) 'DMX was a Gen X icon who gave Black men like me a stronger voice', *CNN*, 10 April, Available from: https://edition.cnn.com/2021/04/09/opinions/how-dmx-changed-1990s-hip-hop-rap-and-me-joseph/index.html [Accessed 30 September 2021].

Joyner Lucas (2016) 'I'm Sorry' [Song]. USA: The Cratez.

Katz, E. (2016) 'Beyond the physical incident model: how children living with domestic violence are harmed by and resist regimes of coercive control', *Child Abuse Review*, 25: 46–59.

Keightley, E. and Pickering, M. (2006) 'For the record: popular music and photography as technologies of memory', *European Journal of Cultural Studies*, 9(2): 149–65, Available from: https://doi.org/10.1177/1367549406063161 [Accessed 19 January 2022].

Kerig, P.K., Wainryb, C., Twali, M.S. and Chaplo, S.D. (2013) 'America's child soldiers: toward a research agenda for studying gang-involved youth in the united states', *Journal of Aggression, Maltreatment and Trauma*, 22(7): 773–95. https://doi.org/10.1080/10926771.2013.813883.

Kimmel, M.S. (2002) '"Gender symmetry" in domestic violence: a substantive and methodological research review', *Violence Against Women*, 8(11): 1332–63.

Kimmel, M.S. and Wade, L. (2018) 'Ask a feminist: Michael Kimmel and Lisa Wade discuss toxic masculinity', *Signs: Journal of Women in Culture and Society*, 44(1): 233–54, Available from: https://doi.org/10.1086/698284 [Accessed 19 January 2022].

Kitzmann, K.M., Gaylord, N.K., Holt, A.R. and Kenny, E.D. (2003) 'Child witnesses to domestic violence: a meta-analytic review', *Journal of Consulting and Clinical Psychology*, 71(2): 339–52, Available from: https://doi.org/10.1037/0022-006X.71.2.339 [Accessed 19 January 2022].

Krane, D. and Davies, L. (2002) 'Sisterhood is not enough: the invisibility of mothering in shelter practice with battered women', *Affilia*, 17: 167–90.

Krohn, M.D. and Thornberry, T.P. (2008) 'Longitudinal perspectives on adolescent street gangs', in A. Liberman (ed) *The Long View of Crime: A Synthesis of Longitudinal Re-Search*, New York: Springer, pp 128–60.

Krug, E.G., Dahlberg, L.L., Mercy, J.A., Zwi, A.B. and Lozano, R. (2002) 'World report on violence and health', *The Lancet*, 360: 1083–8.

Lacey, R.E. and Minnis, H. (2020) 'Practitioner review: twenty years of research with adverse childhood experience scores – advantages, disadvantages and applications to practice', *Journal of Child Psychology and Psychiatry and Allied Disciplines*, 61(2): 116–30, Available from: https://doi.org/10.1111/jcpp.13135 [Accessed 19 January 2022].

Lapierre, S. (2008) 'Mothering in the context of domestic violence: the pervasiveness of a deficit model of mothering', *Child & Family Social Work*, 13(4): 454–63. https://doi.org/10.1111/j.1365-2206.2008.00563.x.

Laughey, D. (2006) *Music and Youth Culture*, Edinburgh: Edinburgh University Press.

Leroy Smart (1976) 'Ballistic Affair' [Song], UK: Well Charge.

Levine, M.D. (1975) 'Interpersonal violence and its effects on the children: a study of 50 families in general practice', *Medicine, Science and Law*, 15, 172–6.

Liberty (2021) *Liberty's Briefing on the Police, Crime, Sentencing and Courts Bill for Second Reading in the House of Lords.* [Report] Libertyhumanrights.org.uk, September, Available from: https://www.libertyhumanrights.org.uk/wp-content/uploads/2020/04/Libertys-briefing-on-the-Police-Crime-Sentencing-and-Courts-Bill-Report-Stage-HoC-July-2021.pdf [Accessed 4 February 2022].

Lillywhite, R. and Skidmore, P. (2006) 'Boys are not sexually exploited? A challenge to practitioners', *Child Abuse Review*, 15: 296–310.

Lloyd, J. and Firmin, C. (2020) 'No further action: contextualising social care decisions for children victimised in extra-familial settings', *Youth Justice*, 20(1–2): 79–92, Available from: https://doi.org/10.1177/1473225419893789 [Accessed 19 January 2022].

Local Government Association (2018) *Public health approaches to reducing violence* [Report], Available from: https://www.local.gov.uk/sites/default/files/documents/15.32%20-%20Reducing%20family%20violence_04_WEB.pdf [Accessed 2 March 2022].

Logic ft Alessia Cara and Khalid (2017) '1-800-273-8255' [Song], USA: Visionary, Def Jam.

Lozon, J. and Bensimon, M. (2017) 'A systematic review on the functions of rap among gangs', *International Journal of Offender Therapy and Comparative Criminology*, 61(11): 1243–61, Available from: https://doi.org/10.1177/0306624X15618430 [Accessed 19 January 2022].

LSCB (London Safeguarding Children Board) (2009) *Safeguarding Children Affected by Gang Activity and/or Serious Youth Violence* [Report], London.

Ludacris ft Mary Jane Blige (2007) 'Runaway Love' [Song], USA: DTP, Def Jam.

Maguire, D. (2019) 'Vulnerable prisoner masculinities in an English prison', *Men and Masculinities*, 24: 1–18, Available from: https://doi.org/10.1177/1097184X19888966 [Accessed 19 January 2022].

Maguire, D. (2021) *Male, Failed, Jailed: Masculinities and 'Revolving Door' Imprisonment in the UK*, Cham: Palgrave.

Martinez, T.A. (1995) 'Gang innovation, patriarchy and powerlessness: expanding theory to relfect [reflect] American politics', *Explorations in Ethnic Studies*, 18(2): 145–58, Available from: https://doi.org/10.1525/ees.1995.18.2.145 [Accessed 19 January 2022].

Maruna, S. (2004) *Making Good: How Ex-Convicts Reform and Rebuild their Lives*, Washington, DC: American Psychological Association.

Maruna, S. and Matravers, A. (2007) 'N = 1: criminology and the person', *Theoretical Criminology*, 11(4): 427–42, Available from: https://doi.org/10.1177/1362480607081833 [Accessed 19 January 2022].

Maslow, A. (1943) 'A theory of human motivation', *Psychological Review*, 50(4): 370–96.

McAuley, R. (2007) *Out of Sight: Crime, Youth and Exclusion in Modern Britain*, Cullompton: Willan Publishing.

McGavock, L. and Spratt, T. (2017) 'Children exposed to domestic violence: using adverse childhood experience scores to inform service response', *British Journal of Social Work*, 47(4): 1128–46, Available from: https://doi.org/10.1093/bjsw/bcw073 [Accessed 19 January 2022].

McGee, C. (2000) *Childhood Experiences of Domestic Violence*, London: Jessica Kingsley Publishers.

McGuffey, C.S. (2005) 'Race, class, and gender reaffirmation after child sexual abuse', *Gender & Society*, 19(5): 621–43, Available from: https://doi.org/10.1177/0891243205277310 [Accessed 19 January 2022].

McGuffey, C.S. (2008) '"Saving masculinity:" gender reaffirmation, sexuality, race, and parental responses to male child sexual abuse', *Social Problems*, 55(2): 216–37, Available from: https://doi.org/10.1525/sp.2008.55.2.216 [Accessed 19 January 2022].

McLaughlin, K.A. and Sheridan, M.A. (2016) 'Beyond cumulative risk: a dimensional approach to childhood adversity', *Current Directions in Psychological Science*, 25(4): 239–45, Available from: https://doi.org/10.1177/0963721416655883 [Accessed 19 January 2022].

McNaughton Nicholls, C., Cockbain, E., Brayley, H., Harvey, S., Fox, C., Paskell, C., Ashby, M., Gibson, K. and Jago, N. (2014) *Research on the Sexual Exploitation of Boys and Young Men* [Report], Nuffield Foundation, August, Available from: https://www.nuffieldfoundation.org/sites/default/files/files/cse_young_boys_summary_report.pdf [Accessed 19 January 2022].

Mejía, X.E. (2005) 'Gender matters: working with adult male survivors of trauma', *Journal of Counseling and Development*, 83(1): 29–40, Available from: https://doi.org/10.1002/j.1556-6678.2005.tb00577.x [Accessed 19 January 2022].

Messerschmidt, J.W. (2005) 'Men, masculinities, and crime', in M.S. Kimmel, J. Hearn and R.W. Connell (eds) *Handbook of Studies on Men and Masculinities*, Thousand Oaks, CA: SAGE, pp 196–212.

Messerschmidt, J.W. (2018) *Hegemonic Masculinity: Formulation, Reformulation, and Amplification*, London and New York: Rowman & Littlefield.

Miles, C. and Condry, R. (2015) 'Responding to adolescent to parent violence: challenges for policy and practice', *The British Journal of Criminology*, 55(6): 1076–1095 https://doi.org/10.1093/bjc/azv095 [Accessed 28 March 2022].

Motzkau, J. (2020) 'Children as victims', in D.T. Cook (ed.) *The SAGE Encyclopedia of Children and Childhood Studies*, Thousand Oaks, CA: SAGE Publications, pp 412–15.

Mshweshwe, L. (2020) Boys' transition to manhood: a missed opportunity for masculinity transformation: implications for domestic violence', *Youth & Policy*, 2 July, Available from: https://www.youthandpolicy.org/articles/boys-transition-to-manhood/ [Accessed 8 November 2021].

MSPTU (Modern Slavery Police Transformation Unit) (2018) *Modern Slavery Police Transformation Programme Annual Report to 31st March 2018*, March.

Mulholland, H. (2018) 'Youth work cuts leave young people out in the cold', *The Guardian*, October, Available from: https://www.theguardian.com/society/2018/oct/31/youth-work-cuts-young-people-councils [Accessed 19 January 2022].

Mullender, A. (1996) *Rethinking Domestic Violence*, Abingdon: Routledge.

Mullender, A. Hague, G., Imam, U.F., Kelly, L., Malos, E. and Regan, L. (2002) *Children's Perspectives on Domestic Violence*, London: SAGE.

Mullins, C.W. (2006) *Holding Your Square: Masculinities, Streetlife and Violence*, Cullompton: Willan Publishing.

Neal, M.A. (2013) *Looking for Leroy*, New York and London: New York University Press.

Newburn, T., Jones, T. and Blaustein, J. (2018) 'Framing the 2011 England riots: understanding the political and policy response', *Howard Journal of Crime and Justice*, 57(3): 339–62, Available from: https://doi.org/10.1111/hojo.12268 [Accessed 19 January 2022].

Neville, F.G., Goodall, C.A., Gavine, A.J., Williams, D.J. and Donnelly, P.D. (2015) 'Public health, youth violence, and perpetrator well-being', *Peace and Conflict: Journal of Peace Psychology*, 21(3): 322–33. https://doi.org/http://dx.doi.org/10.1037/pac0000081.

NLSCB (Newham Local Safeguarding Children Board) (2018) *Serious Case review – Chris: Overview Report*, LSCB.

Oakley, A. (1972) *Sex, Gender and Society*, San Francisco: Harper & Row.

O'Brien, K., Daffern, M., Meng Chu, C. and Thomas, S.D.M. (2013) 'Youth gang affiliation, violence, and criminal activities: a review of motivational, risk, and protective factors', *Aggression and Violent Behavior*, 18: 417–25, Available from: https://doi.org/10.1016/j.avb.2013.05.001 [Accessed 19 January 2022].

Oliver, R., Alexander, B., Roe, S. and Wlasny, M. (2019) *The Economic and Social Costs of Domestic Abuse*, Research Report 107, London, January, Available from: https://assets.publishing.service.gov.uk/government/uploads/system/uploads/attachment_data/file/918897/horr107.pdf [Accessed 19 January 2022].

OMI (2013) 'My Old Lady' [Song]. Jamaica: Errol Jackson.

ONS (Office for National Statistics) (2016) 'Homicide: findings from analyses based on the Homicide Index recorded by the Home Office covering different aspects of homicide', Available from: https://www.ons.gov.uk/peoplepopulationandcommunity/crimeandjustice/compendium/focusonviolentcrimeandsexualoffences/yearendingmarch2015/chapter2homicide#relationship-between-victim-and-principal-suspect [Accessed 19 January 2022].

ONS (Office for National Statistics) (2019) 'Suicides in the UK: 2018 registrations', 3 September, Available from: https://www.ons.gov.uk/peoplepopulationandcommunity/birthsdeathsandmarriages/deaths/bulletins/suicidesintheunitedkingdom/2018registrations [Accessed 20 January 2022].

Överlien, C. and Hydén, M. (2009) 'Children's actions when experiencing domestic violence', *Childhood*, 16(4): 479–96, Available from: https://doi.org/10.1177/0907568209343757 [Accessed 19 January 2022].

Pearce, J.J. and Pitts, J.M. (2011) *Youth Gangs, Sexual Violence and Sexual Exploitation: A Scoping Exercise for the Office of the Children's Commissioner for England* [Report], Bedfordshire, University of Bedfordshire.

Pease, B. (2019) *Facing Patriarchy: From a Violence Gender Order to a Culture of Peace*, London: Zed Books.

Peled, E., Jaffe, P.G. and Edleson, J.L. (1995) *Ending the Cycle of Violence: Community Responses to Children of Battered Women*, Thousand Oaks, CA: SAGE Publications.

Phillips, C. (2020) 'The pains of racism and economic adversity in young Londoners' lives: sketching the contours', *Journal of Ethnic and Migration Studies*, [online] 30 November, 1–18, Available from: https://doi.org/10.1080/1369183X.2020.1850246 [Accessed 19 January 2022].

Phoenix, A. (2004) 'Schooling everyday cultures: 11–14 year old boys and constructions of masculinities', in E.B. Silva and T. Bennett (eds) *Contemporary Culture and Everyday Life*, Durham, NC: Sociology Press, pp 130–48.

P!nk (2002) 'Family Portrait' [Song], USA: LaFace, Arista.

Pinkey, C. and Robinson-Edwards, S. (2018) 'Gangs, music and the mediatisation of crime: expressions, violations and validations', *Safer Communities*, 17(2): 103–18.

Pitts, J. (2013) 'Exploitation and gang affiliation', in M. Melrose and J. Pearce (eds) *Critical Perspectives on Child Sexual Exploitation and Related Trafficking*, London: Palgrave Macmillan, pp 23–4.

Pizzey, E. (1974) *Scream Quietly or the Neighbours Will Hear*, Harmondsworth: Penguin Books.

Popcaan (2013) 'Unruly Prayer' [Song]. USA: Dinearo.

Porr, C., Mayan, M., Graffigna, G., Wall, S. and Vieira, E.R. (2011) 'The evocative power of projective techniques for the elicitation of meaning', *International Journal of Qualitative Methods*, 10(1): 30–41, Available from: https://doi.org/10.1177/160940691101000103 [Accessed 19 January 2022].

Portas, J. and Sharp-Jeffs, N. (2021) *The Economic Abuse Threat Facing Girls Women in the UK: 6 Moments That Matter* [Report], London, Available from: https://survivingeconomicabuse.org/the-economic-abuse-threat-facing-girls-women-in-the-uk-new-report-reveals-the-six-key-life-moments-when-women-are-most-vulnerable-to-abuse/ [Accessed 19 January 2022].

Postmus, J.L., Hoge, G.L., Breckenridge, J., Sharp-Jeffs, N. and Chung, D. (2018) 'Economic abuse as an invisible form of domestic violence: a multicountry review', *Trauma, Violence, and Abuse*, 21(2): 261–83, Available from: https://doi.org/10.1177/1524838018764160 [Accessed 19 January 2022].

Presser, L. (2016) 'Criminology and the narrative turn', *Crime, Media, Culture*, 12(2): 137–51, Available from: https://doi.org/10.1177/1741659015626203 [Accessed 19 January 2022].

Public Health England (2019a) *Collaborative Approaches to Preventing Offending and Re-offending in Children (CAPRICORN)* [Report], London, Available from: http://www.scie-socialcareonline.org.uk/collaborative-approaches-to-preventing-offending-and-re-offending-in-children-capricorn/r/a110f00000THhVYAA1 [Accessed 19 January 2022].

Public Health England (2019b) *A Whole-System Multi-Agency Approach to Serious Violence Prevention: A Resource for Local System Leaders in England* [Report], Available from: https://assets.publishing.service.gov.uk/government/uploads/system/uploads/attachment_data/file/862794/multi-agency_approach_to_serious_violence_prevention.pdf [Accessed 19 January 2022].

R. Kelly (2002) 'The World's Greatest' [Song], USA: Jive.

Radford, L., Aitken, R., Miller, P., Ellis, J., Roberts, J., and Firkic, A. (2011) 'Meeting the needs of children living with domestic violence in London', Refuge/NSPCC research project.

Raisborough, J., Frith, H. and Klein, O. (2013) 'Media and class-making: what lessons are learnt when a celebrity chav dies?', *Sociology*, 47(2): 251–66, Available from: https://doi.org/10.1177/0038038512444813 [Accessed 19 January 2022].

Ralston, K.M. (2020) '"If I was a 'real man'": the role of gender stereotypes in the recovery process for men who experience sexual victimization', *Journal of Men's Studies*, 28(2): 127–48, Available from: https://doi.org/10.1177/1060826519864475 [Accessed 19 January 2022].

Ray, L. (2018) *Violence and Society* (2nd edn), London: SAGE.

Renzetti, C. (1999) 'The challenge to feminism posed by women's use of violence in intimate relationships', in S. Lamb (ed) *New Versions of Victims: Feminist Struggle with the Concept*, New York: New York University Press, pp 42–56.

Richards, L. and Safelives (2009) DASH risk model, Available from: www.dashriskchecklist.co.uk [Accessed 19 January 2022].

Roberts, G. (2021) 'County lines gangs have changed tactics during COVID – and their victims are getting even younger', *Sky News*, 28 March, Available from: https://news.sky.com/story/county-lines-gangs-have-changed-tactics-during-covid-and-their-victims-are-getting-even-younger-12258744 [Accessed 4 November 2021].

Roberts, Y. (2021) 'The perpetrators: inside the minds of men who abuse women', *The Guardian*, 7 November, Available from: https://www.theguardian.com/society/2021/nov/07/the-perpetrators-inside-the-minds-of-men-who-abuse-women [Accessed 7 November 2021].

Sacks, G. (2008) 'DV Conference Report #3: 12 year-old boys in abusive families aren't allowed to go to shelters with their mothers, but instead go into foster care' [Blog], Available from: http://glennsacks.com/blog/?p=1819 [Accessed 1 September 2017].

Sandberg, S. (2009) 'Gangster, victim or both? The interdiscursive construction of sameness and difference in self-presentations', *British Journal of Sociology*, 60(3): 523–42, Available from: https://doi.org/10.1111/j.1468-4446.2009.01254.x [Accessed 19 January 2022].

Sanghani, R. (2015) 'Nicola Sturgeon: "We'll never have gender equality until we stop domestic violence"', *The Telegraph*, 9 October, Available from: http://www.telegraph.co.uk/women/womens-politics/11922942/Nicola-Sturgeon-Domestic-violence-is-stopping-gender-equality.html [Accessed 19 January 2022]

Saunders, D.G. (2002) 'Are physical assaults by wives and girlfriends a major social problem?', *Violence Against Women*, 8(12): 1424–48.

Schinkel, W. (2010) *Aspects of Violence: A Critical Theory*, Basingstoke: Palgrave Macmillan.

Schwöbel-Patel, C. (2018) 'The "ideal" victim of international criminal law', *European Journal of International Law*, 29(3): 703–24, Available from: https://doi.org/10.1093/ejil/chy056 [Accessed 19 January 2022].

Segal, L. (1990) *Slow Motion: Changing Masculinities Changing Men*, London: Virago.

Sharp-Jeffs, N. and Kelly, L. (2016) *Domestic Homicide Review (DHR) Case Analysis* [Report], London, Available from: https://static1.squarespace.com/static/5ee0be2588f1e349401c832c/t/5efb6ce1d305a44006cb5ab9/1593535715616/STADV_DHR_Report_Final.pdf [Accessed 2 March 2022].

Shaw, C.R. (1930) *The Jack-Roller*, Chicago: University of Chicago Press.

Shepard, M. and Pence, E. (1999) *Coordinating Community Responses to Domestic Violence: Lessons from Duluth and Beyond*, Thousand Oaks, CA: SAGE Publications.

Shuker, L. (2013) 'Constructs of safety for children in care affected by sexual exploitation', in M. Melrose and J. Pearce (eds) *Critical Perspectives on Child Sexual Exploitation and Related Trafficking*, London: Palgrave Macmillan, pp 125–38.

Specht, J.A. (2013) 'Mental health in schools: lessons learned from exclusion', *Canadian Journal of School Psychology*, 28(1): 43–55, Available from: https://doi.org/10.1177/0829573512468857 [Accessed 19 January 2022].

Spencer, C., Griffin, B. and Floyd, M. (2019) *Vulnerable Adolescents Thematic Review (Report for Croydon Safeguarding Children Board)*, February, Available from: http://ow.ly/POix30oc5s4 [Accessed 19 January 2022]

Spencer, L. and Scott, J. (2013) 'School meets street: exploring the links between low achievement, school exclusion and youth crime among African-Caribbean boys in London', *ISER Working Paper Series*, pp 2013–25.

SSCB (Sheffield Safeguarding Children's Board) (2020) *Serious Case Review: Archie: Final Report*, LSCB.

SSCP (Southampton Safeguarding Children Partnership) (2021) *Child Safeguarding Practice Review concerning a Child Referred to as Liam* [Report].

Stark, E. (2007) *Coercive Control*, Oxford: Oxford University Press.

Stark, E. and Hester, M. (2019) 'Coercive control: update and review', *Violence Against Women*, 25(1): 81–104, Available from: https://doi.org/10.1177/1077801218816191 [Accessed 19 January 2022].

Stockport Safeguarding Children Board (2016) *Serious Case Review: 'Jaiden': Final Overview Report*, LSCB.

Sullivan, M.L. (2006) 'Are "gang" studies dangerous? Youth violence, local context, and the problem of reification', in J.F. Short Jr and L.A. Hughes (eds) *Studying Youth Gangs*, Oxford: AltaMira Press, pp 15–36.

Swain, J. (2005) 'Masculinities in education', in M.S. Kimmel, J. Hearn and R.W. Connell (eds) *Handbook of Studies on Men and Masculinities*, Thousand Oaks, CA: SAGE, pp 213–29.

Taylor, J. and Shrive, J. (2021) *Public Perceptions and Attitudes towards Women who become Pregnant or Have Children Conceived in Sexual Violence* [Report], VictimFocus, Available from: https://irp.cdn-website.com/f9ec73a4/files/uploaded/Exploring%20the%20experiences%20of%20women%20who%20become%20pregnant%20or%20have%20children%20from%20sexual%20violence%20FINAL%20.pdf [Accessed 19 January 2022].

Tonsing, J.C. (2019) 'Understanding the role of patriarchal ideology in intimate partner violence among South Asian women in Hong Kong', *International Social Work*, 62(1): 161–71, Available from: https://doi.org/10.1177/0020872817712566 [Accessed 20 January 2022].

Tracy Chapman (1988) 'Behind the Wall' [Song], USA: Elektra.

Trickett, J. (2017) 'Jon Trickett: one in six refuges have closed since 2010 – the Tories must do more to protect vulnerable women', *LabourList*, 27 March, Available from: https://labourlist.org/2017/03/jon-trickett-one-in-six-refuges-have-closed-since-2010-the-tories-must-do-more-to-protect-vulnerable-women/ [Accessed 22 September 2021].

Tyler, I. (2013) *Revolting Subjects: Social Abjection and Resistance in Neoliberal Britain*, London: Zed Books.

UK Faculty of Public Health (2016) 'The role of public health in the prevention of violence: a statement from the UK Faculty of Public Health', Available from: https://www.fph.org.uk/media/1381/the-role-of-public-health-in-the-prevention-of-violence.pdf [Accessed 2 March 2022].

UK Parliament (2019) 'How is the government implementing a 'public health approach' to serious violence?', *House of Commons Library*, 22 July, Available from: https://commonslibrary.parliament.uk/how-is-the-government-implementing-a-public-health-approach-to-serious-violence/ [Accessed 14 June 2021].

UN Women (2020) 'The shadow pandemic: violence against women during COVID-19', Available from: https://www.unwomen.org/en/news/in-focus/in-focus-gender-equality-in-covid-19-response/violence-against-women-during-covid-19 [Accessed 24 November 2020].

UNICEF (United Nations Children's Fund) (2006) *Behind Closed Doors: The Impact of Domestic Violence on Children* [Report], Body Shop International.

University of Cambridge (2021) Stormzy Scholarship for Black UK Students, Available from: https://www.undergraduate.study.cam.ac.uk/stormzy-scholarship [Accessed 24 September 2021].

Unnamed Local Safeguarding Children Board (2019) *Serious Case Review No: 2019/C7991 Published by the NSPCC On Behalf of an Unnamed Local Safeguarding Children Board: Overview Report*, Available from: https://library.nspcc.org.uk/HeritageScripts/Hapi.dll/filetransfer/2019AnonymousGraceLisaCareyOverview.pdf?filename=AA58F75CEDE68892A73FB681FE246B8371684F102152F0AA780A14959D3BCE5767137B3B2A935011CBAEC3068664FF681AA6D2524E357BAB96C006752CCD756759AD77BD1E389823A55CFAAE74B2EE64F46C611AD1724BE1AC50776135EAAAAFFECACF7BE0247BFC24B132894BF73BFE7824E77DDFBE38C859EED94484776921CA35A9CE3E82C3F9476CCCBB0DB06E8F09D37DA68AB15F4DE20FBC2720AE0E91&DataSetName=LIVEDATA [Accessed 2 March 2022].

Violence Reduction Unit (2011) *Glasgow's Community Initiative to Reduce Violence* [Report], Available from: http://www.svru.co.uk/wp-content/uploads/2020/02/CIRV_2nd_year_report.pdf [Accessed 20 January 2022].

Volpe, J.S. (1996) 'Effects of domestic violence on children and adolescents: an overview', *American Academy of Experts in Traumatic Stress*, 11, Available from: https://www.aaets.org/traumatic-stress-library/effects-of-domestic-violence-on-children-and-adolescents-an-overview [Accessed 2 March 2022].

Volpp, L. (2005) 'Feminism versus multiculturalism', in N.J. Sokoloff (ed.) *Domestic Violence at the Margins: Readings on Race, Class, Gender, and Culture*, London: Rutgers University Press, pp 39–49.

Walby, S. (2020) 'Varieties of gender regimes', *Social Politics*, 27(3), Available from: https://doi.org/10.1093/sp/jxaa018 [Accessed 20 January 2022].

Walby, S. and Allen, J. (2004) *Domestic Violence, Sexual Assault and Stalking: Findings from the British Crime Survey* [Report], London.

Walklate, S. (2004) *Gender, Crime and Criminal Justice* (2nd edn), Cullompton: Willan Publishing.

Walklate, S. (2011) 'Reframing criminal victimization: finding a place for vulnerability and resilience', *Theoretical Criminology*, 15(2): 179–94, Available from: https://doi.org/10.1177/1362480610383452 [Accessed 20 January 2022].

Walsh, C. (2018) 'Addressing serious male youth violence: missed opportunities within the UK Serious Youth Violence Strategy', *Youth & Policy*, 10 October, Available from: https://www.youthandpolicy.org/articles/addressing-serious-male-youth-violence-missed-opportunities-within-the-uk-serious-youth-violence-strategy/ [Accessed 8 November 2021].

Welsh, B.C., Braga, A.A. and Sullivan, C.J. (2014) 'Serious youth violence and innovative prevention: on the emerging link between public health and criminology', *Justice Quarterly*, 31(3): 500–23, Available from: https://doi.org/10.1080/07418825.2012.690441 [Accessed 20 January 2022].

West, C. and Zimmerman, D.H. (1987) 'Doing gender', *Gender & Society*, 1(2): 125–51.

Westside Gunn ft Tiona D (2014) *Never Coming Homme* [Music video], YouTube, Available from: https://www.youtube.com/watch?v=IwzyylvETJ4 [Accessed 20 January 2022].

White, J. (2020) *Terraformed: Young Black Lives in the Inner City*, London: Repeater.

WHO (World Health Organization) (2002) *World Report on Violence and Health*, Available from: https://apps.who.int/iris/bitstream/handle/10665/42495/9241545615_eng.pdf [Accessed 20 January 2022].

WHO (World Health Organization) (2018) 'Adverse Childhood Experiences International Questionnaire (ACE-IQ)', Available from: https://www.who.int/violence_injury_prevention/violence/activities/adverse_childhood_experiences/introductory_materials.pdf?ua=1%0Ahttp://www.who.int/violence_injury_prevention/violence/activities/adverse_childhood_experiences/en/ [Accessed 20 January 2022].

Williams, D.J., Currie, D., Linden, W., Donnelly, P.D. (2014) 'Addressing gang-related violence in Glasgow: a preliminary pragmatic quasi-experimental evaluation of the Community Initiative to Reduce Violence (CIRV)', *Aggression and Violent Behavior*, 19: 686–91.

Williams, P. (2015) 'Criminalising the other: challenging the race–gang nexus', *Race and Class*, 56(3): 18–35, Available from: https://doi.org/10.1177/0306396814556221 [Accessed 20 January 2022].

Williams, P. and Clarke, B. (2018) 'The Black criminal other as an object of social control', *Social Sciences*, 7: 1–14, Available from: https://doi.org/10.3390/socsci7110234 [Accessed 20 January 2022].

Wilson, D. (2003) '"Keeping quiet" or "going nuts": some emerging strategies used by young Black people in custody at a time of childhood being re-constructed', *Howard Journal of Criminal Justice*, 42(5): 411–25, Available from: https://doi.org/10.1046/j.1468-2311.2003.00297.x [Accessed 20 January 2022].

Wolfe, D.A., Jaffe, P., Wilson, S.K., and Zak, L. (1985) 'Children of battered women: the relation of child behavior to family violence and maternal stress', *Journal of Consulting and Clinical Psychology*, 53(5): 657–65.

Wolfe, D.A., Jaffe, P., Wilson, S.K., Kaye, S., and Zak, L. (1988) 'A multivariate investigation of children's adjustment to family violence', in G.T. Hotaling et al. (eds) *Family Abuse and Its Consequences: New Directions*, Thousand Oaks, CA: SAGE, pp 228–41.

Wolfe, D.A., Crooks, C.V., Lee, V., McIntyre-Smith, A., and Jaffe, P. (2003) 'The effects of children's exposure to domestic violence: a meta-analysis and critique', *Clinical Child and Family Psychology Review*, 6: 171–87.

Women's Aid (2022) 'What is a refuge and how can I stay in one?' *The Survivors Handbook* [online], Available from: https://www.womensaid.org.uk/the-survivors-handbook/what-is-a-refuge-and-how-can-i-stay-in-one/ [Accessed 17 March 2022].

Wroe, L.E. and Lloyd, J. (2020) 'Watching over or working with? Understanding social work innovation in response to extra-familial harm', *Social Sciences*, 9(4): 37, Available from: https://doi.org/10.3390/socsci9040037 [Accessed 20 January 2022].

Yates, J. (2010) 'Structural disadvantage: youth, class, crime and poverty', in W. Taylor, R. Earle and R. Hester (eds) *Youth Justice Handbook*, Cullompton: Willan Publishing, pp 5–22.

Young, T. (2009) 'Girls and gangs: "shemale" gangsters in the UK?', *Youth Justice*, 9(3): 224–38, Available from: https://doi.org/10.1177/1473225409345101 [Accessed 20 January 2022].

Young, T. (2016) *Risky Youth or Gang Members? A Contextual Critique of the (Re)discovery of Gangs in Britain* [Report], London Metropolitan University.

Young, T., Fitzgibbon, W. and Silverstone, D. (2013) *The Role of the Gamily in Facilitating Gang Membership, Criminality and Exit: A Report Prepared for Catch22*, London.

Young Dolph (2017) '100 Shots' [Song], UK: Buddah Bless.

Youth Violence Commission (2018) *Interim Report: July 2018*, Available from: https://publications.parliament.uk/pa/cm/cmallparty/171108/knife-crime.htm [Accessed 20 January 2022].

Index

References to figures appear in *italic* type;
those in **bold** type refer to tables.

'1-800-273-8255' **43**, 131
2Pac 39–40, **42**, 82
2Pac ft Danny Boy 113
'5 Cs' 141
'100 Shots' **42**, 106

A
abuse
  economic 71
  and music 47
  physical 48, 57
  sexual 52–3, 60
acceptance, and gangs 75
adultification 16, 31
adverse childhood experience (ACE) 14, 28, 29, 143
adversity 31, 32
African racial identity 61
age limitation policies 20, 21, 166
agency 73–4, 75, 155, 161
age of exposure 19
aggressive invulnerability 35
Akon **42**, 85
alcohol abuse 50, 56–7, 91
Alexander, Claire 25, 30
Allett, N. 33
alpha male 81
alpha victim 32, 141–2
Amnesty International 23
Andell, P. 41
anger 53–4, 58, 66, 76–8, 82, 100, 117, 129, 164
  expressed through violence 60
  and fighting 8, 75, 79
  residual 128, 166
  in school 154
anti-youth violence initiatives 118
authenticity 120, 121

B
Back, L. 34–5
Baker, H. 21

'Ballistic Affair' **42**, 84
'Beautiful Boy' **43**, 48
Bentley et al 17
bereavement 103–5
Bernard, C. 21
Bertin, Baroness 137
Black, Minority Ethnic, and Refugee (BAMER) families 21
Black and Minority Ethnic (BME) groups 146
Black Atlantic 34
Black boys 3–4, 31, 79, 154
Black diaspora 40
Black families 60–2
Black hegemonic masculinity 93
Black male violence 7
Black masculinity 21, 30, 35, 62, 165
Black men
  considered dangerous 21
  and criminality 164
  in gangs 25
  and hyper-masculinity 40
  on being 'The Man' 92
  systematically stigmatized and rendered invisible 7
  and victimhood 30
Black people, on Gangs Matrix 23–4
Black urban subculture 41
Black urban young people 16
Black women 21–2, 99
Black young people 31
Blair, M. 28
blood donation 119–20
blues music 35
Bob Marley and the Wailers **42**, 70, 115, 126
Boullier, M. 28
boxing 166
breadwinner role 71, 72–3
bullying 53, 57, 66, 78–9, 88, 154

C

Callaghan et al 18, 34
CAPRICORN ('Collaborative approaches to preventing offending and re-offending by children') 141
Caruth, C. 157
Case, S. 30
cathexis 11, 34–5, 97, 99, 101, 102, 158
  and becoming a father 122
  and power and fear 111
  and sexual violence 59, 60, 157, 160
  and the way women are viewed 106
Centre for Social Justice 27
'Changes' **42**, 82
Chard, A. 28
charity work 115, 118–20
chavs, White 92–3
Chicago Cure Violence 140
child abuse 57, 63
child-in-need 19
child protection 18–19, 31, 136
children, seen as offenders 29–30
Children's Commissioner for England 26, 136, 155
child sexual exploitation (CSE) 75–6, 159–60
Christie, Nils 30
Clarke, B. 25
clothes, and a sense of self-esteem 72
Cockbain et al 159
'code of the street' 79, 107, 110, 120, 125, 128, 129
coercive control 5, 108
'Collaborative approaches to preventing offending and re-offending by children' (CAPRICORN) 141
Collier, R. 101
Commission for Young Lives 16
complicit masculinity 127–8
Connell, R.W. 4, 5, 6, 7, 92, 157, 164
  and cathexis 11, 60, 97, 101, 106, 160
  on Black masculinity 21
  on protest masculinity 9, 110
contagion 137, 141
contextual safeguarding 31
coping mechanism 19, 74, 79, 91
  and music 34, 37, 38, 39, 77
Cormega **42**, 76
Council of Europe Convention on preventing and combating violence against women and domestic violence ix
county lines 32
COVID-19 shadow pandemic 167–8
Crenshaw, K.W. 3, 10
Crest Advisory 28
crime, and gangs 25
criminality 24–5, 31, 41, 95, 164
criminology 11–12

cross-generational transmission of violence 19–20
Croydon Children's Services 28
Cure Violence 138, 142–3
cycle of violence 19–20, 23, 27

D

Dave 47
Davies, L. 22
Davis, J. 31
Dawes, Karen 142
Dempsey, M. 155
DeNora, T. 34, 37
Densley, J.A. 25–6
Densley et al 26
deprived areas 24
Depzman **43**, 103
Desert Island Discs 33
desistance 113, 118, 120, 164
Deuchar, R. 90, 125
Deuchar et al 166–7
Devlin **43**, 98
DMX 37, 39, 41, **42**, 51, 65
dog, as metaphor 66, 79
domestic abuse (DA)
  and school exclusion 153
  and sexual exploitation 159
  and SV 136–7
Domestic Abuse Bill 5
Domestic Abuse Commissioner 136–7
Domestic Abuse Stalking and 'Honour'-Based Violence (DASH) 21, 168
domestic sphere 58, 65
Donovan et al 153–4
dos Santos, A. 36
drill music 40
drug dealing 66–7, 71, 73, 74, 96, 163
drunkenness 50, 56–7, 91
Duluth model of DVA 10
DVA (domestic violence and abuse)
  and alcohol 50
  and anger 53–4
  and Black families 60–1
  in childhood 17–23
  and child maltreatment 47–8
  and CSE 159
  difficult to decipher 56
  an expression of a patriarchal society in which violence against women is normalized and tolerated 9
  form of protest masculinity 63
  and gangs 26–9
  hidden 55
  and invisibility 16, 17–23
  lack of control or ability to intervene 49
  and male violence 139
  and music xi, 34
  neglect and physical abuse 48
  and powerlessness 54–5

INDEX

and pressure to protect 58–9
and public health approach 142
and public violence 163
and rape 59–60
and 'Runaway Love' 53
and school 154, 155
and Serious Case Reviews 146–53
shadow pandemic 167
and SV 135, 136
and terrorism 57
and vulnerability 8–9
witnessing 19–20
and women 4–5
Dying to Belong: An In-Depth Review of Street Gangs in Britain 27

E

economic abuse 71
Ending Gang and Youth Violence 27
ethnicity 24, 60–2, 164
ethnic minority groups 119, 155
ethnic penalty 25
exclusion 127
  school 150, 153, 154, 155
existential vulnerability 8–9
experience of DVA 18, 19, 61, 95, 105, 161
  and anger 164
  and *Dying to Belong: An In-Depth Review of Street Gangs in Britain* 27
  and race 60
  and school 153, 154
experts-by-experience 118, 119
exploitation 32, 67, 75–6, 156–7
exposure to DVA 18, 19, 59

F

family 100, 101–2, 103, 122–4
fatherhood 122–4
fear 58, 59, 81, 110–12, 140, 163, 165, 167
Feldman, Allen 78
Ferrell, J. 41
fighting 69, 75, 79, 91, 107, 163
financial control 71–2
financial gain 94–6
Firmin, Carlene 31
forgiveness 120, 125
Frankenberg, R. 93
Fraser, A. 142

G

Gadd et al 22–3, 31, 105
gang prevention 118
gangs 16, 23–8, 97–9, 151–2
  definition 12–13
  and drug dealing 73–5
  and financial gain 72, 94–6
  and homophobic culture 130–1
  identity 128
  involved in as well as exploited by 137
  and love 100–1, 102

and music 41, 44
and protest masculinity 164–5
and public health approach 141
and race 93–4, 164
and school 154
and sexual exploitation 159, 160
and stigmatization 139, 153
ties to 102–3
and violence 81–2
Gangs Matrix 23, 24, 138, 152
gay liberation movement 7
gay masculinities 131
Gebo, E. 141
Gelles, R.J. 110
gender
  performativity 5–6
  and victimization 138
gender-based violence ix, 9, 29
gender dynamics 19, 107
gendered coping strategies 19
gender identity 60
gender inequality ix, 5, 9, 22–3, 29, 167
gender regime of patriarchy 10
gender relations 9, 10–11, 57, 160
gender stereotypes 75
gender trauma 9
'Ghetto' **42**, 85
Gilligan, J. 140
Gilroy, P. 34–5, 61
Gilson, E.C. 8, 91, 103, 164
Gordon, Avery 126
Gordon, J.E. 139
Gough, B. 123, 130
grace 124
grime artists 40
grime music 40, 41, 44
grooming 32, 73–4, 75, 161
Grundetjern et al 123
Gunter, A. 13, 79, 154

H

Hague, G. 168
Hall et al 23
Hallsworth, S. 13
Harding, Simon 7, 10, 154
hardness 78, 88
harm 4, 17, 18, 26, 31, 49, 125
  on-road 88
  protection from in refuges 149
  and women 5
haunting 126
Havard et al 110
Hayward, K. 92
healthy masculinity 130
hegemonic masculinity 6, 7, 9, 30–1, 73, 130, 167
  Black 93
  and breadwinner role 72

195

and Connell 92
and control over financial resources 71
and disassociation from family 101
distinction between 'a man' and 'The Man' 80
idealized qualities of 166
and music role models 38
and protest masculinity 162
and testosterone 131
hegemony 6, 9
heroic masculinity 102, 110
Hester, M. 18
high-risk DVA 18
high risk of homicide/femicide 21
hip-hop 34, 35, 40
  '1-800-273-8255' 131
  'Changes' 82
  'I Ain't Mad At Cha' 113
  'I Miss You' 51
  'Lesley' 47
  'Mother's Son' 98
  'Never Coming Homme' 64
  'Runaway Love' 53
  'The Saga' 76
  'Slippin' 65
'At Home Shouldn't Mean At Risk' 167–8
homicides, gang-related 24
homophobic culture 130–1
homosexuality 131
hooks, bell xi, 4, 7, 10, 35
Hutchings, K. 90
Hydén, M. 18
hyper-masculinity 40
hypervisibility, and gangs 16, 23–6

I
'I Ain't Mad At Cha' **42**, 113
Iantaffi, A. 9
ideal offenders 105
ideal victim 30, 161
identity
  gender 60
  minority racial and ethnic 60
  professional and gang 128
  racial 61
  and refugees 72, 78
IDVAs (independent domestic violence advocates) 20–1
'I Miss You' 37, **42**, 51
'I'm Sorry' **43**, 124
inequality 126–7, 140, 164
  gender ix, 5, 9, 22–3, 29, 167
intergenerational transmission of violence 19–20, 61
interior selves 35
intersectionality 10, 16, 102, 161, 164
invisibility, and DVA 16, 17–23
invulnerability 7, 35
Irwin-Rogers, K. 74, 142, 154

Istanbul Convention ix
Iwamoto, D. 40

J
The Jack-Roller 11–12
Javaid, A. 160
Jefferson, T. 78, 88
Joseph, P.E. 38

K
Keightley, E. 36
Kelly, L. 18–19
Kelly, R. **42**, 68
Kerig et al 90–1
Kimmel, M.S. 130
King, B.B. 35
Kitzmann et al 19
knife crime 53, 76, 103, 135, 141, 142
Krane, D. 22
Krug et al 139

L
Lacey, R.E. 29
language, siloed 16
'Lesley' **43**, 47
Liberty 136
Lillywhite, R. 160
Lloyd, J. 31, 152
Local Government Association 139, 156
lockdowns 167–8
Logit ft Alessia Cara and Khalid **43**, 131
London Gangs Matrix 94
London riots, 2011 24
Longfield, Anne 16
love 101, 102, 111–12
Lucas, Joyner **43**, 124
Ludacris ft Mary J. Blige **43**, 53
lyrics xi, 34, 37, 41, 68, 77
  '1-800-273-8255' 131
  2Pac 40
  Depzman 103
  'My Old Lady' 49
  'The Saga' 76

M
Maguire, D. 8, 89
male domination 10, 24, 160
male violence 5, 9, 10, 20, 110, 143
  and hooks on 7
  SV and DVA 139
'The Man,' becoming 80, 81, 92
'a man,' being 80, 81
marginalization 93, 127, 140, 155
marginalized men 9, 101, 159, 161
Marley, Bob 37–8
Marsh, N. 31
martial metaphors 90–1
Maruna, S. 118, 120
masculine capital 6, 7
masculine dominance 7

INDEX

masculine identity 59, 61, 78, 120, 163
masculine power 60, 110
masculine role models 38–40
masculinity 5, 25, 38–9, 59–60, 65, 119, *145*, 160
  Black 21, 30, 35, 62, 165
  complicit 127–8
  and Connell 4
  and distinction between 'a man' and 'The Man' 80
  and fatherhood 123
  heroic 102, 110
  on-road 7
  and prison 89
  subordinate 8, 63
  and trauma 166
  vulnerable 8
  and war 90
  see also hegemonic masculinity; protest masculinity
Maslow, A. 121
May, Teresa 24
McAuley, R. 25
McGavock, L. 28–9
McGee, C. 48, 57
McGuffey, C.S. 9, 159
McMahon, Coleen **43**, 48
McNaughton et al 75–6, 159
'means-end' perspective 10
Mejía, X.E. 165–6
memories, music anchor to 36–8
mental health 153
Messerschmidt, J.W. 6, 7
Minnis, H. 29
minority racial and ethnic identity 60
mixed-race identity 61
mixed-race people 60
money
  difficulty earning away from crime 127
  strong motivation for gang involvement 72, 75, 94–5
moral code 125
moral panics 24, 30
mother figure 99–100
'Mother's Son' **43**, 98
Mshweshwe, L. 166
Mullins, C.W. 7
multi-agency safeguarding hubs (MASH) 31
murder 55–6, 104–5
music x, xi, 4, 47, 68
  and cathexis 34–5
  as coping mechanism 34, 77
  localized creation 40–1, 44
  tracks **42–3**
  see also hip-hop; lyrics
music elicitation 33–4, 35–40, 76–7, 157
musicians, as masculine role models 38–40
'My Old Lady' 34, **42**, 49

N

narrative criminology 11–12
National Youth Agency 156
'Natural Mystic' **42**, 126
Neal, Anthony 3–4
needs, hierarchy of 121
neglect 7, 48, 57, 144, 150
'Never Coming Homme' **42**, 64
Neville et al 140
Newburn et al 24
nutter 7–8, 81, 87, 88–90

O

O'Brien et al 25
offenders
  ideal 105
  young 29–30, 89
OMI 34, **42**, 49
omnipotence 7
'One Love/People Get Ready' 36, **42**, 115
on-road
  definition 13
  and drug dealing 73–4
  and harm 88
  and hypervisibility 23–6
  and protest masculinity 65, 96, 164
  and school 154
on-road masculinity 7
organized crime groups 32
Överlien, C. 18

P

pandemic, shadow 167–8
the past
  looking back at 120–2
  and music 36, 41
patriarchy 9, 10, 71, 165, 167
Pearson, C. 18
Pease, B. 140
peers
  acceptance by 79
  domination over 163
  feared by 81
  power over 65
  and power relations 78
  and violence 103–5
performativity of gender 5–6
perpetrator/victim overlap 22–3, 29–32, 105
Phillips, C. 89
physical abuse 48, 57
Pickering, M. 36
Pitts, J. 160
planetary humanism 34–5
Polak, Lord 137
police 23–4
Police, Crime, and Sentencing Bill 135–6, 137, 138
poor people 24–5
Popcaan **42**, 106

197

popular music 36
Porr et al 34
poverty 25, 71–3, 93
power 60, 62, 96, 110, 111
  among peers 65
  and anger 78
  making money 72, 95
  and production relations 163–4
  and public violence 79
powerlessness 54–5, 56, 59, 60, 62, 110, 163
  in light of mother's abuse 57–8, 63, 150
power relations 10, 55, 59–60, 73, 96
  and grooming 74
  and peers 78
  and religion 125
  subordination 62
  unequal between men and women 63
Presser, L. 12
pride 119, 123, 129, 163, 167
prison 85, 87, 89, 113, 114, 123
private sphere 58, 65, 96, 164, 165
private violence 76, 77, 135
production relations 10–11, 73, 96, 127, 164
protect, pressure to 58–9
protest masculinity 7–8, 38, 63, 65, 79, 89, 111
  and 2Pac 39, 40
  and complicit corporate masculinity 128
  and gender relations 9
  and marginalization 127
  and move from subordinated masculinity 81, 163
  and the nutter 88
  on-road 96
  and peers 78
  rite of passage for young men 131
  and sexual violence trauma 158
  and vulnerable masculinity 95, 101, 110, 162, 164–5, 166
public health approach 26, 135, 137, 139–42, 143
Public Health England 135, 139, 140–1
public sphere 96, 164, 165
public violence 77, 79, 107–8, 135, 163
Punishing Abuse 28

R
R&B music 35, 68
race 30, 60–2, 93, 164
racialization 31
racism 21–2, 89, 93–4, 126
Raisborough et al 92
rape 49–50, 59–60, 70, 156, 157, 158–9, 160
rap music 35, 38, 41, 44, 77, 106, 124
rappers 38–9
Ray, L. 63, 110
'Reality' **43**, 103

refugee identity 61, 78
refugees 72
refuges viii–ix, xii, 20, 21, 22, 149, 166
reggae 34, 70, 84, 106, 115
reintegrative shaming 120
religion 124–6
Renzetti, C. 105
resilience, and vulnerability 8
respect 65, 78
restorative justice 120
risk 17, 21, 28, 31, 142, 143
robbing 67, 83–4
role models 38–40
Rosser, Lord 137
'Runaway Love' **43**, 52, 53
Russell, Lord 137

S
safeguarding 26, 31
safe spaces 155–6
'The Saga (The Remix)' **42**, 76
Sandberg, S. 56
Santos, A. dos 36
school 79, 150, 153–6, 168
Schwöbel-Patel, C. 30
Scott, J. 154
second-wave feminist movement 166
Segal, L. 22
self-esteem 72, 110
self-harming 86, 91
self-identity 61, 72, 166
self-narratives 12
Serious Case Reviews (SCRs) 144, 146–53, 167
serious violence (SV) 26, 28, 135–6, 137, 138, 139
'Serious Violence Strategy' 135
sexual abuse 52–3, 60
sexual exploitation 67, 75–6, 156–7, 159–60, 161
sexual violence 9, 59–60, 156–60
shaming 75, 120, 124, 125
Sharp-Jeff, N. 18–19
Shuker, L. 159
siloed language 16
single-parent families 27
Skidmore, P. 160
'Slippin' **42**, 65
Small Acts (Gilroy) 62
Smart, Leroy **42**, 84
social field theory 7
social housing 24
social learning theory 19, 31
softness 78
songs 35–6, 37, 38, 39, **42–3**, 64, 77
  '1-800-273-8255' **43**, 131
  '100 Shots' **42**, 106
  'Ballistic Affair' **42**, 84
  'Beautiful Boy' **43**, 48

INDEX

'Changes' **42**, 82
'Ghetto' **42**, 85
'I Ain't Mad At Cha' **42**, 113
'I Miss You' 37, **42**, 51
'I'm Sorry' **43**, 124
'Lesley' **43**, 47
'Mother's Son' **43**, 98
'My Old Lady' 34, **42**, 49
'Natural Mystic' **42**, 126
'Never Coming Homme' **42**, 64
'One Love/People Get Ready' 36, **42**, 115
'Reality' **43**, 103
'Runaway Love' **43**, 52, 53
'The Saga (The Remix)' **42**, 76
'Slippin' **42**, 65
'Three Little Birds' 37–8, **42**, 70
'Unruly Prayer' **42**, 106
'The World's Greatest' **42**, 68
Spartans 90
Spencer, L. 154
Spencer et al 28
Spratt, T. 28–9
Stark, E. 5
Sternberg et al 19
stigmatization 7, 12, 16, 29, 31, 155
  and gangs 13, 25, 139, 153
stop and search 24
Stormzy 40
structural inequality 126–7, 164
Sturgeon, Nicola 5
subordinate masculinity 8, 38, 62–3, 65, 81, 96, 163
suicide 73
Sullivan, M.L. 26
surveillance 138, 146, 152
Sutherland, Superintendent John 27
SV prevention duty 135–6

T

terrorism 57, 66
testosterone 131
Theoretical Criminology 11–12
'Three Little Birds' 37–8, **42**, 70
ties, to gangs 102–3
toxic masculinity 130
trap 95–6
trauma 157, 162, 165, 166, 168
trip-hop 35
true self 120–1
Tyler, I. 93

U

'Unruly Prayer' **42**, 106
UN Women 167

V

victimization 75, 105, 137–8, 157, 160
victim/perpetrator overlap 22, 29–32, 105

violence 10, 31, 41, 165
  cycle of 23, 27
  and gangs 81–2
  gender-based ix, 9, 29
  intergenerational transmission of 19–20, 60–1
  male 7
  peer 65, 103–5
  public 77, 79
  and public health approach 139–40
  school 150, 153, 154
  sexual 156–60
  and vulnerability 8, 162–3, 167
  against women 107–10
Violence Against Women and Girls (VAWG) Strategy 136, 161
violence reduction units 135
Volpp, L. 21
vulnerability 7, 8–9, 75, 121, 130, 157–8, 166
  and Gelles 110
  and Gilson 91, 103
  and power 162–3
  and violence 167
Vulnerability and Violence 28
vulnerable adolescent (VA) 28
vulnerable masculinity 8, 38, 95, 101, 110, 111, 166
  at root of discontent 162
  shadow self 164

W

Wade, L. 130
Wagner, C. 36
Wales Violence Reduction Unit 142
Walklate, S. 8
Walsh, C. 137
war, as metaphor 90–1
Westside Gunn ft Tiona D **42**, 64
White, Joy 40, 41
White chavs 92–3
whiteness 62, 93
White supremacist capitalist patriarchy 4, 10
Williams, P. 25, 155
Wilson, D. 89
witnessing DVA 19–20, 59
Wolfe et al 19
women
  and DVA 4–5
  and gang-involved men 97–9
  and harm 5
  and heroic masculinity 102
  viewed with reverence and value 106–7
  violence against 107–10
Women's Aid Federation England ix
working-class boys, Black 31
World Health Organization (WHO) 139–40
'The World's Greatest' **42**, 68
Wroe, L.E. 31, 152

Y
Yar, M. 92
Yates, J. 29–30
Young, T. 13
young Black men 30, 40
Young Dolph **42**, 106

young offender 29–30, 89
youth clubs 156
youth justice system 27–8
youth offending and risk management support services 23
youth services 155–6

www.ingramcontent.com/pod-product-compliance
Lightning Source LLC
Chambersburg PA
CBHW051541020426
42333CB00016B/2040